Praise for

# EMT

"Ivey has an uncanny ability to recall detail and to relate it
with due respect to what is appropriate and what isn't. . . . Her
first-person account of the events is refreshing. This, coupled
with her ability to help the reader know her fellow technicians
as she does, makes you feel you're there working her calls. . . .
Ivey keeps you riveted to each page."

*Emergency*

"Painfully descriptive at times, the work is not gruesome.
Genuinely humorous at times, the writing is guardedly serious.
It's a book about a person's life, after all. But more importantly
for Ivey, it's a book about many people's lives and what it
takes to save them."

*Orange County Review*

"A wonderful book! So well-written, and so very human . . . It
is a book that every American should read, since it so
beautifully captures the essence of the volunteer spirit."

Conover Hunt
Coordinator
Julian Stanley Wise Foundation

"Candid . . . Honest."

*Salem Times-Register*

# EMT:

## Beyond the Lights and Sirens

## Pat Ivey

IVY BOOKS · NEW YORK

ISBN 0-8041-0711-4

This edition published by arrangement with Diamond Books, an imprint of Eakin Publications, Inc.

1. *Emergency Care In The Streets* by Nancy Caroline, M.D. 2nd Ed. Little, Brown and Company, Boston. Page 9.
2. *Do Not Go Gentle Into That Good Night*. Dylan Thomas: Poems of Dylan Thomas. Copyright 1952 by Dylan Thomas. Reprinted by permission of New Directions Publishing Co.
3. Newspaper article on Julian Stanley Wise by Brian O'Neill, *Roanoke Times and World News*, Roanoke, VA.

Portions of this work previously appeared in the following publications:
   *The Orange County Review*, Orange, VA.
   *Virginia Lifeline*, Official Publication of Virginia Association of Volunteer Rescue Squads

**Manufactured in the United States of America**

First Ballantine Books Edition: January 1991

*This book is dedicated to my children—*
*David, Matt, and Jennifer*


*And to the men and women on volunteer rescue squads—*
*who give so freely of their skills,*
*their time, and their love—*
*so that others may live.*

*There are close to half a million
Emergency Medical Technicians.*

*We all have a story to tell.
This is mine.*

# Acknowledgments

I am grateful for my associations with the following emergency services personnel: the fire and rescue organizations of Orange County, Spotsylvania County, Culpeper County, and the city of Fredericksburg; the ER staffs of Mary Washington Hospital, Culpeper Memorial Hospital, and the hospitals of the University of Virginia and the Medical College of Virginia; Emergency Physicians Dr. Sam Heard, Dr. Thomas Flaherty, and Dr. Warren Parmelee; and Dr. Robert Kravetz and Dr. M. David Schenck, teachers, friends.

A number of individuals gave me support in a variety of ways and to them I offer my thanks: Mrs. Ruth Wise, for sharing with me memories of her husband, Julian Stanley Wise; Richard Dillard, author and professor of English at Hollins College, VA, for his professional advice; for the inspiration he gives to us all, Fredericksburg Rescue Squad volunteer Sam Perry, who continues to serve his community after almost fifty years; Debbie Christie and Margaret Powers, for the gift of their friendship; Joe Broderick, for his continuous moral support; my parents, Edna and Al Follmar, for teaching me that giving is better than taking; and Richard Curtis and Rob Cohen of Richard Curtis Literary Associates, for believing in my book.

And I remember with appreciation my creative writing professor at the University of North Carolina, Chapel Hill: the late Manly Wade Wellman who reaffirmed my belief in the power of words and the magic of writing.

Finally, I want to thank the members of the Lake of the Woods Volunteer Rescue Squad, without whom this book could never have been written.

Present and past members of the Lake of the Woods Volunteer Fire Department and Rescue Squad who appear in the book:

| | |
|---|---|
| Purvis Beanum | Sally Kelley |
| John Beery | Betty Law |
| Bill Belt | Ed Law |
| Pia Boot Van der Heiden | Suzanne Lawrence |
| Jay Broderick | Jack Lemay |
| Joe Broderick | Kathi Lemay |
| Mara Bueng | Paul Lewis |
| Phyllis Burbank | Jean Lodge |
| Howie Crain | Bob Luckett |
| Linda Dickerson | Joseph Maiden |
| Millie Droste | Bud Morley |
| Norm Ensrud | Joanie O'Brien |
| Dick Ferguson | Buzzy O'Toole |
| Woody Fox | Al Potter |
| Kathy Gates | Lou Potter |
| Bob Grim | Marcus Wallace |
| Joyce Grim | Bill Werber |
| Harry Haas | Carmie Witzke |
| John Harkness | Ken Witzke |
| Pat Ivey | Cliff Wolff |
| Mac Johnson | |

With few exceptions, rescue squad volunteers are identified by their real names. Patient's names and distinguishing characteristics have been changed.

Chronology and circumstances have been rearranged in some instances. Dialogue, while not always verbatim, is true to the character of the speaker and the nature of the episode. Descriptions of all emergency cases involving the Lake of the Woods Volunteer Rescue Squad are drawn directly from actual calls.

# Chapter 1

His hands lay still by his sides, palms up, his small fingers curled slightly. I knelt beside him and placed my hand gently on his chest and felt his struggle for each breath. His eyes were half closed, his lids fixed, his pupils sluggish. Cerebrospinal fluid, watery and clear, drained from his nose and right ear. I didn't know his name then and so when I leaned closer to him, so close I could feel his sweet breath on my face, I simply called him, "Baby." But there was no response.

I glanced at the overturned and shattered car, then turned my attention back to him. There was no blood to wipe away. There were no lacerations to bandage, no broken bones to splint, but when I moved my fingers through his blonde hair I felt the deep depression in his skull.

Lonnie had intended to go to the store before her children awoke. Paula was five now and Jesse was three, and she felt she could occasionally leave them alone while they slept since it was only a fifteen minute trip to the store and back.

She enjoyed taking them with her when there was a little extra money, when she could buy them Starbursts or a fudge bar or one of the toys which hung by the register—checkout temptations, she called them—Silly Putty or ball and jacks. But today her husband had left her only enough for the milk. She knew Jesse would probably make a scene and she'd have to spank him

1

and then they'd both be angry for the better part of the morning. That's why she wanted to go alone.

She changed from her gown into jeans and sweatshirt and was running a comb through her dark curly hair when she heard them laughing. She dropped her comb on her dresser and crossed the narrow hallway to their room. When she opened the door their laughter abruptly stopped, and she saw the movement under the covers.

"Do you have that puppy in bed with you?" she asked them. Her velvety Virginia accent padded her words and stretched them out so each word nudged the next.

The children exchanged a sober glance. "Yes, ma'am," Paula answered.

"Get him out," Lonnie said. "And go back to sleep."

"I don't want to go back to sleep," Jesse objected, dropping the beagle pup on the floor. "I'm hungry." The puppy darted under the bed.

"I'm hungry too," said Paula.

"Well," Lonnie sighed, "we've got to go get some milk first."

Jesse slid off the bed onto the floor and the puppy was there to meet him. "Can I get something?" he asked, scooping the beagle up into his arms.

"Not today, honey," she told him. "Put the dog down so you can get dressed."

"I can't get anything?" he whined.

She pulled his pajama top over his head, then smoothed his tousled hair. "Jesse, there's only enough for the milk."

"Then can I take Rascal with me?"

"Can we, Mama?" Paula asked.

She looked at their upturned faces.

"All right," she said. "We'll all go to the store."

It was 8:00 when they took their places in the car. Jesse sat next to the window with the puppy on his lap, Paula in the middle beside their mother. The car was old. There were no seatbelts.

"Keep Rascal over there, Jesse," Lonnie said as she backed out of the driveway. "Don't let go of him."

Jean Lodge, Joe Broderick, and I were on rescue squad duty that day. By 8:00 we'd been on for 2 hours of our twelve-hour shift. So far, it had been a quiet morning. No calls. I took my pager from its charger and clipped it onto my belt, then finished the last of the breakfast dishes.

I opened the freezer door and studied my selection, trying to decide what to have for dinner. Both Dave and Matt had football practice after school and wouldn't be home until late. Jennifer would get off the bus at her friend's house and I'd pick her up at six when my duty ended. David would be home by 6:30. We often ate in shifts, especially during football season. I decided on meat loaf and took out two pounds of hamburger.

At her home, Jean switched on her TV, waiting for 9:00 and "Donahue," then took out her stationery to write a quick note to her grandson in Florida.

Joe had been at his hardware store since seven, gathering information from the store's computer for the upcoming inventory.

I closed the freezer door. Jean uncapped her pen. Joe jotted down the stock numbers of storm doors.

The tones went off.

"ATTENTION LAKE OF THE WOODS RESCUE SQUAD MEMBERS," our dispatcher announced. "WE HAVE A REPORT OF A 10-50 PI ON ROUTE 624. THREE VICTIMS, TWO CHILDREN, ONE UNCONSCIOUS."

A 10-50 is a wreck. PI indicates personal injury. Our dispatcher repeated the message, but by then I was already in my car hurrying toward the fire and rescue building. Joe was closest. He had the ambulance out of the bay when Jean and I arrived.

We were on the road in three minutes.

"Medic 29 to LOW," I spoke into the radio. "We're en route to the scene. Tone out for a second unit."

I replaced the radio and turned to Joe. "If our information is correct, we'll need both units."

Joe drove the ambulance skillfully, carefully accelerating over the narrow winding road. Trees stood like sentries on either side. Above us, their limbs touched, forming a golden archway. Pavement gave way to gravel as we moved deeper into the country. Gravel surrendered to dirt when we turned onto Route 624.

Our information was correct.

Jean went to the little girl sitting in the grass next to the road-way. She was softly whimpering and appeared dazed and dis-oriented. Jean held her for a few moments before she began bandaging the large laceration on the back of her head.

The mother was on the ground near the girl. Joe knelt beside her. She was having difficulty breathing. Her ribs were fractured, one lung punctured. Joe suctioned blood from her mouth, then placed the oxygen mask on her face.

I went to the boy.

Later, in the hospital, Lonnie would remember clearly all that preceded that trip to the store, but her recollections of the accident were blurred. It was Paula who told about Rascal jumping onto the floor and crawling under her mother's feet, and when her mother had reached to grab the beagle pup, the car swerved off the road and overturned.

I watched the boy's chest rise and fall rapidly. His breaths were labored. Suddenly, they stopped. I pressed my mouth over his and breathed.

And he breathed on his own—one breath, then another—slowly at first, but gradually accelerating and increasingly labored. Then again he stopped, and again I breathed into him.

I knew it was Cheyne-Stokes respiration: the bizarre breathing pattern that accompanies a severe head injury.

The cycle continued.

Our firemen were now on the scene and I called to them to bring me a short backboard. We carefully eased him onto it and carried him to the ambulance.

Bill Werber and Cliff Wolff arrived with our second unit. They would transport the mother; we would take the children.

Inside the ambulance I placed electrodes on the boy's chest, then connected the leads to the cardiac monitor. I saw the EKG of a healthy three-year-old. His heart was strong. It was the blood and swollen cerebral tissue pressing against his brainstem and irreversibly damaging his respiratory control center that was taking him from us.

I breathed for him.

Joe moved in beside me.

"Stay with him," I said. "Watch his breathing."

I had asked the firemen to help Jean get the girl on a backboard. She should have already been in the ambulance. We were losing time.

I stepped off the ambulance and saw the sock lying in the road. It must have fallen there when we moved him. Almost subconsciously I picked it up and put it in the pocket of my jacket.

The girl was more alert now and was terrified. She screamed over and over for her mother. Jean had tried to restrain her on the backboard, but it was impossible.

"I'm going to have to just pick her up and carry her," I said to Jean.

Firemen were hosing down the area around the car where gasoline had spilled onto the ground. Jeff, one of our firemen, was holding a beagle puppy.

Cradling the girl securely in my arms, I started to step onto the ambulance when suddenly she cried, "Rascal!" I turned and paused as Jeff approached us. The beagle was barking and squirming in his arms.

"Is this your puppy?" he asked her.

"That's Rascal," she said, rubbing the puppy's ears.

"Will you let me keep him for you until you come home?" he asked. "I'll take good care of him."

She studied Jeff carefully before she nodded. "Yes."

"Okay." Jeff smiled at her.

She had quieted. I carried her into the ambulance and placed her in Jean's lap, then moved next to Joe.

"Let's go," I said to him. As he moved up front into the driver's seat, I told him, "Expedite."

Before we turned onto hard surface, while we still moved over the back country roads, I could hear Jean and the child talking. Their voices were soft. Jean positioned her so that her back was to her brother, so that she couldn't see me breathing into his mouth.

"What's your name?" Jean asked her.

"Paula," she said in almost a whisper.

"Carla?" Jean asked.

5

"No, Paula."

"That's a pretty name," Jean said to her. "Even prettier than Carla."

"What's your name?"

"My name is Jean."

"That's a pretty name, too," the child said.

"How old are you, Paula?"

She held up her hand and spread her fingers. "Five."

"What's your brother's name?" Jean asked her.

Paula turned toward him. That was the only time she looked our way. She watched for a brief moment, then turned back to Jean.

"Jesse," she said. "His name is Jesse."

When we left the dirt and gravel roads and moved onto asphalt and into traffic, Joe switched on the siren. The undulating wail filled the space around us. Jean held Paula closer.

As we neared the hospital, Jesse's condition worsened. The cycle shortened. I became his every breath.

In the trauma room at Mary Washington Hospital, two doctors labored over him. They inserted an endotrachial tube into his airway and injected Mannitol into his veins in hope of reducing the swelling in his brain. He remained unresponsive. They called for the helicopter and twenty minutes later he was flown by Medstar to Washington Children's Hospital for emergency surgery.

We called the hospital that night and again the next morning to check on his condition. It remained unchanged.

Thirty-six hours after the accident, Jesse died.

It was later, when I was cleaning out the pockets of my jacket, that I found Jesse's red sock. I looked at it, so small in my hand. It was new.

"For God's sake, Pat," David said to me, "throw it away."

"I can't," I told him.

I couldn't throw the sock away and couldn't return it, so I tucked it away in my dresser drawer. As time passed, it was pushed farther and farther to the back.

Almost two years have gone by since that day and from time

to time, during spring cleaning or when I'm searching through that drawer for something else, I find the sock.

And I remember Jesse and pause for a moment.

Then I think of us, the rescue squad.

"He never had a chance," the hospital nurse had told me on our last phone call about Jesse.

"I know," I had said.

I did know and had known from the very beginning. From the moment I saw him there on the road, from the instant I saw his hands and his eyes, before I felt the deep depression in his skull, and before I tried to breathe life into him, I had known.

But we try. Even if it means hoping when there is no hope, wishing on a starless night, we try.

# Chapter 2

"I COULD NEVER work on a rescue squad."

Even before she spoke, I knew she was watching me. She sat at the Formica-topped table in the ER nurses' lounge, clean and crisp in her white uniform.

I poured coffee into a Styrofoam cup, adding sugar and cream. The mixture was grey and smelled like charcoal.

I muffled a yawn. "Why not?" I asked her.

"I like knowing there's a doctor nearby," she said. "And I have to work in a controlled environment."

I smiled at her. "Then you really wouldn't have liked it out there tonight." I raised the cup to my lips, then lowered it. "What time do you fix a fresh pot?"

"Probably not until about 3:00," she said. "I don't drink it myself."

"Well, don't start drinking it now," I told her.

I walked into the bathroom, switched on the light and poured the coffee into the sink. It left a grey ring at the mouth of the drain. I turned on the faucet to rinse it and glanced in the mirror.

"Good Lord."

I reached up to the right side of my head and felt the blood and vomitus matter in my blonde hair. I tried picking it out, then cupped my hand under the running water and splashed it on my hair, but that just seemed to stir up the smell.

My blue eyes were bloodshot and swollen and ached with fatigue. My whole body was sore and the sight of my image, looking much older than forty, just made me feel worse. The fluorescent light exposed every line and blemish on my face.

"It's hopeless," I said aloud. I washed my hands and returned to the lounge. The nurse had gone.

I walked into the hall. Joe and Norm Ensrud had finished changing the sheets on the gurney. I took a nasal cannula from the supply shelf to replace the one we had used and walked behind them as they pulled the gurney down the hall toward the loading dock.

"Sounds like a Saturday night," Joe said.

The ER sounds never blend together, but rather are like musical instruments in a homemade band, always a little off-key and disjointed. There is no harmony. Low pitched moans, short yelps, the occasional clanging of a dropped bedpan make it difficult to accurately locate any one particular sound.

Voices are easier to define: the paging of hospital personnel over the intercom, "Respiratory therapy, ICU, STAT," quick snatches of conversations between doctors, "I still think the arrhythmia is a result of the amount of digoxin he's taking"; and from the waiting room where the walk-ins converge, "His fever's worse," "I've been sitting here over an hour," "She just broke out in this rash," "I think it's broken."

Unless they are especially shrill or vulgar or interesting or frightening, we move oblivious through the sounds and around the voices like people subconsciously aware of the Musak, but unable to recall what songs were played.

"Smells like a Saturday night, too," Norm said.

"I think that's Pat you smell," Joe told him, looking back at me and grinning.

"Very funny," I said.

We walked past the front desk and the triage nurse.

"Hey, Lake of the Woods," she said. "Please don't bring us any more like that last one."

"There can't be any more like him," I told her.

His car had been airborne for fifty feet before it crashed into the woods, coming to rest at a forty-five degree angle, its left

9

side resting on a tree. Inside the car, our patient had been hurled into the back seat.

Marcus Wallace, one of our squad members, lived near the scene of the accident and had responded direct.

"He keeps blacking out," Marcus told us. "We're going to have to get in there, and the doors on this side are jammed. Pat, can you get in from the other side?"

"I'll try."

If a patient is trapped in a vehicle following an accident and if entry can be gained, a squad member gets into the vehicle until the patient can be removed. I have crawled through front, side and rear windows to bandage and splint, to monitor a patient's heart rhythm, to start an IV, to comfort, to make patients feel less frightened, less alone, and to be with them when the harsh, grinding noises of extrication explode around them.

But this night would be different.

Norm and Joe and I walked through the underbrush to the opposite side of the car. "How come no one ever asks you all to do this?" I asked them.

Joe patted my shoulder. "It pays to be tall."

Our crash truck arrived along with the firetruck, and the spotlights were turned on, illuminating the scene.

Joe checked the size of the tree on which the car rested, then pulled hard on the back fender of the car.

"It's secure," he told me.

Because of the angle of the car, its door was at my shoulder level. "You're going to have to help me get in," I said to him.

He cupped his hands. "Put your foot here." He boosted me up and into the car.

Inside, it was hard to keep my balance. I had barely two feet of room and kept sliding to the right, against our patient. Finally, I knelt facing him, but still had to brace myself against his left arm.

He appeared to be in his early twenties. "I'm Pat," I said. "I'm here to help you. What's your name?"

"Larry," he mumbled, and I could smell the alcohol. "Get me out of here," he said, leaning hard against me, pushing me into the corner of the back seat.

"We're going to," I told him, placing my hands against his arm to keep him off me.

Marcus reached inside the opposite window and handed me a cervical collar, a precautionary device, in case a victim has injured his cervical spine. I leaned around Larry to get it.

"I'm going to need some help getting this on him," I said. "Can somebody reach in from the back?" The back window was shattered.

Marcus called to Norm. He climbed onto the trunk and lay across the window frame. I handed him the front section of the collar. I would fit the back piece on Larry, then Norm would attach the front with the Velcro tabs.

John Harkness, who had arrived with the firetruck, leaned in where Marcus had been. "We're going to have to take this door off," he said.

"I know."

"You okay?" he asked.

"So far," I told him.

Norm moved his hand in front of Larry to try to get the collar on his neck, but he rolled toward me, pinning my right arm under him.

"Forget the collar, Norm," I said. "We just can't do it."

"I want to get out of here," Larry said.

"We're getting you out," I told him. I pushed against him with my left hand, moving him enough to free my arm.

Joe stuffed the tarp inside the car. I reached for it and pulled it over Larry and me. The extrication was about to begin and the heavy tarp would protect us from broken glass and sharp pieces of metal. The generator was fired, and I wrapped my arms around Larry and held him while the firemen moved the Hearst tool within inches of us.

The back of his head was pressed against my face and I could feel his blood, warm and sticky, on my cheek and forehead. He began to strain against my hold. "Let me go," he insisted.

I tried to tighten my grip on him, but he was too strong. I had no room to move. My legs, still folded under me, were beginning to cramp. The tarp was heavy over our heads, and I was damp with perspiration. His breaths were rapid, and the smell

11

of alcohol combined with the acrid odor of his blood made our limited space even more oppressive.

He pulled away suddenly, breaking my grasp. He gasped once, then vomited. I felt it splatter in my hair and on my face. He vomited again and I was momentarily afraid that I would vomit too. I lifted the corner of the tarp, turned my head away from him and took several deep breaths.

He was sitting straight up now. He looked from side to side. "Shit!" he said. "I gotta get out of here."

I tried to ease away from him but there was nowhere to go.

"Joe," I called out the back window. "Norm!"

But no one could hear me over the noise of the generator.

I saw Norm standing on the perimeter of a group of bystanders. His attention was focused on the firemen cutting away at the car. Larry and I were on the opposite side of the car, still obscured by darkness, so Norm never looked my way.

Even above the noise of the generator, I could hear the blood pounding in my ears. He was trapped in the car and so was I.

I sat perfectly still. Larry hadn't reacted to my calling for help. I watched him spit several times, then wipe his arm across his mouth. Suddenly he groaned loudly and began hitting the roof of the car with his fists. I closed my eyes.

Then the door popped and the generator was still.

"Get the backboard," I heard Joe yell to Norm.

Larry stopped punching the roof and leaned back against the seat. For the moment he was quiet.

I opened my eyes and saw Joe's face in the open space where the door had been.

"Pat," he said, "what do you need?"

"Out," was all I could tell him.

On the hospital loading dock, Norm and Joe lifted the gurney back onto the ambulance.

"Look at that mess," Joe remarked. "You think it'll keep until Saturday?"

"I think if we leave it this way, Saturday's crew will kill us," Norm said.

"I'll do some cleaning on the way back," I told them, "if you'll stop somewhere and get coffee."

12

"That's a deal," Joe said. He and Norm got up front. I climbed into the back.

It was 2:00 in the morning. There was very little traffic. Joe drove below the speed limit. There were no quick accelerations or sudden turns, unlike the trip into town. I could easily move around in the back.

I used paper towels to sweep the dirt and leaves into a pile by the door. I picked up the soiled bandages, the sleeves of Larry's shirt which we cut off so I could start the IVs, unused pieces of bandages, a chemical ice pack, now warm and flaccid, and dropped it all into a plastic bag.

I sat down in the jump seat which backs up to the cab. Joe and Norm faced forward, I faced the rear. I pulled off my tennis shoes and propped my feet up on the gurney as Joe pulled into the 7-11.

"You still awake?" he asked me.

"Just barely."

"Stay there," he said. "I'll bring you some coffee."

I had not yet told Joe and Norm about how frightened I was in the car with Larry. There hadn't been time. Once we got him out of the car and into the ambulance we were too busy, for only then were we able to give him any real medical care. He was bleeding internally and his blood pressure was dangerously low. At that point he was quite subdued. I started the IVs and we put MAST trousers on him.

Halfway to the hospital, he began to lash out at Joe and me, verbally and physically.

"Step on it, Norm," I called to him and I felt the sudden acceleration of the ambulance.

We finally had to restrain Larry. He had taken several swings at Joe and although he now lacked the strength to hurt us, we were afraid he would pull the IVs out. So Joe tied his arms to the sides of the gurney.

The emergency room personnel could hear him yelling when we pulled up to the loading dock.

"Here you go," Joe said. "Three creams, two sugars."

I took the cup from him. "You're a lifesaver, Joseph."

13

He smiled. "I guess that's why I'm out here in the middle of the night instead of in bed where I should be."

He was exhausted. I could see it in his eyes. He moved slowly toward the front and took several sips of coffee before he turned the key in the ignition. I could hear Norm snoring softly. He'd been asleep since we pulled away from the loading dock. Usually we discussed our call on the trip home, and this one would have lasted the full twenty miles and more in its recounting, but talking would take effort and effort requires energy, and that night energy was in short supply.

The whole squad was running double duty because membership was low. That happens every few years. Then it builds up again, but the growth seemed to be taking longer this time.

Twenty-four hour coverage is a necessity and many areas, suffering from the loss of volunteers, have already converted to paid personnel. Ambulance service has changed drastically over the last fifteen years, from the old days of "scoop and scoot" to the highest level of pre-hospital patient care. Lifesaving efforts once performed only in the confines of a hospital are now being carried out on the scene by emergency medical personnel.

To provide this definitive patient care requires enhanced skills which can only be acquired through intense training, and many people think the time involved just isn't worth it.

My friend Bob Luckett, who worked on an ambulance in Alexandria as a paid paramedic and volunteered his time on our squad, once said to me, "You people must be either the craziest people in the world or the most dedicated to do all that work and not get paid."

"A little of each, I guess," I told him.

I finished my coffee, leaned back and watched the lights of Fredericksburg slowly fade as we moved west on Route 3, toward home.

Home is Lake of the Woods, in Wilderness, Virginia. Located in largely rural Orange County, Lake of the Woods is a planned recreational-residential community built around a 500-acre lake. Eleven years ago David and I moved here with my sons from a previous marriage, Dave, seven, and Matt, five, after deciding that life in the city of Alexandria was not conducive to childraising. The next year our daughter Jennifer was born.

Here, the children have trees to climb, and a lake in which to fish and ski and sail. There is room to grow. We need only to walk to the back of our yard to pick wild strawberries and blackberries. In the spring, dogwood and redbud trees bloom and the surrounding woods are thick with ferns and wildflowers.

"Medic 29 to LOW," I heard Joe call our dispatcher. "We've returned to station."

And the response, "10-4, Med 29, return to station at 0253."

Joe replaced the radio. "Rise and shine, you guys. We're home," he said. "Norm. Pat."

"I'm awake," I told him. "I think we ought to just move Norm to the gurney and leave him here for the next call."

"I hear you plotting," Norm said. "Don't even mention another call. My back can't take it."

"Is your back bothering you again?" I asked him. Everyone on the squad has occasional back problems. We call it an occupational hazard and try to remember to bend our knees when we lift the gurney. But Norm's was more serious. He was almost sixty and had undergone back surgery just three months ago.

He nodded. "I can feel it."

Joe backed the ambulance inside the bay.

"Well," Norm said, "it's been an experience."

"I've got to tell you about my experience in the car sometime," I said to them.

"Anytime but now," Joe said. "I'm sure it's memorable but if you tell me now, I wouldn't remember any of it. Wait until I've had some sleep. I would like to know where you got that cologne, though."

Norm laughed. "Good night, good people."

"Night, Norm," I said. "Take care."

Joe started on the paperwork.

I swept out the pile of dirt and got the disinfectant and paper towels and started on the floor.

Joe leaned inside the ambulance. "I'm all finished," he said. "You need any help?"

"No, thanks. I'm almost through."

"Okay," he said. "I'm off. Good night, Pat."

"Night, Joe. Sleep fast."

"Yeah." He smiled. "You too."

After I finished the floor, I checked supplies and restocked where there was a shortage. I added several icepacks and six rolls of the four-inch gauze: then made sure the lock was secure on the cabinet containing our IV and drug boxes.

I stepped off the ambulance and closed the heavy doors behind me, and glanced at my watch, 3:20. By now, there would be freshly brewed coffee in the emergency room lounge. I thought about what the nurse had said to me, "I could never work on a rescue squad."

I certainly couldn't argue with her reasons. After all, there is no doctor in the next room on whom we can call for help, and we often must work in an environment which is anything but controlled. From a midnight auto accident to a call for a shooting victim, we never know what we will encounter or under what conditions we will have to work.

Her reasons were valid. Just seven years earlier I had made that same remark, yet my reasons had no logic, no validity. I couldn't even verbalize them. They were so deeply rooted in my past I lacked the words to give them meaning.

Seven years ago, on an early spring day, a sixteen-year-old boy drowned in the lake. His small rowboat had capsized, hitting him on the head when it overturned. Unconscious, he went down. A life jacket would have saved him.

Several weeks later I received a call from Lou Potter. She and her husband, Al, were members of the rescue squad. I was a den leader for our Cub Scout pack and Lou wanted to talk to my boys about water safety.

I liked Lou. She was easy to be with and interesting and caring. She spoke at our next meeting, and afterwards, as she prepared to leave she said to me, "Pat, you're home during the day. We really need daytime people on the squad. Why don't you give it some thought?"

I smiled and shook my head. "Lou," I told her, "I could never work on a rescue squad."

"Well, maybe not until Jennifer starts school," she replied.

16

"No," I said. "You don't understand. I mean I *can't* do it."

"Why not?" she asked.

I hesitated. "It's hard to explain," I told her. "Just believe me. That's one thing I could never do."

"Okay," she conceded, "at least for now. But I'm not going to give up on you."

And she didn't.

I smiled to myself, remembering, as I switched off the light in the bay and headed home.

# Chapter 3

IT WAS A beautiful evening with just enough breeze to keep the mosquitoes away. David and I and the children had joined Brian and Lynda Hall for a cookout on their farm three miles from Lake of the Woods. The Halls' children, Justin, eight, and Jenny, three, were the same ages as Matt and Jennifer and they had become close friends. Dave had invited his best friend, Billy, to go with us.

"Don't go down to the pond without one of us," I told each of them. It had been only two months since the drowning at Lake of the Woods and I felt the pond was the only danger they would encounter on the farm. "We'll go fishing after supper if you want to."

After the cookout we all sat for a while at the picnic table, happy, full, and content. Brian and David challenged Dave and Billy to a game of badminton. Matt and Justin had already made plans to go exploring in the woods. We cautioned them to be back before dark. Then Lynda and I and the girls walked the short distance to the pond.

The fish were biting and Jenny and Jennifer squealed with delight at each catch. At 8:15 a cloud cover abruptly moved in, turning twilight to dusk. The breeze subsided and the mosquitoes found us. We gathered our fishing gear and walked to the house with Jennifer and Jenny carrying the bucket of fish between them.

"You girls are going to help clean those fish, aren't you?" I asked them.

"No!" they screamed, quickly putting the bucket down on the back steps and dashing into the house.

Lynda laughed. "We'll clean them in a few minutes. Let's have some coffee first."

Brian had a fresh pot of coffee waiting for us. We poured ours and joined him and David at the kitchen table.

"Where are the boys?" Lynda asked.

"Watching TV," David said. "Please don't ask them about the game. They clobbered us."

"Are Matt and Justin with them?" I asked.

"No," Brian answered. "They're probably at the barn."

"Mama," Jennifer called to me from Jenny's room, "where's my Dressie Bessie doll?"

"It's still in the car," I answered. "I'll get it."

I walked out into the darkness and shivered at the sudden breeze, and the chill on my bare arms. I went to the car, found the doll, closed the door and stood listening. It was too quiet.

"Matt," I called, facing the barn. "Justin." There was no answer, no sound at all.

I walked to the fence where they'd cut through to go into the woods and called to them again. "Matt. Justin." Silence.

I took the doll to Jennifer, then returned to the kitchen. "I can't find Matt and Justin," I said. "Did anyone see them come back?"

David glanced at Brian, then looked at me. "No."

Brian peered out the window into the darkness. "They're probably building a fort out in . . . "

"They're not in the barn," I interrupted. "I called them and no one answered."

"Maybe they're hiding," Brian suggested.

"You know them better than that," Lynda told him.

She got up from the table. I reached for my jacket and followed her outside. Under the porch light the fish glistened, their vitreous eyes staring blindly at some fixed point in the night sky. We walked to the fence and called again. David and Brian, helped by Dave and Billy, circled the property, stopping every

19

few minutes to call. Jennifer and Jenny sat close together on the back steps, holding hands.

Lynda and I drove down the road adjoining their property as far as we could imagine the boys might have wandered. We stopped frequently, getting out of the car to call to them.

I cupped my hands around my mouth. "Matt."

Lynda faced the opposite side of the road. "Justin."

The trees bordering the road were tall and dense. There were no echoes. The only sounds were those of cicadas and whip-poorwills.

An hour later we returned to the house. Brian met us in the driveway.

"We couldn't find them," he said. "I've called the rescue squad."

"Why?" I asked. "Why a rescue squad?"

"We need more help, Pat," he said, and I could hear the desperation in his voice. "They must still be in the woods and we can't cover it all by ourselves. We've got to have some help."

"Where are the others?" Lynda asked him.

"Inside with David," he said, turning back toward the house. Lynda followed.

I stood alone.

Brian had called the rescue squad, and they were on their way. "Oh, Matt," I whispered into the night.

Unwanted, unbidden memories stirred within my mind, memories of another night so many years ago.


It was the September of my seventh year.

I slept on a day bed in the living room of my grandparents' home. French doors separated me from the foyer where the staircase led to the second floor and to the room where my grandfather lay dying.

I was awakened by unfamiliar sounds and opened my eyes to see a single light penetrating the darkness, falling across the living room floor and casting mosaic shadows on the fireplace mantel.

I eased up slowly. Resting on one elbow, I looked toward the light's source, into the foyer and beyond to the staircase where men were descending. They carried my grandfather on a stretcher. Everything appeared chalky, alabaster: the light, the men's jackets, my grandfather's face, the sheet over my grandfather's frail body. My father followed the men down the stairs. Behind him came my mother and my grandmother. And they were crying.

I pulled the curtains aside and watched out the window. The men carried my grandfather onto the front porch and down the sidewalk to the ambulance crouched under the streetlight. I watched the men ease the stretcher inside and close the doors.

The ambulance pulled away and traveled down the tree-lined street where I had walked so often with my grandfather, his hand holding mine. My father, his arms around the shoulders of my mother and grandmother, waited there with them until the ambulance rounded the corner. Then they retraced their steps back into the house and on into the kitchen. They talked in muffled voices I couldn't understand. I smelled coffee brewing and smoke from my father's cigarette and lay back and pulled the quilt up to my face, holding the warm, familiar material against my skin.

I heard my mother's footsteps and closed my eyes, feigning sleep, afraid to hear what she might tell me. I sensed her above me, heard the rustle of her robe as she leaned over to softly kiss me. More footsteps crossed the room, my father's.

"I'm going to the hospital now," he whispered to my mother. "I'll call you when I know something. Mama's still in the kitchen. See if you can get her to go back to bed."

They walked away, my father toward the front door, my mother back to the kitchen. I heard him drive away and waited for the kitchen light to go out, waited for the sound of footsteps going up the stairs. When daybreak lightened the green of the curtains and softened the shadows in the room, they were still there, and they were still there when the phone rang.

For the next several years when other children screamed with excitement at the sound of sirens and ran to see the flashing lights, I covered my ears and silently begged the ambulances not to come to my house. One had taken my grandfather away, and he had not come back.

I knew that since that night I had an aversion to the sight of illness or injury. Yet there had been no other emergency, no need to call an ambulance for someone in my family. So I had not known the old illogical fear was still there, still strong. But it was.

I felt tears, cold on my cheeks, and wiped them away.

I looked again toward the woods where the lush evergreens and the tall hardwoods grew, where the thick underbrush reached out to entangle and to snare. I walked again to the fence. The woods, looming darker now, led to the Rapidan River, where unexpected cuts in the high banks, often hidden by dense growth, dropped down to the rough waters.

Maybe this time, I thought. "Matt! Justin!" I called. The breeze whipped my words away and then threw them back to me.

It was then that I heard the siren. I turned and saw the red flashing lights as the ambulance rounded the curve and started down the open stretch of road which led to the farm. Brian and David stood waiting, then walked to meet the people as they got out.

The red light atop the ambulance continued to rotate silently, casting its beams into the night, so that where I stood, beyond the light's perimeter, seemed even darker.

Hesitantly I approached them and saw John Beery. His son was in Dave's class at school. "Hi, Pat," he said, looking up from a map he was studying.

"Hi, John," I responded, walking closer. David came to me and put his arm around my shoulder. I saw Howie Crain and Ed Law, both neighbors, friends. Each smiled and spoke to me. Ed squeezed my hand.

Then more help arrived from Lake of the Woods and Mine Run and Richardsville.

They gathered information from us and assembled in small groups with maps and flashlights and radios. John was in charge and he sent them into the woods to look for our sons.

At 11:00, still others arrived with food and coffee. Fresh teams headed out as the first ones trickled back for sandwiches and drinks and a brief rest. One search party radioed from deep in the woods that they couldn't get back out through the heavy underbrush. John sent in a brush truck to cut a path for them.

At 1:30 A.M., John called for the Virginia Search and Rescue Dog Association unit. When Bill and Linda Dickerson responded with their German shepherds, we gave them articles of the boys' clothing and they began their trek into the woods. Several years and 180 search missions later, Linda would tell me that the terrain they covered that night was the roughest they have ever encountered.

John conducted the search from the picnic table where, what seemed like an eternity before, our families had sat together. I stayed on the bench beside John, waiting, with Jennifer asleep in my arms. Lynda had put Jenny to bed and was helping in the kitchen, where more food had arrived. Brian and David and the two older boys were in the woods with the search parties.

At 3:00, John radioed the dispatcher and asked him to contact the rescue helicopters in Richmond. They were to respond at dawn.

Someone brought me a blanket. I wrapped it around Jennifer. On the opposite hillside the fluorescent collars of the search dogs gleamed. Coffee was handed to me. Jennifer stirred. Night passed.

The first sign of dawn came at 5:15. As the golden rays of sunlight reached above the horizon, word came that the helicopters were fueled and ready.

At 5:55, Matt and Justin were found.

They were one mile from the farm, huddled together between two downed trees. They were cold and hungry and scratched, but they were safe. They were alive.

They had ventured too far into the woods and had been trapped by the sudden darkness. They'd lost their way, moving in the wrong direction until they were too tired and too afraid to continue. They had heard rescuers call to them and had responded, but were not able to make themselves heard. Disoriented by the intensely dark night, they could not determine from which direction the calls had come.

They refused to be carried back. They walked out of the woods and down the hill to the farmhouse.

Cheers shattered the morning silence.

Several days later I talked with Ed Law. As we discussed that long night, he told me that after dark it's almost impossible to find anyone in such surroundings.

"Well, why," I asked, somewhat surprised, "why did all of you stay?"

Just as surprised, he asked me, "Do you think we could have left you?"

So we wrote a note of thanks and made a donation to the Lake of the Woods Volunteer Rescue Squad. But how can "thank you" be enough when "thank you" is what you say to someone who passes you the salt or holds the door open for you when your arms are full?

We had called for help and these people had responded. They came and they calmed our fears with their knowledge and assurance. They gave us hope with a touch, a look, with simply being there.

They had come with lights and sirens and had been faceless strangers to me until I left my pocket of darkness and walked into the light where they stood.

# Chapter 4

I TIGHTENED THE jib as we rounded the last mark. "Let it out," David yelled. "We're getting backwinded." I loosened the sheet and ducked my head as the boom swung across. We tacked once more and headed for the finish line.

John Beery and his wife, Yvonne, had introduced us to the sport of sailing shortly after our long night together on the Hall's farm. At John's prodding, we'd bought a secondhand daysailer, joined the Lake's sailing club and entered the fall racing series.

The sudden blare of the horn resounded over the open water as we crossed the finish line. "I think we did it," David said, smiling broadly. When the results were tallied, our handicapper announced that of the twelve boats in the race, we had finished first and the Beerys second.

We docked in the marina next to them. John was quietly lowering his sails. "Hey, Beery," David said, "what happened to you? Did you have your anchor down?"

John growled back at him, "Who taught you everything you know?"

"Kind of reminds you of the kids, doesn't it?" I said to Yvonne.

"John takes his sailing very seriously," she told me. "He grew up on Long Island. His father was a sailor."

I smiled. "Well, David's from Arkansas and his father's a minister, but I think the Long Island sailor is rubbing off on him."

"Preacher's kid, huh?" John said. He was kneeling on the dock, folding his sails. "You gotta watch out for those."

John was overweight and balding. He was opinionated, competitive, and argumentative. He lacked grace. He could appear aloof. But he was funny. He had a dry sense of humor and laughter that crackled.

"Not this preacher's kid," I said, wrapping my arms around David's waist. "Come on, skipper," I told him, "let's get this champion vessel stripped of her sails and get something to eat."

David turned to John and Yvonne. "Come join us."

After supper our children played in the park adjoining our property and the four of us took our coffee out on the deck. We sat in lawn chairs with our feet propped up on the railing. The trees around us were still full, but there were spaces between the branches where I could look up and see the stars. I reached out and took David's hand.

"Good race today, guys," John said to us.

"Thanks, John," I said. "It was fun."

"One of these days," David told John, "I'm really going to beat you."

"You beat me today."

David shook his head. "No, not in handicap. I'm going to be the first across the line."

John laughed. "Bullshit."

"What is that noise?" I asked. "That beep-beep."

John's feet hit the deck. "Where's my pager?"

"I thought you left it at home," Yvonne said.

"No, it's in my jacket," John said, standing up.

"Do you have to go?" she asked.

"I don't know yet," he answered her. He opened the sliding door and went inside. Seconds later he returned with his jacket in one hand, his pager in the other. "Structure fire," he said. "Gotta go."

"Did it say that?" I asked him, but he was already halfway down the steps.

"Can one of you take Yvonne and the kids home?" he yelled up at us as he got into his car.

"Sure," David answered him.

John switched on his emergency flashers, pulled quickly out of the driveway and was gone.

"Yvonne," I said, "how did he know it was a structure fire? Did that information come over the pager?"

"Yes," she sighed. "The dispatcher sets off the tones and then gives the announcement."

"I wish I could have heard it," I said. "All I heard was 'beep-beep.' "

"I've been hearing 'beep-beep' for five years now," Yvonne said. "When we sit down to eat, when we're sound asleep and, worse, when we're making love."

"Talk about coitus interruptus," David said, grinning.

Yvonne continued, ignoring David. "He's the assistant fire chief now and I think he feels he has to respond to all the fires."

"And rescue duty on top of that," I said.

"Yeah, every fourth night. Most members don't do both but you know John. And now that he's a cardiac technician, he ends up running more than just his one night."

"That's a lot of time to give away. For nothing," David said.

"He doesn't look at it that way," Yvonne remarked.

"I don't think he's giving it away for nothing either," I told David.

He shrugged. "What does he get for it?"

"Quite a lot, I imagine."

Yvonne nodded. "Yes, I think he does. Pat," she said, "he's determined to get you on the rescue squad."

"I know he is. He doesn't let up. Lou's still after me, too. She called me last week to tell me an EMT class is starting in October." I shook my head. "I don't understand why they're so insistent."

"I think it all began the night the boys were lost," she said. "You were so calm."

"I didn't feel very calm."

"John said you weren't one of those hysterical women who just make it harder for everyone else."

I laughed. "John has such a way with words."

"Pat," she said, "everyone feels comfortable with you. You're good with people."

"Not if they're bleeding," I told her, then turned to David. "Right?"

"Yes, take her word for it, Yvonne," he said. "In an emergency, she's useless."

I looked back at him. "Useless?"

He nodded. "Totally."

We finished our coffee, then David took Yvonne and her two children home. Jennifer came out on the deck and crawled into my lap.

"Tired?" I asked her.

She sat up straight. "No!"

I smiled at her. "Good," I said. "I wanted you to look at the stars with me. Lean back against me and rest your legs on mine."

We sat quietly. Soon I heard her breathing deepen. I touched my lips to her hair, then rested my head against hers.

Useless.

"Useless," I said aloud. The word itself sounded offensive.

But I knew he was right.

I certainly had been useless with the boys. When Dave, at two, was bitten in the mouth by a dog, the emergency room nurse had taken one look at me and asked me to stay in the waiting room while they sutured him. Matt was five years old when an older boy, practicing golf swings with a nine iron, hit him near the left temple. David covered the wound with a dark towel before taking him to the emergency room.

"So Matt couldn't see the blood?" I asked David later.

"No," he answered. "So you couldn't."

But it wasn't just with my children. It wasn't only with family and friends. It was anyone.

When I was a junior in high school my mother would sometimes drop me off on her way to work at a nearby elementary school. One early fall morning as our car neared my school, a boy ran into the street just as a delivery truck was passing by.

Whether the boy had simply misjudged the distance or the truck had suddenly slowed was unknown, but he ran into the truck's sharp rear side. The driver, unaware of the accident, drove away. At that moment, the only people who could help the boy were my mother and me.

My mother hurriedly parked the car and rushed to help him. "Come on, Pat," she said to me.

I eased my door open, got out and slowly walked toward him. Blood flowed from his mouth and from a deep cut on the side of his head. His legs were jerking sluggishly, like a slow motion of a warped film. When I finally stood over him, he looked up at me. His lips were moving, but his words were indistinct. I turned away.

"Pat," my mother spoke to me. She was kneeling beside him, quietly talking to him. She had pressed her scarf against the laceration on his head, but the blood was seeping through her scarf between her fingers.

"Pat," she said again, louder. "Go to school and tell Mr. Miller to call an ambulance."

I had been given a command, something on which my mind could focus, a direction to take me away from him and the crowd of curious spectators now gathered around him. I walked the short distance to school and entered the cool, locker-lined hallway.

The bell rang as I walked past the principal's office and on to my first period classroom. I sat down at my desk and rubbed my hands across the comforting smoothness of its wood.

Soon I heard sirens. I glanced out the window and caught a glimpse of the red flashing lights as the ambulance passed. Someone had called. Someone else.

The boy was in the hospital a long time. I saw him when he returned to school. His hair was short and the long red scar clearly visible and when his eyes met mine, I looked away.

I didn't tell my mother that I hadn't gone to Mr. Miller's office. She would have asked why and I wouldn't have known how to answer her.

So many times I have wished I could have that day back again.

David and I sailed each weekend until ice formed in the shallow water of the coves. When winter settled around us, the children and I built a snow family in the front yard, complete with a dog and two cats. In the evenings we gathered around the living room fireplace.

"What can we do?" Jennifer asked one night. She was nestled in my lap, watching the fire. I looked down at her. Almost four. In a matter of months she would start nursery school. I wondered where the time had gone, and why so fast.

"You are getting so big," I said to her.

She sat up and faced me. "What can we do, Mom?"

I smiled at her. "Want to do something sloppy?"

"Yeah. What?"

"If you can get the paper away from Daddy," I whispered to her, "we can papier-mâché."

She grinned and nodded, then slowly eased herself off my lap and walked to David. Leaning against his chair, she glanced back at me, reached out and grabbed the newspaper from him.

"I got it, Mom," she squealed.

David watched as she ran into the kitchen. "What is she doing?" he asked.

"She's going to cut up the newspaper so we can papier-mâché," I told him.

"Oh, no!" He shook his head.

"Just kidding," I said, mussing his hair as I headed toward the kitchen. "You want to do something sloppy?"

"Not if you mean papier-mâché," he laughed.

Jennifer gave his newspaper back to him, then gathered a stack of old ones from the magazine rack. She asked Dave and Matt if they wanted to help, but absorbed in "Dungeons and Dragons," they also passed.

"We'll practice with a bowl," I told her. "Then we'll do a balloon. You want to cut or mix?"

"Mix," she said.

"I was afraid of that. Just try to get as much flour in the mixing bowl as you get on you."

I found my scissors, sat down at the table and started cutting the newspapers into strips. My attention was more on Jennifer than on what I was doing, then halfway through the second paper the word *squad* caught my attention, but not before I had already sliced the article into three pieces.

30

"Daddy, come see what I'm doing," Jennifer called.

David walked into the kitchen. "You're a mess," he said as he laid his newspaper on the counter. "It's all yours, sweetheart." He looked at me. "Are you doing papier-mâché or working a puzzle?" he asked.

"I'm just trying to read this article," I told him.

"Wouldn't it have been easier to read before you cut it up?"

"Now, why didn't I think of that?" I responded.

I had two-thirds of it, enough to see that the subject was the need for volunteers on area rescue squads. Some squads had serious problems because of the shortage, especially during daytime hours.

I picked up my scissors and continued cutting.

By the end of the evening, all five of us had made something out of the papier-mâché. We went through a whole bag of balloons and five pounds of flour and left an assortment of oddly-shaped creations on all the kitchen counters.

"We've got to stop," David said, "before we start on each other."

I gathered everyone's dirty clothes and put them in the laundry basket. When I took off my jeans, the two pieces of newspaper fell out of the back pocket. I picked up the strips off the floor and started for the trash can, but instead, I pulled open my desk drawer and dropped them inside.

That September Jennifer started nursery school. I used the first several mornings of my free time to thoroughly clean the house. I was amazed at the number of crayons I retrieved from under the sofa and chair cushions. On the third morning I finished the bathrooms, which were last on my list, and still had thirty minutes before it was time to pick up Jennifer. The house was clean. Plans for my Cub Scout meeting the next day were complete. My spaghetti sauce simmered on the stove.

I poured myself a cup of coffee, carried it onto the deck, and sat down in the old rocking chair I'd used for each of the children. I sat quietly, feeling the warmth of the cup against my hands.

"So," I said aloud, "what now?"

I could renew my teacher's certificate. It would be easy with two colleges close by, easy and predictable, for that's what former teachers do when their children are all in school. Security meant knowing what to expect. My life was secure and easy and predictable, like the seasons and their progressions.

Was that still enough?

Was I being moved through life, I wondered, instead of setting my own course? Too many baby steps and too few giant ones? "Mother, may I?" played on the front sidewalk that ran between the maple trees long ago, with home base far, far away. Baby steps were safer, but you couldn't win the game. Giant steps were harder, riskier, but they got you there.

And was I in any way giving enough back to life for what it had given me? My life was good. Many lives were not. If life is a barter, was I then a cheater, giving too little for all that I was taking?

I looked into the surrounding woods. Leaves were gently falling in the soft breeze. Before long the branches would be covered with snow. I thought of those nearby woods where Matt and Justin were lost and about the people who had given so much of themselves that night.

"We really need people during the day," Lou had told me.

"John is determined to get you on the rescue squad," Yvonne had said. "You're good with people."

It would be hard. It would be risky.

I carried my empty cup into the house, switched off the burner and picked up the car keys. Jennifer was grinning broadly and waving to me as I pulled up in front of the nursery school.

I gave her a big hug and kiss. "How was school?" I asked, tightening her seat belt.

"It's getting better," she said. "I think I'm going to like it. I got to paint today."

"Great! We're going to paint in Scouts tomorrow. You want to help?"

"Sure, Mom," she said, sounding quite the authority on painting.

"Want to go get a Slurpie?" I asked her.

"Yeah!"

It was a short distance to the 7-11. As we approached our turn I saw, just beyond the intersection, the lights of the ambulance and two cars that had collided.

Jennifer craned her neck to see. "Look," she said, pointing, "it's a wreck."

"Yes," I said. I pulled into the 7-11 parking lot and parked facing the accident. I saw Lou there, leaning over the patient on the gurney. She was holding his hand and talking to him.

"Jennifer," I spoke softly. "I want to do that."

She turned and looked at me. "Do what?" she asked.

"What Mrs. Potter's doing. See her?"

"Yeah, Mom, I see her. That'd be neat. Can I have my Slurpie now?"

I gave her hand a squeeze. "You bet."

On our way home Jennifer and I stopped by John's office to return his sailing manuals. He was on the phone when we walked in and motioned for us to sit down. Jennifer threaded paper clips into a necklace.

When he hung up, he glanced at the books. "All through with them?" he asked.

"For quite a while," I confessed. "Sorry it took me so long to return them." I looked around his office. "Where's your pager?" I asked. "There was a wreck at Routes 3 and 20."

"I didn't even bring it today. I've got too much work to do. Was it bad?"

I shook my head. "No, it didn't look bad. I think they only had one patient."

He was grinning at me. "You looked, huh? There must not have been any blood."

I gave him a good-natured scowl and stood up. "Thanks for the manuals," I said, placing them on his desk. "They were a big help. David says we're going to beat you in every race."

"Bullsh . . ."

"John," I interrupted. I took Jennifer's hand and turned to go.

He followed us to the door. "Well," he said, "now that you know everything there is to know about sailing, you ready to join the rescue squad? I mean anybody who can ride a trapeze on a sailboat can face a little blood.''

I stopped and looked back at him. "Yes," I nodded. "I think I am."

"Is this a joke?" David asked me when I told him. I sat on the floor folding clothes still warm from the dryer.

"No, I'm serious," I told him. "I want to see if I can do it."

He sat on the sofa facing me. He shook his head slowly. "Pat, this isn't something you can just try, you know, like golf or sailing. What would you say to a person in a wreck if you got there and couldn't do anything? 'Sorry, fellow, I thought I could help you but I can't.' Honey, why don't you try something else, if you just want to do something?''

"I don't want to just do something," I said. "I want to do this."

He sighed. "Did you let John talk you into it?"

"No, not John or Lou or anybody. It was my decision, mine. Look, David, I can't really explain it," I admitted, "but I just believe that IF I can do it, I will be good at it."

"Pat, you can't even look at blood. You won't be able to bandage somebody with your eyes closed."

"And that's another thing," I said. "I've always accepted that fear like . . . well, like I've accepted the color of my eyes. It was a part of me and there was nothing I could do about it."

"I like the color of your eyes," he said.

"Thank you." I got up and sat next to him on the sofa. I took his hand. "David," I said, trying to find the words to explain this thing that was still somewhat of a mystery to me. "I think I can give more. I want to be more. I want to go beyond where I am."

He looked at me. Then he shrugged. "Go for it."

I leaned against him. "Thank you for understanding."

"I'm not so sure I do," he said.

"That's okay," I told him. "I'm not sure I do either."

Several days later my mother called. My parents were still residents of Salem, Virginia, my hometown. We discussed the children and the latest events in each of our households. Then I told her about my plans.

The line was so still I thought we'd been disconnected.

Finally, her voice broke the silence. "You're going to join the rescue squad?"

"Yes." I nodded to her across the miles.

"The rescue squad?" she asked again.

I heard the extension phone lifted and my father's voice. "Hi, honey. How's everything?"

"Great."

"The kids?"

"They're fine. They'll be sorry they missed your call. The boys are exhausted from this weekend's campout and Jennifer is still trying to adjust to her nursery school schedule. They're all sound asleep."

"Give them our love. Tell them we're coming to see them next month."

"Don't forget your baseball glove again," I told him.

He laughed. "Don't worry. I won't make that mistake twice. Uh, did I hear Mom say somebody joined the rescue squad?"

"Her," my mother said. "Pat."

"You?" he said to me.

"Me," I told him. "But I haven't joined yet."

"Second thoughts?"

"No. I just have to get my application in. I start the EMT class in two weeks."

"EMT?"

"Emergency Medical Technician," I explained.

"Emergency Medical Technician," he repeated. "Sounds serious."

"Yes," I agreed. "It does."

"Well," he said, "I'm sure you'll be good at it."

I smiled to myself. "I hope so," I told him.

We said our goodbyes and I returned to the living room.

"Was that your folks?" David asked.

"Yeah."

"How are they doing?"

"Fine," I said. "I imagine they think I've lost my mind."

He looked up from his book. "Or going through a phase."

"I think that I am a little old for a phase," I told him.

I walked back to our bedroom, sat down at my desk, and looked at the application to become a member of the Lake of the Woods Rescue Squad. It was complete. I folded it and slipped it into the envelope addressed to Rescue Captain Joseph Maiden.

I still had the envelope in my hand when David came in. He stood in front of me. "Pat, I've got to admit I have trouble imagining you doing this, but . . . " He hesitated.

I looked up at him. "But?"

"I think you can do it," he said. "I think you'll be good at it."

"Thank you."

I appreciated his thoughtfulness, his expression of confidence, but silently I questioned his sincerity, just as I had questioned my father's. They knew my history.

It was months later that I realized they had been right.

I was good at it.

# Chapter 5

TWENTY-FIVE PEOPLE STARTED the Emergency Medical Technician class with me. Seven months later, sixteen finished. I understood what drove the others away. Quitting crossed my mind more than once.

It had been fifteen years since I'd had to retain information more complicated than a baby's formula, phone numbers and simple directions. I'd majored in English in college and had once memorized long passages from *Hamlet*. Now I forgot the recipe ingredient while reaching for the measuring cup.

To add to my difficulty, I was faced with studying the very subject for which I had always had an aversion, but neither of these was the pivotal reason for my wanting to quit.

The Tuesday evening prior to my second class I secluded myself in the bedroom, pulled out the old card table and laid out my textbook, workbook, glasses and pens and sat down. David was at an Optimist Club meeting. The children were in the living room watching the "A-Team."

I was on the second page of the chapter on chest injuries when Jennifer burst into the room. "Matt has my doll and he won't give it to me," she wailed, pushing her way onto my lap, knocking my notebook to the floor.

"Matt," I yelled, "give her the doll. Now!"

I kissed her and gave her a quick hug, then eased her off my lap and leaned over to retrieve my workbook. She gave me a backward glance and walked out, leaving the door ajar. I got up and closed it.

Twenty minutes later Matt opened it.

"Can you hem my pants now?" he asked me, his arms folded across his chest.

I looked over my reading glasses at him. "Why now?"

"You said you'd do it by Wednesday and tomorrow's Wednesday."

"So it is," I sighed. "All right. Get your pants and my pins," I told him. I marked my place and closed the book.

By the end of the evening I had read four pages, completed one page of my workbook, hemmed a pair of pants, retrieved a doll and tucked three children into bed.

"This isn't going to work," I muttered to myself as I sat back down at 11:15 to try to finish the chapter.

David was putting on his pajamas. "What?"

"I said I don't think this is going to work. I get started and then there's an interruption," I told him. "Now it's quiet and I'm too tired to read."

"You just have to organize your time," he said, getting into bed. "That's all."

"Sounds so simple."

"It is. Now, come get in bed with me and you can get organized tomorrow."

"In a minute," I told him, concentrating on a diagram of the lungs. "I didn't know the right lung has three lobes and the left lung has just two."

"Very interesting," he said, rolling onto his side. Soon I heard him snoring.

I took off my glasses and laid them on the table. I closed my book, slowly. The pages slid across my fingers.

I got up from the table, undressed, then switched off the light and got into bed, moving close to David.

He stirred, turned over and put his arm around me. "That's more like it," he said.

He wasn't used to sharing me, not even with a textbook. Nor were the children.

I wanted to go beyond where I was, not abandon it. I had

always been and would continue to be there for each of them, but realized I also had to be there for me.

They weren't used to sharing me and I wasn't used to the guilt.

I worked on organizing my time, fitting my study hours around David's schedule and the children's. I looked forward to my weekly classes at Germanna Community College. It felt good to be back in a classroom. It was also exhilarating to discover that my brain would still function after all.

I was amazed at how little I knew about the human body. The more I learned the more I wanted to know. I combed bookstores and libraries searching for additional books on anatomy, illnesses and injuries.

I was so euphoric over my newly acquired knowledge that I often forgot that this class was a means to an end and not an end in itself.

My application to join the rescue squad passed from Captain Joseph Maiden through the Personnel and Grievance Committee to the Fire and Rescue Board of Directors and then to the membership. It was quite a process to become a volunteer.

"Congratulations!" Captain Maiden called to give me the news. "You are now a member of the rescue squad."

"I am?" I said.

"You sure are," he told me. "Now, when can you start running?"

"Running," is a part of the squad idiom. A rescue call is a "run" and when you go on a call, you are "running." I wasn't ready and I told him, "Not until I finish the class."

"You don't have to wait till then, Pat," he said. "You can run now."

"I know but I think I'll have to wait until the class is over."

"Well, you'll have to start coming to training meetings." His voice sounded flat. "They're on the third Tuesday of each month."

I assured him I would, thanked him for calling with the news and hung up. I knew he wanted me to start right away, but I couldn't run days until Jennifer started kindergarten and David didn't want me to be on night duty. So as far as the Captain was concerned, I was dead weight.

It was months later when he admitted to me, "You know, I never thought you'd amount to anything." Then he slipped his arm around me and added, with that crooked smile of his, "But I think I was wrong."

We had three weeks of CPR instruction, then had to undergo a rigid examination. I was first in line and felt very confident. The CPR instructor had me start over four times and when I was finally through with the test, my mouth felt like cotton.

That same night we were also tested on the procedures to use on victims of upper airway obstruction, or choking. These patients are often referred to as "café coronaries," because while eating they suddenly slump over as if suffering a heart attack. If we suspect they are choking we ask, "Can you talk?" If they can, their airway is open. If they can't, we begin the procedure.

One evening while Christmas shopping in a nearby mall, the children and I stopped for some ice cream. The four of us were sitting together going over some of our Christmas lists and enjoying the much needed break when I heard a man at the adjoining table ask his wife if she was all right. I glanced back and saw his expression of concern. His wife was seated directly behind me.

"Are you choking?" he asked her. I turned around and saw her nod.

"Mama, it's dripping," Jennifer said. I picked up my napkin and handed it to her, then turned back around.

"Ask her if she can talk," I said to the man.

I waited, poised, ready to move, while he asked her. The woman coughed, then turned to me and nodded. She could talk. "Thank you," she said.

I smiled at them and turned back to the children.

Dave was red-faced. "Mom," he said, then leaned closer to me and whispered, "why did you ask her if she could talk?"

"That's what we're taught," I started to explain. "She could talk. That meant her airway was open. She wasn't choking."

"Can Matt and I go to the arcade?" he asked.

He hadn't really wanted to know my reason for asking the question but rather why I, his mother, had done such a thing in a public place.

I looked at my watch. "Meet Jennifer and me at the pet store in half an hour. Do you have some quarters?"

He nodded back to me.

I turned to Jennifer and wiped the chocolate ice cream off her face. "Do I embarrass you, too?" I asked her.

"I don't know," she said. "What does that mean?"

"Come on." I took her hand, smiling down at her. "Let's go see Santa Claus."

Before class the next week I told our instructor, Mark Hood, about what had happened. When class began he asked me to repeat it. I didn't understand why he felt it was significant enough to share.

"The thing that is important," he said when I was through, "is that Pat didn't hesitate to try to help that woman."

I thought back on it and realized that he was right. I hadn't hesitated. My response had been automatic. That split second when I turned to the woman to help her was the first time my knowledge overshadowed my fear.

That same involuntary reflex would again and again cause my head to turn, my hands to move, my feet to hit the floor, and my brain to come awake from a deep sleep because someone was hurt or sick or dying.

But that night was the beginning.

The weeks went by quickly. Robins appeared. Winter had passed.

In class I had a perfect attendance and was maintaining a high "B" average. I had attended all the monthly squad meetings and training sessions. By late March we had covered all the body systems. Our vocabulary stretched from alveoli to zygoma. We'd learned to take a patient's vital signs; pulse, blood pressure, and respirations. I was saturated with medical knowledge and performing well in classroom patient-rescuer simulations. My confidence soared.

Then Mark told us it was time to do our twelve hours of work in the emergency room at Mary Washington Hospital.

I still had not been on a rescue call. I'd never been responsible for a real patient. I hadn't even been close to one.

The scenarios we practiced in class were hypothetical. The emergency room was real.

I was first to go, but not alone. Linda Dickerson was my partner for the first six-hour shift. Linda and I had enjoyed becoming re-acquainted after that long night she and Bill spent with their search dogs looking for Matt and Justin.

We picked a Monday night because it sounded safer than the weekend. What we didn't know was that there is no safe time in an emergency room.

We were supposed to wear our rescue squad jumpsuits. I called Joseph several days before I was scheduled to work and told him what I needed. When I stopped by his house he gave me summer and winter uniforms and a jacket.

"These are really nice," I told him. The jumpsuits were white with blue lettering on the back: LAKE OF THE WOODS RESCUE SQUAD. The orange jacket had identical lettering.

"They're used but they're in good shape," he told me. "They don't even have any bloodstains on them. But it won't be long," he said. "Will it, Pat?"

I wasn't going to do anything else to shake his confidence in me.

"No," I agreed. "It won't be long."

"We will ask you to get the patient's chart and do the vitals, pulse, respiration, blood pressure, and temperature." The emergency room nurse gave us our instructions. "Replace the chart when you're through," she added. "Any questions?"

I had a million. I shook my head. "No."

"Are you as nervous as I am?" I asked Linda.

"At least," she answered. "Let's try to stay together. Okay?"

"Just try to lose me," I said.

I glanced at the clock. "It's already 5:15," I told her. "We only have five hours and forty-five minutes left."

We wandered through the corridors. There were only two patients in the fourteen-bed ER. "That's what has me worried," I told Linda as we passed the ambulance entrance, "anything that comes through there."

We walked into the nurses' lounge. Linda headed for the bathroom. "Hurry up," I asked her and sat down to wait.

"Pat." I heard the nurse's voice. She entered the lounge. "Pat. That's your name. Right?"

I hesitated, then nodded.

"I've got a patient for you," she said.

I glanced at the bathroom door.

"Come on," she insisted.

I followed her out of the lounge and into the nurses' station. She removed a clipboard from a hook on the wall. "Chart's on here," she said. She pointed to a curtained off area. "Bay 1."

She pushed the clipboard toward me.

I took it from her.

Please, God, don't let me mess up, I silently prayed as I walked toward Bay 1. I eased the curtain open. The strong odor of whiskey greeted me. I stepped inside and closed the curtain behind me and faced my first patient.

"Good evening, sir," I said, approaching him. I had always imagined patients lying down. This one was sitting up, facing me.

"I would like to take your vitals," I told him. My voice was shaky, my throat like sandpaper.

He looked at me. Under heavy lids, his eyes were half closed.

"Honey," he slurred, "you can take anything of mine you want."

Reluctantly, I took his hand, found his pulse and counted, then recorded it, 84. I could feel his eyes still on me. I wrapped the blood pressure cuff around his arm, inflated it, put my stethoscope in my ears, slowly turned the gauge to release the pressure and waited, listening. 140/80. I wrote it on the chart.

My hands were shaking so badly I was afraid I might break the thermometer on his teeth. "Under your tongue, please," I said, hoping he would think he was the one with the tremors.

"I'll put it anywhere you want me to, cutey-pie," he said around the thermometer.

I picked up the chart and tried to focus my attention on it while I waited for the thermometer to register. Respirations! Damn! I'd forgotten the respirations. We'd been taught to take patients' respirations immediately after taking their pulse, while we're still holding their hands. That way, they don't know we're monitoring their breathing. Often, if they know what we're doing they become conscious of their breathing and we don't get an accurate count.

But I refused to take his hand again. Instead, I looked at his chest, watching it rise and fall, counting, and hoping he wouldn't notice: 16. I recorded it and pulled the thermometer from his mouth. Normal. I wrote that down and turned to go.

"Did you see something you like, honey?" For a drunk, he didn't miss a thing.

I kept my back to him. "I'll check on you in a few minutes" was all I could think to say.

"I'll be waiting," he called to me as I pulled open the curtain. I hurriedly closed it with a great sense of relief.

Linda was coming down the corridor and I walked to meet her.

"Pat," she said, "I had the sweetest little lady. She'd hurt her foot and I got to take her to X-ray."

"You get the sweet lady," I told her. "I get the drunk."

"You had a drunk patient?"

Before I could even begin to tell my story, our nurse reappeared.

"You two can check on a girl with a possible appendicitis in Room 4," she said. She handed me the chart. "Get her undressed."

The girl had severe pain in her lower right quadrant. She was nauseated and had a temperature of 101 degrees. Classic signs of appendicitis. We helped her undress and slipped one of those awful hospital gowns on her. She was obviously frightened so we stayed with her while the doctor waited for the results of her blood test. After my first patient, it was a pleasure to be with her. I told Linda, "As long as we're behind a closed door, maybe our nurse won't find us."

I was wrong. The door opened. "Could I see you for a minute?" she said. She was looking at me.

I walked out into the corridor with her.

"Did you do something with Mr. Saunders?" she asked.

"Who?"

"Mr. Saunders," she repeated. "Bay 1. Did you move him?"

"No. I didn't move him," I told her. "Isn't he still there?"

She shook her head. "No," she said. "He's gone."

"Could he have just left?" I asked. "Just walked out?" I'd always thought that once that plastic band was on your wrist, you were hospital property.

"He could have," she said, almost smiling. "A lot of them do." She shrugged and walked away.

I started to laugh. When Linda joined me several minutes later, I told her, "Please don't tell Mark that I lost my first patient. Literally."

At 8:30, we took a coffee break in the lounge. We sat with two of the nurses, and their attitude toward us had warmed. I could understand their initial reservations. After all, this was their territory and we had invaded it. Each year they had to put up with a barrage of EMT students, some well prepared, some not. They had to learn us individually.

"You two are doing a good job tonight," one of them said.

Linda and I smiled in appreciation.

I was glad she hadn't seen me with my first patient. I wondered what had become of him. I pictured him sitting on a curb somewhere trying to gnaw the plastic band off his wrist.

The door suddenly opened. "CODE BLUE coming in," the nurse announced. Fredericksburg's Rescue Squad was bringing in a patient in cardiac arrest. Linda and I followed the nurses hurrying out of the lounge.

The doors to the ambulance entrance opened and squad members wheeled the gurney into the corridor toward the cardiac room. One member was kneeling on the gurney doing CPR. Cardiologists were summoned over the hospital intercom.

Inside the cardiac room, orders were given. Hands moved. A nurse squeezed the ambu bag to ventilate the patient. Another nurse started an IV. Arterial blood was drawn to measure blood gases. Machines were wheeled in. Electrodes were applied to the man's chest.

Paddles were charged. "Everybody clear," the doctor ordered. The paddles were placed firmly on the man's chest, and fired. His body jumped from the electrical current. "Again, at 400. Everybody clear." A second firing. "Continue CPR."

I was surprised that the squad member continued to do the CPR. I thought that rescue squad work ended at the Emergency Room entrance. I just assumed that he would be relieved by hospital personnel. I was wrong.

More orders were given, words I didn't recognize or understand, then. "Ventricular fibrillation." "Epi." "Bicarb."

They all focused their attention on the small monitor screen. What they saw there looked to me like nothing more than scribbling, but they made sense of it. "He's converted," the doctor said. They were smiling.

As quickly as he had been wheeled in, the patient was taken away, down the corridor to the intensive care coronary unit. People moved in step beside the gurney, holding IV bags, ventilating, watching the EKG monitor. Linda walked behind them.

I was alone in the room. I looked around. One of his slippers had dropped from the gurney. It was corduroy, dark brown, worn. I picked it up from the floor and placed it on a cart. I hadn't seen his face, not clearly. The oxygen mask had covered it. Nor did I know his name. But neither had most of those working so desperately to salvage his life.

By 10:30, the rooms and all the bays were full. Patients on gurneys and in wheelchairs lined the corridor. Linda and I worked alongside the nurses, and independently. We had proved ourselves. They trusted us. They knew we were there to learn and to help.

At 11:00, as we were preparing to leave, our nurse said to us, "I wish you all could stay. We really could use you."

"I wish we could, too," Linda said.

We couldn't. I had David and the children, lunches to pack

and cookies to bake for Jennifer's nursery school party the next day. Linda had Bill and four children at home.

"We'll be back," I told her.

Everyone was asleep when I got home. I packed the boys' lunches and mixed the cookie dough. Then I opened the refrigerator door and set the bowl of cookie dough inside.

"It'll keep until morning," I said to myself.

I eased into bed, careful not to wake David. I was exhausted, but unable to sleep.

I had done it. I had gone beyond where I once was, taking giant steps.

# Chapter 6

I HAD ONE more six-hour shift in the Emergency Room. This time my first patient stayed. I was more relaxed, more confident. The nurses knew my name and I knew theirs. We talked during our breaks and they included me in their in-house conversations, their private jokes, and they gave me greater responsibilities.

Around the middle of the evening a three-year-old was brought in by his mother. He'd fallen against the sharp edge of a table and had a deep cut on his lower lip. To restrict his movement during the suturing, we placed him in a papoose, a restraining device for children.

"Hold his head perfectly still," the doctor told me.

I looked down at the blonde-haired boy as I held his head firmly, yet as tenderly as possible. His mother stayed with him. His arms were enclosed in the papoose, but she held onto his hand. Hoping he could hear me above his cries, I leaned close and talked to him while the doctor put four stitches in his lip.

I thought of Dave and of that night in another emergency room in another city, and hoped that whoever it was who held his head while the doctor sutured his lip had treated him with the same tenderness.

My shift that night began the way my first shift had ended, with the rooms and bays and corridors filled. There were lacerations and stomachaches, broken bones and chest pains. I learned something from every patient and approached each succeeding one with increased knowledge and understanding.

I was everywhere I could be, wanting to be two, three, four places at once. I saw how a word, a smile, a gentle touch could ease patients' fears and slow down an accelerated heart rate.

David was still awake when I returned home that night and listened patiently while I recounted every single detail.

"If it's the last thing I do," David said to John when he and Yvonne stopped by the following evening, "I'm going to beat you across that finish line."

"Why the sudden need for revenge?" John asked him. "We don't even start racing for two months."

"For Florence Nightingale here," he said, pointing to me.

John grinned. "I knew she could do it."

"I haven't done anything yet," I told him.

"Well, you'll make it long before David beats me across the finish line."

I had tried since October to schedule my study time when David was at work and the boys and Jennifer were in school, but as the months passed and studying became more intense, I found I needed more time. The final exam was less than a month away, so I carried my study cards with me to the grocery store and reviewed them while I waited in the check-out line. I propped them against the toaster while I cooked and laid them on the end of the ironing board, until I scorched one of David's shirts.

Joseph gave me a pager and told me that I should start going on rescue calls whenever I could, that I needed to get some experience before going on a scheduled duty crew. So the first week in May when David asked me what I wanted for Mother's Day, I told him, "If there are any calls that day, I'd like to go on them."

"That's going to be kind of hard to wrap," he said.

On Mother's Day the children fixed my breakfast, then piled into bed with David and me and watched my face as I took my first bite.

"Delicious," I told them.

"I found the recipe," Dave said. "It's a Western omelet."

"I cut up the cheese," Matt said.

"And I cracked the eggs," Jennifer announced.

Matt grinned. "That's why it's full of eggshells."

"It is not," she objected.

"Matt!" David said.

"He's just kidding," I told them, then turned to Matt. "Aren't you, kiddo?"

"Yeah," he nodded. "Sorry, Jennifer."

Matt's my middle child. He's twenty-two months younger than Dave, who has always been self-reliant, secure. He's six years older than Jennifer, the baby of our family. Matt's in a tough spot. He requires a little more patience and a few more hugs. I tell him he is the peanut butter and jelly between my two slices of bread.

After I finished my Western omelet, Matt handed me my gift, a new fishing rod and reel.

"I love it," I told them. "We'll dig up some worms this week and catch that big catfish down at the marina." I hugged each of them. "I've got to be the luckiest mom in the world."

"I'll wash the dishes," Jennifer said when Dave picked up my tray. The three of them headed for the kitchen.

"I'll bet they don't argue about that," David said.

It was an hour later when the tones went off. Jennifer and I were sitting on the living room floor working a puzzle. I glanced at my pager, then looked at David.

"Happy Mother's Day," he said.

"Thank you!" I ran into the bedroom and grabbed my uniform. As I pulled it on over my shorts and shirt, I heard our dispatcher's voice on the pager, "ATTENTION ALL LAKE OF THE WOODS RESCUE SQUAD MEMBERS. WE HAVE A RESCUE CALL ON SKYLINE DRIVE FOR A MAN WHO HAS CUT HIS HAND ON A POWER SAW."

"I love you," I called as I ran past David and Jennifer and out the door, hoping the duty crew wouldn't leave without me.

I switched on my car's emergency flashers as I pulled out of the driveway. It was two miles from our home to the squad building. As I approached it, I saw the lights of the ambulance. They hadn't left. I pulled into the emergency parking area and got out.

Ed Law was standing by the ambulance waiting for the rest of his crew.

"Pat," he called to me as I started toward him, "your flashers are still on." I returned to the car and switched them off.

"Can I go with you?" I asked him.

He smiled at me. "Sure you can," he said. "Hop on."

I got in the back of the ambulance. Joyce Grim was already there. Carmie Witzke jumped on and Ed announced we were en route to the scene. I heard the siren's wail.

"This is my first call," I announced to Joyce and Carmie.

Joyce handed me the clipboard. "This is a good way to begin," she said. "When we get there you fill out the call-sheet."

I looked at it and tried to concentrate on it. Name, address, medical history, nature of injury, type of illness, blood pressure, pulse, respirations, state of consciousness, treatment given, et cetera.

"You don't have to memorize it," Carmie laughed.

I was excited and I was scared. I'm inside an ambulance and going on a rescue call, I thought to myself. I'm really going on a rescue call.

We arrived at the scene. Joyce got off and I followed her down the driveway as Ed backed the ambulance in. Inside the carport a man sat on a stack of lumber, holding his hand in a towel soaked with blood. He looked up at us.

"I think I've cut my finger off," he said.

I was suddenly relieved that Joyce had only given me the responsibility for the chart.

Ed unwrapped the towel from the man's hand. I glanced at his finger before Joyce and Ed began to bandage it. It was attached to his hand by only a thin strand of skin.

I busied myself with recording information as it was presented to me, name, age, vitals, location and extent of injury, and estimated blood loss. It sure looked like a lot to me.

En route to the hospital I rode in the back with Ed and Carmie, watching them with the patient, who was extremely good-natured considering the pain he was in. Ed looked at me and said, "I'm sorry to have gotten you out on Mother's Day."

"Oh, that's all right," I assured him.

We arrived at Mary Washington Hospital ER, transferred the man to the stretcher there, and gave the nurse the information on him. Ed and I rolled our gurney back into the hall to change the sheets.

"Hey, I'm really good at this part," I said.

"So this was your first one?" he asked.

"My very first," I nodded. "This is one of my Mother's Day presents."

"Pat," he laughed, "I'm not even going to ask for an explanation."

On our return to the Lake, Ed drove while Joyce and Carmie and I rode in the back. They explained the layout of the rescue unit, showing me where all the supplies were kept.

"We don't go over this enough in class," Joyce said. She and her husband, Bob, were in my EMT class, but they had been running calls for three months. "It doesn't do you any good to know what it is," she added, "if you don't know where it is."

"When I'm studying for the EMT test, I'm not sure we've gone over anything enough," I said.

"When is it?" Carmie asked. She'd been on the squad for two years, along with Ed.

"Two and a half weeks," I groaned. "I should probably be home studying now, but Joe wanted me to run some calls before I start on a crew. You know," I said, "I thought I would really be more scared than I was, but knowing you're not alone makes all the difference."

"That's what you have to remember," Joyce told me. "You'll always have somebody with you on a call," she said reassuringly. "You'll never be alone."

I believed her.

When we pulled into the driveway of the squad building, Ed glanced at me. "Okay, gal, you've got your first one under your belt. You feel like a pro?"

"Yeah," I answered, "at filling out the chart. I'm ready for another one."

Before he could back the ambulance into the bay, the tones

went off again, this time for a small boy who'd been bitten by a snake.

"Pat, this is your fault," Ed said as we turned right on Route 3.

The call was in neighboring Spotsylvania County, which was one of our first-due areas. En route we collected what we'd need for a snake bite—ice packs and tourniquet.

The boy's mother met us at the door. Her face mirrored her anxiety. "He's in the kitchen," she told us, hurrying ahead. We found the four-year-old boy sitting on the kitchen table, staring intently at the snake bite on his finger.

"He followed his older brother to the pond," his mother said. "He said he put his hand in the water and the snake bit him. Is it bad?" she asked.

"I don't think so," Joyce told her. The examination had revealed that the two tiny holes in his finger had none of the characteristics of a poisonous snakebite. There was no swelling or discoloration.

"It doesn't hurt," the child told us. That was another good sign.

Just to be sure, Ed suggested that we take him in to let the ER doctor look at it. The boy's mother rode in the back of the ambulance with him. On the way to the hospital, he wanted to hear the siren, so we turned it on. We made a puppet for him out of a surgical glove, and he laughed at the face we drew on it. By the time we reached the hospital he'd forgotten all about the snake.

"That was a good call," Ed said, as we again started home. This time I rode beside him. "I needed that one," he added quietly.

"You were on the call several weeks ago for the little girl, weren't you?" I asked him.

He nodded.

She was riding a tractor with her older brother. He had failed to notice the tree stump until it was too late. The impact tilted the tractor and the child lost her balance and fell off. In his frantic effort to steer clear of her, the boy turned in the wrong direction and ran over her.

Ed and other squad members performed CPR on her all the way to the hospital.

"That was the worst call I've ever had," Ed said. "She was only six years old. We worked so hard to save her and all the time I knew it was hopeless." We rode along in silence for a while before he said, "But, you have to try."

I looked over at him. His eyes were focused intently on the road ahead. His brow was furrowed, his lips slightly pursed, his concentration fixed on the memory of the child. There was no way I could really understand what that day must have been like for him. Not then. Not before Jesse. But I could share his loss and grief.

He sighed, glanced at me and smiled. I smiled back at him.

Ed was fifty-eight years old. He'd worked for thirty-one years as an oceanographer in Washington, D.C. before his retirement. I had known Ed and his wife, Betty, for several years. He'd been there the night Matt and Justin were lost.

The only time Ed ever looked fifty-eight was on early morning calls, but then we all did. His hair was thick and dark. He was trim. His eyes were soft, expressive, and he was quiet and gentle.

The day had warmed and we stopped for a Coke. We were halfway to the Lake when we heard the tones go off for the third time that day. A call for a possible broken ankle.

"If we hurry, we can make it," I said eagerly.

"Damn, Pat," Ed frowned at me. "Haven't you had enough for one day?" He radioed the dispatcher and told him to tone out for a second crew. We were too far away to respond.

"But Mother's Day comes just once a year," I told him.

That night Lou called me. "Hey gal," she said, "Ed just told me you went on the calls today."

"I did!"

"So, how did it go?"

"Lou, it was really something."

"Ed enjoyed having you along," she said.

I thought for a moment, then asked her, "Lou, when I go on a team, do you think it could be Ed's?"

"I think that can be arranged."

On May 27, eighteen days after that unforgettable Mother's Day, we took our exam. It included a 100-question written test and a practical exam conducted by the EMS state representative from Richmond. We had to demonstrate for him our skills in bandaging, using oxygen, and assessing patients.

Anything over seventy was passing. The highest grade was ninety-three. I got an eighty-nine.

"Congratulations, folks," Mark said as we prepared to leave our classroom for the last time. "You are all EMTs."

Our patches and certificates would not be presented to us for another month, but that night it didn't matter. I knew what I had done.

I had no concept, however, of what lay ahead for me, down unfamiliar roads, in homes of strangers, and of friends. I sometimes wonder if I had known, if I could have cracked open the door to the future and seen what was on the other side, whether I would have slammed it shut and turned away.

My parents were there when I returned home late that night. They had traveled from Salem to take care of the children while I accompanied David to Dallas, Texas. He was the executive director of a national trade association and his annual convention was scheduled to begin the day after my exam.

They were all waiting up for me—David, my parents, Dave, Matt, and Jennifer. They could see it in my face. I didn't have to say it, but I did.

"You're looking at an Emergency Medical Technician!"

The next day as David and I took our seats aboard the plane bound for Dallas, I said to him, "Don't you feel safe having me with you?"

"Don't know how I made it before," he laughed.

It was a good week. We saw friends we hadn't seen for a year. The last planned activity was a trip to a ranch for horseback riding, a barbecue, and a rodeo. We stuffed ourselves on ribs and the trimmings and then tried to work a little of it off by square dancing.

At dusk the rodeo began. David and I sat in the bleachers

watching the last of the calf roping. The evening was warm and clear, and as I sat there with my arm through his, I found myself wishing for a few more days.

Loud cheers drew my attention back to the ring, where the bronco riding was now going on. As the riding continued, the announcer told of the next event, a donkey race. He called David's name to ride one of the donkeys and I laughed as he walked down from the stands.

"That's what you get for being such a loyal Democrat," I called to him.

The last bronco rider stayed on his horse only a few seconds before being thrown. From where I sat, it looked as if he hit the fence, but he got up and walked out of the ring unassisted.

The donkey races began and as I watched a friend of ours trying to keep his seat, David returned to the bleachers. He motioned for me to come with him.

"Oh, no." I shook my head. "I'm not riding any donkey."

"Pat. Come here," he insisted.

Again I shook my head, but he wasn't giving up. He still gestured for me to come with him.

"Come on. They think that guy broke his arm."

I stood up. "What guy?"

"The rider who hit the fence," he explained. "Come on!"

But where is the ambulance, I thought to myself. There should be an ambulance at a rodeo, an ambulance with crew members and padded splints, with clean fresh cravats and sterile bandages and sparkling tape.

"Where is the ambulance?" I asked David as I stepped down from the bleachers.

"There isn't one," he said over his shoulder as he walked away. I had to hurry to catch up with him.

"Well, there should be an ambulance!"

I followed him to the back of the announcer's stand. There in the dark, crouched down holding his arm, was the bronco rider. Two of his rodeo friends were with him.

I looked around.

There was no ambulance.

There was only me.

When Joyce assured me I'd never be alone, she had not considered rodeos in the dusty flatlands of Texas, nor had I.

I approached the three men. "I'm an EMT," I said. "Can I help?"

"Yes, ma'am," one of them said. "I think Shorty here has broke his arm again."

I took Shorty's arm in my hands. I could feel the break, several inches above the wrist.

"Could we have some kind of light here?" I asked.

One of the men had parked his car close by. He moved it to face us. The heavy silver snaps on the cuffs of Shorty's sleeves sparkled in the glow of the headlights. I tried to unsnap them and couldn't. I would have to cut the sleeve off.

"Do you have any scissors?"

"No." They shook their heads.

"A knife?" I questioned them. Rodeo people surely had knives.

"No, ma'am, no knife either."

No ambulance. No knife.

Shorty groaned in pain.

"We'll need some splints," I told his friends. "Boards, newspapers, or magazines will do."

One man hurried away, then reappeared within minutes with two boards he had broken from a fence. I took one and felt its ragged end.

"Could you even that up a little?" I asked. He knocked the heavy splinters away with his hand.

I couldn't get to Shorty's pulse for the snaps on his shirt. I couldn't even get to the fracture. I placed the boards on either side of his arm. "I need something to tie the boards," I said to the man who had gotten them for me.

He took off his shirt, pulled his undershirt over his head and began tearing it into strips and handing them to me. Shorty was barely able to stand as I wrapped the strips around the boards. "Could you all move the car closer so we can let him sit down?" I asked the men. "I need another piece of your shirt, a larger piece, for a sling." He handed me what was left and somehow I fashioned a sling out of it.

We walked Shorty to the car and put him in the back seat. I supported his arm until he was in as comfortable a position as possible. When I released it, there was blood on my hand.

"We'll take him to the hospital," the man told me.

"It's a compound fracture," I said. "Take it easy with him."

"Same as last time, Shorty," he yelled into the back seat.

Shorty groaned.

"Where is the hospital?" I asked.

"Dallas."

"That's two hours away," I said.

"Yep, right far." He got into the driver's seat. "Thank you, ma'am," he said. The door closed and the car pulled away into the darkness.

My EMT book emphasized the importance of checking the distal pulse before and after splinting. I couldn't even get to the distal pulse. Clothing should be removed from the area of any suspected fracture. There were no scissors, no knives. If it's a compound fracture, the site must be covered with a sterile dressing. Even if I could have gotten to the site of the injury, there were no sterile dressings.

It hadn't been anything like the textbook. I had broken all the rules. But I had taken care of Shorty.

"I did my best, Shorty," I said to the darkness.

I watched the car climb the hill. I watched until there was nothing to see but dust settling on the road, hazy and indistinct in the moonlight.

# Chapter 7

OUR WORKING SPACE is limited, our boundaries narrow and tight. The floor measures forty-five inches in width, a fraction over three yards in length. The gurney fits into locks set squarely in the center, allowing us only eleven inches of room on either side.

In summer it's never cool enough. During the winter months the heater blows so hard we shed our jackets and still perspire.

Not one of us can stand erect. I'm only five-foot-three. Still, I must bend my head.

To the right of the gurney is a long bench, room for a second patient. Beneath the bench are splints of all sizes and the CPR board. On the walls, shelves and cabinets provide specific places for supplies and equipment. In an emergency, we can't afford to lose time searching.

A cabinet to the left of the gurney holds the lifepack, the cardiac monitor and defibrillator. Basic first aid supplies, band-aids, ice and heat packs and bandages, the OB kit and two body bags are stored in the cabinet next to the lifepack.

Our two radios are near the lifepack. We use the HEAR radio for simply informing the hospital we are en route, briefly describing our patient's chief complaint and present condition, our treatment and ETA, estimated time of arrival. The MED radio is for advanced life support calls, when we need to transmit EKG strips to the hospital for the ER physician to monitor.

Next to the radios is the main oxygen outlet, suction cannister and tubing. Above, smaller cabinets contain extra nasal cannulas, face masks and ambu bags.

Our seating space consists of the bench, a small seat opposite it and another by the radios.

The jump bag is on the floor. It holds stethoscopes, various-sized blood pressure cuffs, scissors, penlights, additional paper for recording EKG strips, our drug protocol manual and the EOA tube. It's called a jump bag because when we jump off the ambulance, it goes with us.

At the front of the unit is a larger cabinet. The trauma box fits on one shelf. When we arrive at the scene of a 10-50, the first person off grabs that. In it is a collection of the same basic first aid supplies which are on the unit. Below the trauma box a locked cabinet contains our IV and drug boxes.

In the past six years, within that small space, I have been a participant in victories and in defeats. I have watched lives slip away, but I have also seen life sustained. Because, if a life can be saved, we can do it.


Once a year I return to the Cub Scout Pack. I am no longer a den leader. I go, instead, in my white uniform. My Emergency Medical Technician patch is on the left sleeve, my cardiac technician rocker just beneath it. On my right sleeve is a Lake of the Woods Volunteer Fire and Rescue patch. Over my front left pocket is the American flag and to the right, my nameplate and the star of life.

I talk to the Scouts about what they can do in an emergency. We bandage imaginary wounds and splint imaginary fractures. Then I take them outside to the ambulance. They gather in groups of five and I lead them through. I show them our equipment and explain how we use it to save lives.

Each group sits inside the ambulance with me. They ask questions. They tell me about accidents they have had. When I finish answering their questions and listening to their stories, I give each of them a band-aid from the supply shelf.

Then I tell them about Julian Stanley Wise.

"This all began with a dream he had," I tell them.

"When he was asleep?" one of them will ask.

I smile. "No, the kind of dream you have when you're awake, an idea, a wish you really want to come true, one that takes a lot of work.

"Almost eighty years ago, when he was your age, he saw a boat capsize in the Roanoke River, here in Virginia. The two men in the boat drowned. There were other people on the riverbank too, but no one could help the men."

"Why not?"

"Because they didn't have a boat or any ropes. The men were in deep water far out in the river and there were no strong swimmers in the crowd."

"Was he a Cub Scout?"

"No, they didn't have Cub Scouts then. But he became a Boy Scout and he learned first aid just like you.

"He never forgot how helpless he felt that day on the river and when he grew older he decided that what was needed was a squad of men trained to rescue people. In 1928, he started the very first volunteer rescue squad."

Once, one of the boys looked across at me and asked, "Were you on the rescue squad then?"

I laughed and before I had a chance to answer, his friend nudged him and said, "Of course she wasn't. She said it was a squad of men. So she couldn't have been on that one."

Until his death in 1985, Julian Wise worked to promote the volunteer rescue squad concept. His idea caught on around the state, the nation, and the world. That first rescue squad included ten young men. Today, close to a half a million EMTs continue the service Julian Wise began.

When I joined the Lake of the Woods Volunteer Rescue Squad, it was just over a decade old. The LOW squad, like Julian Wise's, stemmed from a desire to serve and to save. Wise's squad responded to six calls during its first year. Our calls totaled thirty.

The Lake of the Woods Volunteer Rescue Squad began with a Chevy Carryall and a first aid box. Now, sixteen years later, we operate with two fully-equipped Advanced Life Support units, one Shock Trauma unit and a crash truck.

Our service area includes Lake of the Woods' 2,600-acre property in Orange County and adjoining sections of Orange, Culpeper, and Spotsylvania Counties. We are located midway between two area hospitals, Mary Washington Hospital in Fredericksburg and Culpeper Memorial in Culpeper. Because our average ETA to either hospital is close to thirty minutes, Medivac helicopters are also available to us, primarily the chopper from the University of Virginia Medical Center in Charlottesville.

We have three levels of training, the basic Emergency Medical Technician—Ambulance, the second level EMT—Shock Trauma, and the EMT—Cardiac Technician. A Shock Trauma technician is trained to start IVs and administer certain drugs. The Cardiac Technician is the highest level of training. The CT's responsibilities include IV infusion, EKG interpretation, the administration of cardiac drugs, and defibrillation.

In October of 1981, I joined the squad with steps as faltering and unsure as a baby's first. I couldn't imagine saving the life of another human being.

The night I attended my first business and training meeting I walked quietly into the room. Squad Captain Joseph Maiden introduced me. The people, many of whom I already knew, smiled and welcomed me. There was warmth in their handshakes and in their eyes, but I knew they were watching me. I was a member but not yet one of them.

There was nothing personal in their attitude toward me. That is just the way it was and is and will continue to be. In the past six years I've watched many new people walk through that door and face us and I know they see the same thing in me that I saw in those veterans I faced that first night.

We must all prove ourselves. Some don't, but most do.

We are all of different backgrounds. We are men and women, young and old, black and white. We are single, married, separated, divorced. We are laborers, firemen, homemakers, accountants, lawyers, data processors, nurses, teachers. We have different tastes in food, music, books and politics.

We've had disagreements, and we've pouted, argued and misunderstood one another. We've been too sensitive, and we haven't been sensitive enough. We've also been petty and jealous and greedy.

We have our bad times, but we have our good times, too. We are a squad, "a small group of people acting together." We understand each other, and we trust, we forgive, and take care of each other. We laugh together and cry together.

We are a squad.

# Chapter 8

"September 10 . . . no calls . . . couldn't eat . . . folks came."

So I began my journal in a crisp new notebook. As the days extended into months and then years, the pages of my notebook filled. My memories were jotted on backs of EKG strips, bandage wrappers, and scraps of paper tucked into my pockets.

But these words were my first.

September 10 was my first day of duty. My name was now on the roster:

**Day Team 3**
Ed Law
Carmie Witzke
Pat Ivey

It was at the bottom, but it was there. From that day on I had no choice. It wasn't a Mother's Day present. I couldn't pick and choose. It was a commitment. If the tones went off, I had to go.

My duty began at 6:00 A.M. I was on for twelve hours. I got up at 5:15, started the coffee, showered, and packed the children's lunches. At 5:50, I slipped on my white uniform. My EMT patch was a bright blue and gold. I clipped my pager to my belt. I looked so new.

I woke the children at 6:45. They watched me while they ate

their breakfast as I puttered about in the kitchen, cleaning the counter several times, checking and rechecking their lunches.

"Mom, you look really neat," Dave said.

I smiled at him. "Thank you."

"But," he added, "you move kinda funny and your shoulders look high."

"My shoulders look high?"

"Yeah, you know, like this," he said, pulling his shoulders up until they were practically even with his ears.

"Oh, I don't look like that!" I told him. Matt and Jennifer laughed.

"You nervous, Mom?" Dave asked.

"No," I replied. "Well," I conceded, "maybe a little."

"I was nervous when I first went to kindergarten," Jennifer said. "That's what my teacher told us. That's why Brent was crying. Because he was nervous. I didn't cry but my stomach felt funny."

I walked over to her and gave her a hug. "Well, I guess I'm feeling what you felt. But it got better for you, didn't it?"

"Yeah," she answered. "But Brent still cries. I don't think it's ever going to get better for him."

"Hey, Jennifer," Dave said. "You should have seen Matt his first day. He didn't cry. He screamed." Jennifer and Dave laughed.

"Shut up, dummy!" Matt scowled.

"Come on, guys," I said. "Jennifer, go wake up Daddy, please."

"Okay," she said. Dave grinned at Matt. His scowl faded a little.

"Nana and Papa will be here when you all get home from school," I told them.

"All right!" Dave said.

Matt's scowl disappeared. "How long are they going to stay?"

"For the weekend. We're celebrating Nana's birthday."

David came from the bedroom. Jennifer held his hand, pulling him down the hall.

"I'll have two scoops of vanilla," he said when he saw me. Everyone laughed at that, including me.

I didn't sit down much that day. Late in the morning I fixed a piece of toast, took one bite, and threw the rest away. I held bathroom trips to a minimum. I moved around a lot and got practically nothing done. I glanced over my note cards from class, refreshing my memory on diabetes, fractures, heart attacks.

At 2:30, my parents arrived. I fixed a pitcher of lemonade and we sat around the kitchen table talking. The timer on the dryer buzzed, startling me.

"You're going to have to try to be less jumpy," my father told me.

"I look at you in that uniform," my mother said, "and I still can't believe you're actually doing this."

"Well, I haven't really done anything yet."

"You earned that patch."

"I have a feeling," I told her, "that was the easy part."

When the children came home from school that afternoon, they headed straight for their grandparents. "Nana, I love kindergarten!" Jennifer exclaimed and spent the next hour recounting every event she could remember from the last two weeks. Dave and Matt grabbed their football and my father, and the three of them went to the park.

David pulled into the driveway at 5:30, and I started supper.

At 6:00, I took off my uniform.

My first day of rescue squad duty was over.

"So you had an easy day of it," David said to me as we sat down to supper.

"Uh, huh," I nodded.

I smiled to myself as I waited for the fried chicken to come my way. I was famished. My head hurt and the muscles in my neck were sore. I was exhausted. Yes, it had been an easy day.


"Tuesday. September 14 . . . no calls," I wrote the night of my next duty day. At the rate I was going my notebook would last a long time.

On Saturday, my third day of duty, I again got up at the crack of dawn. I didn't know then that only rookies begin their duty day this way. I had not yet seen Ed on an early morning call in his pajamas and wearing a cap to cover his tangled hair.

Saturday's day and night crews are responsible for cleaning the rescue vehicles, making sure the gas tanks are full, sweeping the bays, checking the oxygen and medical supplies.

"This is the fun part," Carmie told me as we lifted the gurney off one of the units. We restocked the cabinets, then scrubbed the floor with disinfectant. Ed moved the second unit outside and I swept the bays.

"I'll probably see you later," Carmie said to me as we walked to the parking lot together.

"You think so?" I asked.

"Beautiful day like this," she nodded, "we'll probably get a call."

I drove home slowly, anticipating the sound of the tones coming from my pager at any moment. As I approached the house I saw John's car in the driveway. I carefully backed in past it, edged the rear bumper close to a tree and got out.

John and David were inside talking about the fall sailboat racing series. I fixed a cup of coffee and sat down with them.

"Get them all clean?" John asked.

"Yeah," I answered him. "David, where are the children?"

"Jennifer's in the park with Jenny and the boys are playing basketball."

"Did they have lunch?"

"Dave and Matt fixed a sandwich before they left," he said. "Jennifer didn't eat breakfast until 10:00."

"Okay." I leaned my head back against the sofa cushions and closed my eyes. It was only 12:30 and I was tired already.

"You had a call yet?" John asked me.

My eyes still closed, I shook my head.

"Oh," he chuckled, "I hope I'm here when you do. I really want to see you pick yourself off the ceiling when the tones go off."

I opened my eyes and looked at him. "You are so encouraging."

He got his wish. Half of it anyway.

The tones went off.

I stood up. "See," I announced, "I'm fine."

"I see," John laughed.

"Go get 'em," David called to me as I rushed out the door.

I ran down the driveway, listening to my pager . . . ATTENTION ALL LAKE OF THE WOODS RESCUE SQUAD . . . got in the car . . . MEMBERS, YOU HAVE A . . . turned on the ignition . . . RESCUE CALL ON HARPERS FERRY ROAD . . . and gave it gas . . . SUBJECT HAS BEEN . . . and almost backed into the tree. I had left the car in reverse . . . STUNG BY A BEE.

Ed was already at the firehouse. Carmie pulled in just behind me. Lou would meet us at the scene. If the patient was having a severe allergic reaction, we would need her cardiac technician skill.

We radioed our dispatcher that we were en route. I held the call sheet in my hand. I was the novice. The call sheet would naturally be my responsibility.

We turned onto Harpers Ferry and spotted Lou's car. Ed stopped to let Carmie and me get off, then backed the ambulance into the driveway.

"You do the vitals," Carmie said to me as we walked up the steps. "I sometimes have trouble hearing the blood pressure."

Blood pressures were not my forte either. But I passed the call sheet to Carmie.

"He appears to be okay," Lou reported to us. "No breathing difficulty, but he is allergic to bee stings."

The young man was sitting on the sofa. He smiled at us when we walked in and certainly seemed to be in no distress.

"I think I'm all right," he told us, "but I don't have my medicine with me and I just didn't want to take any chances."

"That was the smart thing to do," I said, sitting beside him and taking his hand for a pulse. I continued with the respirations, then reported both to Carmie.

I pulled the BP cuff out of our jump bag and wrapped it around his arm. Carmie and Ed were talking with the people who shared the house with him. Well, here goes, I thought. I slowly released the pressure in the cuff and listened. I heard it. As clear as a bell.

"125/76," I announced, smiling up at Carmie.

"I'm sure I'm all right," the young man said.

Carmie took a release form from the clipboard and explained it to our patient. It's a document stating that we have offered treatment and transportation to a hospital and that the patient has refused one or both. He read it, signed it, and returned it to Carmie.

"I got the blood pressure," I told Lou as I walked with her toward her car.

"I think we're leaving too soon," she said, more to herself than to me.

Why should she think it's such a big deal to get a blood pressure, I thought as I got back on the ambulance. An EMT is supposed to be able to do that.

Ed looked over at me. "That was an easy one for starters," he said.

I nodded. "Yeah, that was an easy one," I agreed.

As we drove back to the firehouse, Carmie passed the call sheet to me. "Here." She pointed. "You can fill in the mileage and our times when we get them from the dispatcher."

"Oh, I get it back now."

"Hey," she said. "You did great."

"Do you really have trouble with blood pressures?" I asked her.

"Sure," she smiled. "Everybody does sometimes."

Just as we turned into the driveway the tones went off again. "ATTENTION ALL LAKE OF THE WOODS RESCUE SQUAD MEMBERS: YOUR PATIENT WITH THE BEE STING IS HAVING TROUBLE BREATHING. HE IS BEING TRANSPORTED TO THE FIREHOUSE."

Moments later Lou drove in. Right behind her came our patient and his friends.

I could hear his labored breathing as he got on the ambulance. Lou had called Mary Washington Hospital's ER for medical orders to use epinephrine. While she prepared the injection, she asked Carmie to give our patient oxygen. Once again, she transferred the responsibility to me.

"Put him on five liters, Pat," she said as she turned the valve on the main tank. "And turn it on before you put it on him."

69

I rechecked the oxygen flow and then placed the cannula prongs into his nostrils.

"Try to breathe through your nose," I told him.

Lou administered the epinephrine and we headed for the hospital. It wasn't long before the young man's respirations were normal and he was feeling better.

"I'll never go anywhere without my medicine again," he said.

"If you know you're allergic to bee stings," Carmie advised him, "you really can't take any chances. Some people even carry a syringe and a vial of epinephrine with them."

I remembered how surprised I had been when I read in our text that in comparison to the fifteen deaths per year in the United States from poisonous snakebites, there were over 200 from allergic reactions to bees, wasps, and ants.

Lou asked for another blood pressure. I glanced at Carmie. She kept her seat. I reached for the cuff and stethoscope. I had never tried to get a BP in a moving ambulance and as I inflated the cuff I was sure that it would be impossible.

Once again I was surprised. I heard it, turned to Lou, and as if I had done it a thousand times before, I casually announced, "132/78."

Lou nodded. Carmie recorded it.

I was on a roll.

I stood up to check the oxygen just as we turned onto Route 1. "Sharp right," Ed called back. It sure was. I lost my balance, lurched forward, and was prepared to grab hold of the first thing I could reach. I didn't anticipate that my hand would land squarely between our patient's legs.

He groaned.

I apologized and sat down.

Lou and Carmie suppressed their laughter and looked away. I remained seated until we reached the hospital.

My first call filled two entire pages.

My second call came eight days later at 8:30 on a Sunday morning. It was a memorable one because it was my first 10-50.

It's the 10-50's we dread.

We can prepare ourselves for most calls. If it's a broken leg, a severe nosebleed, a laceration, a bee sting, or even a heart attack, we know what we're up against before we arrive at the scene. We can discuss our course of treatment en route to our patient and when we step down from the ambulance, we are armed with the supplies and equipment we will need.

On calls for a 10-50, we must wait.

We know what we'll need from the ambulance, collars, backboards, trauma kit, jump bag. It's what we'll need from ourselves which remains an unknown until we're on the scene. En route to a 10-50, we are quieter, more subdued. The wail of the high pitched siren fills the empty spaces. We are together, but we are alone, insecure and unpoised until the wreckage comes into view.

Then we know.

The reality of what we see so suddenly excludes our earlier imaginings that it sometimes seems that we knew all along what lay before us. Individually, we come to grips with it, and then we step off the ambulance as a team.

But on that Sunday morning in September, on my first call for a 10-50, I was too new, too inexperienced, both as an individual and as a member of a team, to feel anything other than my own fear.

I drove rapidly toward the squad building. Ed pulled in behind me, then Ken Witzke, Carmie's husband.

"I'm covering for Carmie," he said to Ed as we got on the ambulance. "One of the kids is sick."

They got up front. I climbed in the back. My mouth was so dry I felt I couldn't even move my tongue.

"Good morning, Pat," Ed called back to me.

I opened my mouth to return his greeting and somehow got out, "Hi." It was after this call that I started carrying gum to pop into my mouth when the tones went off, just to produce some saliva.

As we came near the scene I leaned forward to look out the front window. I saw a car overturned in the grassy median. I swallowed . . . nothing.

71

A bystander directed us to a police car parked beyond the wreck. Our patient was there.

Ed leaned inside the passenger side. I stepped around him to look. There was no blood, no protruding bones.

She had broken her dentures.

She walked unassisted to the ambulance. She refused to lie on the gurney. I sat beside her. Ken was across from us. "We can go now," he said to Ed. We pulled away from the scene and headed toward Mary Washington Hospital.

"I'm going to take your pulse," I told the woman and reached for her left hand. She was fumbling in her purse with her right hand.

She had no apparent injuries and wasn't complaining of any pain, but we had been taught to always take vital signs. In most cases, the radial pulse is easily located in patients whose cardiac output is adequate. Sometimes it's more difficult to find, but rarely is it impossible. Rarely.

I couldn't feel anything. I looked at her. She was breathing and moving and still searching for something in her purse. I repositioned my fingers and tried again. Nothing. The ER physician would later explain it as unusual anatomical structure. But at that moment, I was somewhat concerned.

"Ken," I said, "would you take her pulse, please?"

He moved over to her right side and took her hand. She sighed, shifted her purse to her left hand and continued fumbling.

Ken tried several times, then moved back to his seat.

I looked at him.

He shook his head. "Dead," he mouthed.

"What?" I asked, sure that I had misunderstood.

"Dead," he mouthed again.

I glanced at the woman to see if she'd heard him. Apparently she hadn't. But she had finally found what she was looking for. From her purse she took a tube of Super Glue and began spreading it on her dentures.

"Are you sure you don't want to lie down?" I asked her.

"No," she snapped at me. "I just want to fix my teeth." Her lips smacked together.

I felt I had to do something, so I reached for the jump bag

and got the BP cuff. "I'd like to take your blood pressure," I told her.

"Well, I don't want you to," she replied.

I looked at Ken. He shrugged.

I glanced out the back and saw we were approaching the hospital. Here we were, arriving with a patient from a 10-50. No collar, no backboard, no vitals recorded on the call sheet. Nothing.

But she had fixed her dentures.

It was on a Monday night two weeks later that David and I sat together in the living room watching the Country Music Awards. He was a Statler Brothers fan. I was rooting for Alabama. I fixed a bowl of popcorn and had just refilled our glasses of Coke when the tones went off. I was not on duty until the next day but I stopped to listen.

It was a 10-50.

I heard the location ". . . near the intersection of Lakeview and Liberty."

"David."

"What?"

"This wreck is right down the street," I told him.

"If you feel like you need to go," he said, "go. Could you hand me my Coke first?"

I handed it to him then ran into the bedroom and switched from my robe to my jumpsuit. I gave him a quick good-bye kiss.

"Cheer for Alabama a little, will you?" I asked him as I started out the door.

"They don't need it," he called back.

I turned off our street, Yorktown, onto Liberty, then took a quick left onto Lakeview. I saw Bob and Joyce's car and the patrol car, with our patrolman, Don Childs, just getting out. I didn't see any wreck.

I approached the patrol car. "Hey, Don," I said. "Where is it?"

He pointed into the darkness, into the trees, then turned his flashlight on the area. I looked but could only see shadowy silhouettes.

I walked through the underbrush. I saw movement, a light, and Bob and Joyce. Joyce was leaning in the car, her arms through the right window, supporting the head of the woman in the front seat. Bob focused his flashlight on her. I looked down into the car. The woman was wearing a rescue squad jacket.

"It's Ellen," Joyce said.

"What happened?" I asked.

"She was unconscious when we got here," Joyce told me. "She came to just a moment ago. Said something about somebody running her off the road."

She was holding Ellen's head, applying pressure with her hand to a deep laceration. Blood covered her fingers.

"Pat," she said, "hold her head. Bob and I will get the door open so we can get closer to her."

I eased my hands under Joyce's to continue the traction. I could feel the warm sticky dampness of the blood. Maintaining the traction on Ellen's head while Bob and Joyce worked around me to open the door was awkward, but finally I could kneel beside the car to get a better hold. I felt shards of glass press into my knees.

I heard the sound of sirens. Within moments the ambulance, fire truck, and crash truck were on the scene.

Bob tried to open the driver's side of the car but the impact had forced the hood back, jamming the left front door, sealing it shut.

"We're gonna have to cut it off," he called to the firemen. They removed the Hurst tool and generator from the crash truck.

Spotlights illuminated the scene.

Ellen was stretched across the front seat. We could clearly see now that her left foot was pinned beneath the brake pedal. Her left leg was broken. She moaned as I said her name.

"Talk to me, Ellen," I told her. "Talk to me." I continued speaking to her, hoping to prevent her from sinking back into unconsciousness.

The generator was fired, a sudden explosion of sound, grinding, persistent. We spread a tarp over Ellen's body and face to protect her from broken glass that could spray across the interior of the car as the firemen cut away the door with the Hurst tool.

"Ellen," I said to her, "talk to me."

"Pat," was all she said, but it was enough.

The door snapped and fell away. The generator was turned off. The silence was equally oppressive.

Bob knelt down to get to the brake pedal, reached to take the crowbar from Howie, and pried the pedal loose from the floor.

Now freed, Ellen's foot moved.

She screamed.

Her scream was as sudden and explosive as the generator's firing. A chill swept over me, but I didn't move. I held on to her as before, talking quietly to her. I watched the others, watched them move, listened to them talk. I was immobilized by my responsibility, but I could watch their actions: careful, thoughtful, and deliberate. I was proud of them and of me. We were in this together.

I was part of a team.

Ellen's head was bandaged. A cervical collar was fitted to her neck. Her leg and foot were splinted. We slid her carefully onto the backboard, then carried her to the gurney.

My work was over.

When I stood, my back ached. My knees hurt from the glass. My hands and fingers were stiff and bloodied. I watched the duty crew load the gurney into the ambulance. They climbed aboard and the doors closed. Moments later it pulled away.

The crowd began to disperse. The wrecker approached and I stepped aside for it. Away from the car and with the scene now well lit, I cringed at the sight of it, astonished that Ellen's injuries were not more serious.

I turned and saw Al Potter walking toward me.

"I just heard about Ellen," he said. "How is she?"

"Her left leg and ankle are broken," I told him. "And she has a bad head laceration. Beyond that it's hard to tell."

"Her car's a mess," he said, watching the wrecker pulling Ellen's car away from the tree.

"Yes," I agreed. "She was lucky she wasn't hurt even worse."

He stood quietly for a moment, then turned back to me. "Was this your first 10-50?"

"No," I said, then thought about it. "Well, I guess it's my first real one."

"How'd you do?"

"Okay," I nodded. "I did okay."

He smiled at me. "I knew you would." He patted my shoulder and walked away.

The confidence was beginning to rub off on me.

The crisp and cool early October night air felt good on my face. I breathed it deeply, turned away and crossed the street to my car.

# Chapter 9

Forty PERCENT OF all heart attack victims die before they reach the hospital. So at 6:55, when the tones went off for "chest pains," on an October Saturday morning, I was aware of the urgency.

I was the first to arrive at the squad building. Being the novice on the squad, I was the only member already up, showered, and dressed before dawn on a Saturday morning.

There were five of us, all cardiac technicians except Ed and me. I knew if five was too many, I would be the one left behind. So I took advantage of my early arrival and quickly got up front and snapped on my seat belt.

Mark got into the driver's seat. Ed, John and Lou piled in the back, and we were off. We found the residence, a small white bungalow, and announced to our dispatcher that we were on the scene.

Our patient was sitting in the living room, his family gathered around him. I took a seat near him, the call sheet in my lap, like a secretary waiting for dictation.

"How are you feeling now?" Lou asked him.

"Well," he drawled, "I'm shaking like a whore in church."

I was tempted to write that down.

Lou asked the man questions about his chest pain, when it started, if the pain was sharp or dull, and if he had a history of heart problems.

Then John explained that he was going to start an IV. I

watched him wrap the tourniquet around the man's arm, wipe the site on his arm with an alcohol swab, insert the angiocath, withdraw the needle leaving the catheter in the vein, attach the line to it and adjust the flow rate.

As attentive as John was to what he was doing, I noticed he kept glancing toward the table behind me. When he finished taping the line to the man's forearm, he turned to the family members.

The EKG monitor was running so I assumed he was going to tell them something about the man's heart. Ed had taken his blood pressure. Mark had talked to the hospital. There was information on his condition. The family was waiting. They looked at John.

He cleared his throat. Then he spoke to them.

"Could I please have some of that caramel candy?" he said.

They relaxed. They smiled.

The man's wife picked three pieces out of the bowl on the table behind me and handed them to John. His daughter gave him three more, then picked up the bowl and insisted he help himself.

They expressed their relief and gratitude through individually-wrapped squares of caramel.

On the way to the hospital, I rode in back with our patient, holding his large hand in mine. He told us the tightness in his chest was gone.

The sense of urgency had passed.

Mark reached into the pocket of his jumpsuit, then asked Lou if she had any gum. She did and shared it with him, taking a piece for herself too. "I didn't get to brush my teeth, either," she admitted.

"Neither did I," said Ed. His striped pajama pants stuck out from the legs of his jumpsuit. "Can I have a piece?"

"Pat?" Lou offered the pack to me.

"No, thank you, Lou. I have some."

Nothing was offered John, in the driver's seat. He had his supply of caramel.

The man eased his hand away from mine. He reached into his

pants pocket, pulled out a tiny bottle, opened it and pressed it to his lips.

"Breath freshener," he announced. He recapped it and put it back in his pocket, then held his hand out to me.

He looked around at us and said, "I can't let you people get ahead of me."

We were still laughing when the ER door swung open for us.

"Chalk up another one, Pat," Ed said to me as we headed home.

"My first cardiac call," I replied.

"Caramel cardiac call," John said.

I laughed. "I stand corrected," I said. "My first caramel cardiac call."

One evening several weeks later, just as we were finishing dinner, the tones went off for a "youth who's been drinking rubbing alcohol." I wasn't on duty, but the dispatcher gave the location, three blocks away.

"That must be Gary," Dave said.

Gary was the son of neighbors of ours. Their younger son, Rick, was in Dave's class at school.

I looked at David. "I think I should go."

"Yeah," he nodded. "Sounds bad."

"Rubbing alcohol," Matt groaned. "Gary's drinking rubbing alcohol?"

"Pretend you didn't hear that," I told him. I gave each of them a quick kiss. "Just stack the dishes. I'll do them when I get home."

When I pulled up in front of the house I saw Gary's eleven-year-old brother on the upstairs porch. "Where is he, Rick?" I called to him as I approached the house.

"In the bathroom."

I entered the house downstairs and climbed the steps to the second floor.

"The ambulance is on the way," I told him.

"I didn't know what to do," he said, his voice breaking. "Mom and Dad went to Washington today. They said they'd be late. I just didn't know what to do."

"You did fine," I told him. "You did the right thing." I put my arm around his shoulders. "Show me where Gary is."

Gary was lying face down in the bathroom, his head wedged between the toilet and the bathtub. His respirations were rapid, shallow.

"Rick, did he fall?" I asked, considering a possible head or spine injury.

"No, he was leaning over the toilet and he just slid down on the floor."

I looked in the toilet. The water was clear. "Did he vomit?"

"I don't know."

"How much of the rubbing alcohol did he drink?"

"About half the bottle. And he drank some whiskey before that. Right out of the bottle. And he said he'd taken some pills too."

"What kind of pills?"

"I don't know," he said softly. "I'm sorry."

"Honey, it's okay," I told him. "You've been a big help. Now let's see if we can move him out of here." I lifted Gary's head and shoulders and Rick took his feet. We had to stop twice to reposition him but finally got him seated in a chair in the living room.

I shook his arm. "Gary!"

"Mmm," he groaned, jerking his arm away. His eyes were still closed.

"The ambulance is here," Rich said. "And Mr. and Mrs. Grim."

"Good." I shook Gary's arm again. "Open your eyes, Gary."

Once more he pulled away. "No!" Bob came in, carrying the jump pack. He pulled out the BP cuff and stethoscope while I filled him in on what had happened. Joyce headed for the telephone to call Poison Control.

"Rick says he may have taken some pills too," I said to Bob. "I'm going to see what I can find."

I stood up. "Rick, would you show me Gary's room?"

"Yes," he said. I followed him down the hall.

Bob, realizing they had forgotten to bring in the call sheet, went back to the ambulance for it.

I looked on Gary's dresser and bedside table but found nothing. "Rick," I asked, "are you positive he took pills?"

"He said he did."

From the living room came the sound of something, or someone, falling. I ran toward the sound. Rick followed me.

Joyce stood by the phone, her eyes fixed on Gary. He lay motionless on his back on the floor, his eyes closed.

"Are you okay?" I asked her as I knelt beside Gary. She nodded weakly. I leaned over to check him. His respirations were unchanged. His pupil reaction was sluggish.

Bob came in with the call sheet. "What happened?" he asked when he reached the top of the stairs.

"He must have come to while I was on the phone," Joyce said. "I had my back to him. I didn't hear him until just before he lunged for me," she continued. "He missed me and fell. His head hit the table."

Rick was standing in the hallway, crying.

"Joyce," I said, "could you call Betty next door and ask if Rick can stay with them until his folks come home?" I looked at him. "Is that okay, Rick?" He nodded.

Joyce made the call, then crossed the room to him. "I'll walk you over there." She took his hand and they went down the stairs.

Bob knelt on the opposite side of Gary, checking his head for an injury. There was swelling on the left side of his forehead. He moaned when Bob moved his fingers across it. I leaned forward to get a better look. His eyes opened. I sat back. He reached out suddenly and grabbed Bob's jacket.

"Who the hell are you?" he said, his words slurred, his voice hoarse, cold.

I took hold of his hand and pried his fingers, one by one from Bob's jacket. Then I stretched his arm out and away from his body until I could rest my knee squarely on his elbow joint. Bob did the same with the other arm.

Then just as unexpectedly as he had come awake, Gary lapsed back into unconsciousness. I looked at Bob.

"I think we're going to need some help here," he said. Even in that potentially dangerous situation I saw a thread of humor in his statement. Comic relief, like Roy Scheider's line in *Jaws*, "You're going to need a bigger boat."

"I'll go to the ambulance, and radio for security," he said.

"Uh, why don't I go?" I suggested. "Okay," he agreed. "But make it snappy." I eased my knee off Gary's arm, slowly, just in case, but he lay still. Then I quickly got up and ran down the stairs and out to the ambulance.

"Rescue 29 to LOW," I called.

Nothing.

"Rescue 29 to Lake of the Woods."

Still no response.

I sighed, glanced back at the house, then tried again. I couldn't hear them but maybe they could hear me. "Rescue 29 to Lake of the Woods. We need security at the scene. Now!"

I stepped out of the ambulance and started back toward the house.

"Pat," Joyce called to me from the side yard. She was returning from the neighbor's home. "What are you doing?"

"Trying to get some help," I told her. "Come on."

Gary had not moved. Neither had Bob.

"I couldn't get them," I told him.

He looked up at me. "What do you mean you couldn't get them?" he asked.

"Nobody answered," I explained. "I told them we need help. Maybe they could still hear me."

"What did Poison Control say to do?" he asked Joyce. "They gave me a whole list of things," she said, "but we have to know exactly what he's taken."

Gary started moaning again. His legs moved. I took his arm and reassumed my knee to elbow position. His eyes opened. He raised his head from the floor and spit at Bob.

The sputum trickled down Bob's cheek. I wanted to reach out and wipe it off, but I was afraid to move. Gary's arms strained against our grip.

"Police are here," Joyce said.

We heard a car door slam and the downstairs door open. Don Childs took the stairs two at a time. He had his handcuffs out. Somehow the four of us forced Gary's arms together so Don could snap the cuffs on his wrists. Gary kicked and spit at us all the way down the stairs. Once he bit into Don's jacket. We lifted him into the ambulance and Don sat on his legs.

We started to the hospital and once again Gary passed out.

"How did you know to come?" I asked Don. "You didn't answer when I called you."

"I didn't hear you," he said. "But every other member of the fire department and rescue squad did and I think every one of them called us."

"That's a nice feeling," I acknowledged.

Gary drifted in and out of consciousness. When he was conscious he was violent, fighting his restraints. There was little we could do, except keep him from hurting himself, or us.

Once when he lost consciousness his head and shoulders slipped off the gurney. I reached out to hold his head, but Joyce grabbed my arm.

"Don't touch him," she said. "Don't even get near him."

"But . . . " I started to object.

"No," she interrupted me. "I don't like seeing him that way either," she said. "But you are too important to me. I won't let you get hurt."

I sat back, away from Gary. I looked at Joyce. "Thank you." I knew what she meant. I had felt the same way when he had lunged at her and when he had grabbed Bob.

"And," she added, "don't ever respond directly to the scene for a call like this."

"But I know him."

"You may have thought so," she said. She pointed at Gary. "Is this the person you know?"

"No," I conceded. "Not like this."

"Don't ever do it again, Pat."

I shrugged. "I'm learning."

"Just don't learn the hard way," she said.


That was my first call with Joyce and Bob Grim. We were together in EMT class and we have moved through the years together.

They were both fifty-one years old when they joined the squad.

They are intense people. Joyce told me that they met at an Arthur Murray Dance Studio. I wish I could have seen them doing the rumba on the dance floor.

Bob is neither a talker nor a toucher. He is quiet and very serious. He doesn't smile very often. I like to be around when he does. His clear blue eyes twinkle. His hair is grey and thick and when he's gone more than a month without a haircut, it begins to curl around his ears and at the nape of his neck.

"I love your hair," I tell him.

"Then it must be time for a haircut," he says to me. With his round face, twinkly eyes, slight paunch, and serious nature, he reminds me of Winnie-the-Pooh. There's something about him that makes me want to tickle him. He's not a toucher, but in the bad times or the really good times, when I hug him he hugs me back.

He is also a perfectionist. He is a building contractor and you can't find a better one. He oversees the construction of his houses as if he and Joyce were going to be the occupants. When his houses are completed, he even sweeps the floors.

Blueprints can be designed to suit the builder. People cannot. It's easier to smooth down the rough edges of wood than to smooth down the rough edges of people.

But he's good. So is Joyce. If I were sick or injured, I would want them with me. I would trust their care. That is what counts.

I left my pager on all day, every day. Sometimes there would be a second call when the duty crew was already out. Additional personnel would be needed and I wanted to be available; however, I worried that at night the noise might keep David awake. So, just before I switched off my bedside light, I turned off my pager.

I spent one day a week as a parent volunteer in Jennifer's kindergarten class. I got to know the children well. Many of them were from Lake of the Woods and it was nice to see them in the neighborhood after working with them at school.

Sarah was one of them. She was an affectionate child. She'd often sit perched in my lap while we worked on numbers and colors. I didn't know her mother and father well. From the way

Sarah spoke of them, though, I knew they must be good, loving parents.

Sarah's mother was twenty-six years old. She was also a diabetic.

In the middle of December at 4:30 on a Monday morning the tones went off.

The duty crew responded.

The next day Suzanne Lawrence told me about the call. Suzanne was Joyce's daughter and one of our cardiac technicians.

"At 4:45, the tones went off again," she said, "for additional help."

Sarah's mother was in respiratory arrest. Sarah sat alone on the living room sofa, watching the people try to save her mother, watching her father cry.

"Why weren't you there?" Suzanne asked me. "My pager wasn't on," I told her. "I didn't know about it."

"You shouldn't turn it off," she said. "You never know what could happen."

Sarah's mother never came out of the coma. She died on Christmas Day and was buried on December 29, my birthday.

I went to the funeral.


"If I keep the pager out of the bedroom," I said to David, "and leave it on, do you think it would bother you? You know the children can sleep through anything."

"You can try it," he said. "But I think you're taking Suzanne's remarks too seriously. You can't be up all night. Besides," he added, "I really don't want you going on night calls."

I got up from my chair in the living room to fix a cup of tea. "You want anything?" I asked David.

He glanced at me from the sofa. "I want you to keep this thing in perspective," he said. "You're not getting paid for this, you know."

"I meant, do you want anything from the kitchen?"

"No, thanks."

At bedtime I left my pager in the living room. I turned up the volume a little and faced it toward the hallway.

I lay awake for a while after David fell asleep. I knew I would not let the rescue squad dictate my life. It was only a part of it, not the whole. I also realized how valuable my work there had become to me. The fact that there was no paycheck did not diminish its importance.

I thought back on a call we'd had several weeks earlier. It was for an eighty-two-year-old cancer patient. I held her hand as we traveled toward the hospital. She was very weak, but we talked throughout most of the trip. At one point she raised her hand, still in mine, and gazed at our hands clasped together.

She turned to me. "You know," she said, "there is something so wonderful about the human hand. It's kind of like . . . like holding the person's heart."

No, I didn't receive a paycheck. I was paid in gold.

# Chapter 10

ANNIE IS HER name. She was patterned after the child of the inventor whose daughter died in an accident. She is the CPR mannequin and we practiced on her on the classroom floor until our palms and our lips were bruised.

With two fingers up from the tip of the sternum—the xyphoid process—I place my hands. Only the heel of one hand is in contact with the sternum. My other hand is atop the first, fingers interlocked. I begin, but this is not Annie.

I am not kneeling on the classroom floor now, but crouched in the back of the ambulance. We are traveling down the serpentine road which leads from Burr Hill to Culpeper Memorial Hospital. Bob is behind me, and his arms encircle my waist to keep me from falling.

It is so different, the feeling of soft moist skin beneath my hands. The chest is supple. The sternum has more give.

I hear a snap and glance at John.

"You broke a rib," he says. "Keep going. It happens."

I continue, reciting the mnemonic four thousand, five thousand . . . John pushes the demand valve and I hear the sudden swoosh of oxygen.

"Stop CPR," he orders. I stop. He stares at the monitor. "Still asystole. We'll try defibrillation."

I look down to make sure my leg is not touching the gurney. "Everybody clear," John announces as he presses the paddles to the woman's chest. His thumbs push the charge buttons. Her body jumps. He looks at the monitor again and sighs. "Start CPR."

We reach the hospital. The nurses meet us at the loading dock. We rush her into the ER.

The doctor pronounces her dead.

This is my first CPR. My first death. I wait for my grief. I stand quietly in the doorway of the cardiac room, waiting. "Multiple trauma coming in," I hear the triage nurse announce. The doctors and nurses move past me, out of the room. They disperse to make ready for the next crisis.

I look at the pale, aged, lifeless body supine on the emergency room stretcher. No requiem fills my thoughts. No sorrow dampens my eyes.

John's hand is on my shoulder. "Let's go home."

On the trip home, Bob drove. John and I were in back. I rewound the cables to the monitor. He cleaned the gel off the paddles.

"Good CPR, Pat," he said. "You'll be sore tonight."

"I didn't feel anything," I told him.

"You don't feel anything while you're doing it. It's later when your muscles start hurting."

"No, not the CPR," I said. "The woman. She was dead and I didn't feel anything."

"We did our best, Pat, but she really never had a chance. She was dead when we got there. There is no telling how long she'd been dead before her neighbor found her and started CPR. They probably should have just called Clyde Johnson at the funeral home."

"I thought I would feel some loss," I told him. "Then I wondered if something was wrong with me because I didn't."

"There's nothing wrong with you," he said. "She was old and very sick. And we never saw her in life, only in death."

He looked away from me for a moment. "It's when they are alive when we get there," he said, then turned back to face me, "and we try so hard and they die anyway. You'll understand," he added. "You'll see." He was right. I understand now, because there was Jesse.

We live in Wilderness, Virginia. Life is peaceful here. Civil War buffs pass this way as they journey from Gettysburg and Harper's Ferry down to Richmond and Petersburg and south toward Appomattox Courthouse. This was the site of the Battle of the Wilderness.

Near Wilderness, other spots on the map are Burr Hill, Mine Run, Lignum, and True Blue. Where else but in the countryside could fire and rescue personnel hear a call such as Orange County's for "a cow stuck in a pond"?

And, there's something about the people.

"It was a good Christmas," the old man said to us as we traveled toward Culpeper Memorial Hospital. He rested on the gurney. The nitro had helped ease his chest pains. "The best," he added. He looked first at Jean, then at me. "Got me two flannel shirts and a chocolate cake," he told us. "Good flannel shirts, too."

There was also the farmer who lost his barn, all his tools, his entire supply of hay, and two calves. I stood by the fence and watched our firemen hose down the hot spots. The barn was completely down when we arrived on the scene. Barns and mobile homes burn quickly.

He walked my way, then stood beside me. "Could have lost everything," he said. "I'm lucky."

I looked at him. Half full, I thought, not half empty.

"It's good you can feel that way," I told him.

He shrugged. "Only way to feel," he said. "I got my tractor out and the horses are okay. My friends say they'll give me hay for the winter. I'll make it."


Away from the hubbub of city life, rural living is for many a dream come true. Unfortunately, if a country dweller is sick or hurt, that dream can become a nightmare. Some patients just can't afford the time it takes to get to a hospital. That is when Pegasus, the winged horse of Greek mythology, comes to the rescue.

Pegasus is the medivac helicopter from the University of Virginia's Medical Center.

The first time I saw the helicopter was during a training program in Orange. It was beautiful, with the blue-winged horse painted against the white background, and PEGASUS in large letters just beneath the side windows.

"Isn't it something?" I said to David when he came to pick me up that day in Orange. We watched the helicopter take off. "It looks like something that could save lives. Doesn't it look like something that could save lives? I mean the whole idea, with the winged horse. They could have just painted the helicopter white and let it go at that, but look at it!"

He was, instead, looking at me. "You sound," he'd said, "like you're having some sort of religious experience."

The first time our squad called for Pegasus was for the victim of a farming accident. The man had been digging post holes when his shirt became entangled in the gears of the auger, pulling him into the sharp rotating metal, tearing into and shredding the flesh below his right arm. It was a terrible sight. One bystander vomited and another passed out.

Our patient was conscious but his pulse was too rapid, his blood pressure too low, both indicators of shock. We called for Pegasus.

The open farmland was a perfect landing zone. Our firemen set up lights and stood by. I started the IV. Jean and Joe monitored his vital signs. John stayed in radio contact with the Pegasus crew.

"Here it comes," he called to us.

I could hear it, the rapid chop-chop-chop of the blades. From where I sat in the ambulance there was no way I could see it. I wanted to throw open the back doors and watch it land. Instead, I remained seated and checked the flow rate of the IV.

Once on the ground, the Pegasus crew boarded the ambulance. We gave them a status report and then we carried the man to the helicopter.

We moved back. The sudden blast of air from the rotating blades showered us with dirt and grass. I blinked, but never looked away. I watched it lift off the ground, watched the blue-winged horse until it crossed over the hill.

They would reach the trauma center before we finished our paperwork. They would save his life.

I glanced at John beside me. "Isn't it something?" I said to him as we turned back toward the ambulance.

"Yeah," he said. "I'd really love to fly in it."

"You mean to work on it?" I asked.

"Yeah."

"Not me," I said.

"Why not?"

"I don't know," I told him. "I just don't think it's for me."

I knew why. I just didn't want to try to explain it to him.

"If your patients are still alive when you get to them," he once said to me, "you and your crew will either love them to death or talk them to death."

I'd laughed, taking him with a grain of salt, but stopped trying to talk with him about anything serious. We are on different wave lengths. That does not mean that he is wrong. It simply means that we are different.

I wouldn't want to work on a helicopter because fifteen to twenty minutes with a patient is not enough for me.

I have never been in an automobile accident. I have never been seriously ill. I've never had my clothes removed, my body touched, examined by strangers. So I cannot know exactly how our patients feel, but I see the apprehension and fear in their eyes. I can feel it in their hands when they hold tightly to mine. I can hear it in their words and sense it in their silence.

I believe that convalescence begins in the ambulance, and with the care given by emergency medical personnel. If, through our treatment, we minister not just to the illness or injury but to the entire person, then we are contributing much more than just a preface to recovery. The twenty minute flight to a trauma center wasn't enough for me.

We once had a call for a thirty-one-year-old woman with heart palpitations. Inside the ambulance, I hooked her up to the monitor. Her EKG was normal. She lay quietly on the gurney as we headed east toward Mary Washington Hospital.

"Are you comfortable?" I asked her.

Her eyes were large and brown and when she looked at me, I could tell she'd been crying. "Yes, I'm fine," she said.

She wasn't. She stared vacantly out the back window. Her right hand rested on her left. Her hands were fair and slender, her nails long and painted a soft pink. She twisted her wedding band with erratic, harsh movements that were incongruous with the delicacy of her hands.

I rested my hand on her arm. "It's going to be all right," I told her.

She turned her gaze on me. "Is it?" she asked.

"Yes."

She looked at Jean as if for confirmation. Jean nodded.

She talked to us then. She told us her husband had left her. She had thought of suicide, had even gathered all of her sleeping pills together and composed a letter to him.

I handed her tissues from the cabinet.

"I was so frightened," she said, "to think how close I came to killing myself. I have a little girl. I don't want to die."

We listened. Her hands grew still. When we reached the hospital she told us she felt like she was ready to go home.

On the call sheets which we're required to complete on every patient, there is a place for "listening." It's in the section "Treatment Given," in the far right hand column between Neck/Spine Immobilization and Traction Applied. It is called Psychological First Aid.


Captain Joe, as we affectionately called him, stepped down. He had been a good leader. When he was pleased with us he'd cluck over us like a mother hen, but he was also stern. He'd once suspended a squad member for responding to a call looking "unprofessional."

"It wasn't just his jeans, all stained with paint," he'd said to us. "His hands were covered with grease." He'd looked around the room, then continued, "You will wear your uniforms. They will be clean. You will look professional."

We did.

We elected Lou to take his place. Captain Joe had kept us on a short leash. Lou lengthened it. She gave us room to move on our own. If we had a call which was especially difficult, she would call us later just to see how we were doing. I never heard her say an unkind word about anyone.

When it came time for me to go on a regular crew, Lou remembered my request. I was assigned to Ed's team. When Carmie left the squad shortly after that to finish her master's in Library Science, Lou put Jean Lodge with Ed and me.

Jean and her husband Warren had lived in Lake of the Woods since 1980. Lou urged Jean to join the squad as a driver, then persuaded her to enroll in the EMT class.

"The thing about Lou is," Jean said to me, "she's so sweet and well-intentioned, you just can't say no to her."

Jean was tall and stately and had four children and nine grandchildren.

"My children can't believe I'm doing this," she'd say. "I can't believe I'm doing this." Yet, she loved her rescue squad work and she was a good EMT. Our young patients would nestle in her lap and snuggle against her neck and twist her necklace around their fingers. Jean still talks about Paula.

The call is for a baby. A baby choking.

Our directions are incorrect and we turn left on Route 3 instead of right. Wasted minutes, costly minutes. We are redirected eastward. Jean makes the turn quickly and even though the Sunday morning traffic is sparse, she switches on the siren.

Our dispatcher updates us as we turn onto the dirt road in Spotsylvania County. "The baby has stopped breathing."

A man and a woman stand outside the small clapboard house. She is crying. He is holding her. "Hurry," he says to us.

Inside, the room is dark and our eyes adjust from the outside brightness. The baby is lying on the sofa, dressed only in a diaper. His eyes are closed, and he is very still.

I wonder to myself why no one is holding him.

Lou gives him four quick breaths. She thinks she feels a brachial pulse. Ed carries him to the ambulance. We hurry behind him. He lays the baby in Lou's lap and calls the hospital.

"Start CPR," the ER doctor tells him.

We put the CPR board under the baby. I move close to Lou.

I hold his small head in my hands and open his airway. Lou begins the compressions, two fingers against his sternum, counting aloud. On the count of five I breathe into his mouth. I taste sweet milk. His chest rises. I hear Lou whisper, "Baby, please live."

A nurse is waiting for us on the ER loading dock. She takes him from us and rushes him into the cardiac room. We follow. The nurse starts an IV. They monitor his heart. The CPR continues.

The baby's grandmother arrives. The doctor asks me to take her to the private room next to the nurses' station and to stay with her until they have time to talk with her.

I find her in the hall and introduce myself. I take her arm and lead her into the small room. There are no pictures, no focal point upon which we can fix our gaze. We sit across from each other at a Formica-topped table. She clasps and unclasps the handles of her purse, nervous, frightened gestures.

"I kept him yesterday and he was fine," she says to me. "He was fine yesterday. Sometimes I keep him when his mama works."

"Where does she work?" I ask, a pointless question to fill the empty space.

"At the laundry," she tells me. She glances toward the door. "She'll be along." She looks back at me. "How sick is he?" she asks. "Is he very sick?"

I am her only link to her grandson. I want to reach out to her, to touch her, but I can't. The table is between us and if I stand to go to her, she will know.

"The doctor is with him now," I tell her. "He will be in to talk to you soon."

It isn't enough for either of us, but we both settle for it.

The nurse comes in. She is holding a clipboard. The grandmother's gaze falls on her, holds her. I excuse myself to return to the cardiac room.

"Stop CPR," I hear the doctor announce. He glances at the clock. "CPR stopped at 1040." He leaves the room. The nurses remove the IV and the EKG electrodes and walk away.

I am now alone with him.

I stand by the gurney. He is so small, not even four months old. I caress the softness of his face. I take his tiny, lifeless hand in mine and whisper, "Baby."

On a subsequent call which took us to Mary Washington Hospital I looked for Dr. Warren Parmelee, director of the Emergency Room. I found him in the lounge, eating lunch.

"Come in Pat," he said.

We talked briefly about the call for the baby. When I turned to go, he said, "Pat, is there something else?" knowing that there was.

I turned back to him. "Is there anything else we could have done, anything that would have made a difference?"

He shook his head. "No," he said. "There was nothing more any of us could have done."

Several days later I received a letter from him which read, "The work you folks did on the baby was top grade. Failure does not imply poor care and none of us enjoys defeat. To be a poor loser when attempting to save a life is good sportsmanship in any rule book."

"You're going to burn out real early in the game," John said to me later, "if you don't stop caring so much."

"No, I won't," I told him.

A smile crossed his face. "You'll get over it," he said. "You run enough calls and you'll stop feeling this way."

"When I stop feeling this way," I said to him, "I'll quit."

# Chapter 11

I woke suddenly to the sound of the tones.

The room was dark. I turned toward the luminous clock, 2:10. I eased quietly out of bed and hurried down the hall into the living room.

". . . third house on the left past Hillside," I heard the voice of the dispatcher. "Possible miscarriage."

"I'll wait," I told myself.

I walked back into the bedroom for my slippers and robe. I heard David's deep breathing. The pager had not awakened him.

The duty crew radioed the dispatcher that they were responding. Minutes later they marked on the scene. I yawned, sat down on the sofa and pulled the wool afghan over my legs. It was so cold. The temperature had plummeted into the teens every night for the past two weeks.

I heard Howie Crain's voice. He asked the dispatcher to set the tones again for "a female member to come to the scene." I was just getting warm under the afghan and thinking that David really hadn't had such a bad idea about night calls.

I got up and ran tiptoeing back down the hall. I pulled my jumpsuit from the closet, dropped my robe and nightgown on the floor and stepped into my jumpsuit and tennis shoes. Pulling up the zipper, I headed for the door, grabbing my jacket from the coatrack on the way.

Shivering from the cold, I switched on the car heater. I felt the frigid air strike my legs and turned it off. I would be at the scene long before the car's engine warmed.

Howie met me at the front door.

"Thanks for coming, Pat. We just need you to check her bleeding. I want to get some idea of how much blood she's lost."

Mac Johnson and Paul Lewis stood behind Howie. They walked with me toward the woman's bedroom, but stopped when we reached the door. She lay in bed, her feet propped on pillows.

I introduced myself. "Is this your first pregnancy?" I asked her. She nodded.

"When did the bleeding first start?"

"About 1:00, when I got up to go to the bathroom," she said. She told me she was six months pregnant and hadn't had any problems until now.

"Is there any cramping?" I asked.

"Just a little."

"Do you have a pad on?"

"Yes."

"I need to look to see how much you're bleeding."

I moved the sheet off her legs. "My hands are cold," I said. "I'm sorry." I slipped her underpants down and looked at the pad. There was blood but there were no clots. I pulled up her underpants and tucked the blanket around her.

"There's not a lot of blood, and it seems to have stopped," I told her. "I know you're concerned, and there's very little I can say to make it better. But this sometimes happens. It happened to me once," I said, "in my first trimester."

"Did you lose your baby?" she asked.

I smiled and shook my head. "No. She's almost six years old now."

I found the crew in the living room. Joyce and Linda were there too.

"Howie, I would estimate only about 10cc's of blood loss and some cramping," I told him. "Do you want one of us to go to the hospital with you?"

He shook his head. "No, I think we'll be okay. I just wanted a woman to, you know, check her."

Joyce and Linda and I started out the door. Linda looked back at Howie. "Get on the radio and call for a woman," she said, "and look what you get."

"Yeah," Howie grinned. "I've got to remember that."

I got home a little after three. I hung my jumpsuit back in the closet, found my gown on the floor and slipped it on. David was still sleeping soundly. I crawled into bed, careful not to let my icy toes touch his legs.

At our next monthly meeting that call was mentioned. Our patient was doing fine. She would, however, have to stay in bed for much of her pregnancy.

Someone asked why it was necessary to call for a woman EMT.

Howie shrugged. "It just seemed to be the best thing to do under the circumstances."

Someone else pointed out that "we are all medical personnel."

"That's true," Suzanne agreed. "But I'd rather have Pat Ivey looking between my legs than Mark Hood or John Beery."

Suzanne's remark and the subsequent laughter pretty much put an end to that topic of conversation.

Yet, beneath the laughter and beyond the discussion of that one particular call, the real topic was respect for human dignity.

I care for every patient, but I don't like all of them. I didn't like Larry. I don't like Gladys, our perennial patient. I feel sorry for her. She gets drunk and falls down and calls us. When we get there, she yells at us. If we had a dollar for every time she's screamed, "Get your damn hands off me," we could make a down payment on a new ambulance.

The only time I ever seriously considered quitting was after a call for Gladys. Instead, I went home and applied ice to the bruise on my arm where she'd hit me.

It's easier to care for the people who really need us, and that includes Larry and even Gladys. But caring doesn't come easy, though, when patients call us at three in the morning for a backache they've had for two weeks, or when people use our ambulance as a taxi and we find them waiting on the front porch, suitcase in hand, flanked by friends or relatives who drive to the hospital, often in front of us.

There was the golfer who'd been struck in the forearm by a ball. "Could you come back and get me after I finish my game?" he'd asked us. "It hurts, but I've never had a score this good."

"No," I told him.

And the woman who had said, "I don't like this a bit," as I placed the electrodes on her chest. I switched on the monitor and watched her electrocardiogram cross the screen, sinus tachycardia.

"Not many people like to be in the back of an ambulance," Jean told her.

"Is my car badly damaged?" the woman asked. It was the fourth time she'd asked that question.

"Three flat tires," Joe answered her.

She strained to see out the back window. "How did it happen?"

"I don't know," I said. "Looks like you crossed the median and ended up on this side of the highway. Which way were you heading?" She pointed west. "Yeah," I nodded. "That must have been what happened."

Jean bandaged the laceration on her head and put an ice pack on it.

"Have you had anything to drink?" Joe asked the woman.

"A few," she said. "Look, you people are really pushing me around."

"You had a wreck," I told her. "Your pulse is very fast and you have a head injury. We advise you to let us take you to the hospital, but we can't make you go." I pulled a transport refusal slip from the clipboard. "If you sign this, you're free to get off the ambulance."

"Is my car badly damaged?" she asked.

I looked at Jean. Jean sighed and shook her head.

"Three flat tires," Joe said.

"Is that a cop out there by my car?"

I nodded.

The policeman opened the back door of the ambulance. He looked at me. "Can I ask her some questions?"

"Sure. Go ahead," I said.

"Is my car badly damaged?" the woman asked him.

"Three flat tires," he said. "Can you tell me what happened?"

"No," she answered.

"Have you been drinking?"

"A few."

"What's a few?"

She shrugged. "Two, maybe three martinis."

The policeman didn't bat an eye. I wrote it down on the call sheet.

"I don't want to stay here," she told the policeman.

Again I handed her the refusal slip. I showed her where to sign it. She looked at it, then at me. "What does it say?" she asked.

"That we offered you transportation to a hospital and you refused it."

"That's all it says?"

"That's all," I told her.

She signed it and handed it to me. I unhooked the cables from the electrodes and pulled the electrodes off her chest. "If you start feeling bad later on," I told her, "such as sleepiness, headache, or nausea, we advise you to see a doctor."

The policeman held the door open for her as she stepped off the ambulance.

Three martinis.

Two beers.

A couple of drinks.

Just one glass of wine.

About half a pint of whiskey.

We've heard them all.

Vehicular accident as a result of alcohol intoxication. Many are single vehicle accidents. Larry hit a tree. She crossed the median and ended up in the eastbound lane. But many, too many, involve another vehicle and its occupants.

"Two beers," he mumbled, answering our question.

Blood oozed from a laceration on his forehead. He was pinned in the car, the steering wheel pressed against his chest.

The damage to the other car was worse, as were the occupant's injuries. Barely conscious, she was dangerously close to choking on blood, broken teeth, and pieces of her tongue. Her left arm was broken in three places. Her spleen was ruptured. Both hip joints were fractured. We suctioned and controlled the bleeding, splinted, cut her out of the car, started two lines of Lactated Ringers, and called for Pegasus.

We transported him by ambulance. In addition to the laceration on his head, he had two fractured ribs and a broken ankle.

Neither of them died, but I'm not sure it can be said that she truly survived the accident. She was a high school history teacher returning home from work that day to her husband and ten-month-old baby boy. She stayed in the hospital for three months and is still in physical therapy. She feels she can no longer teach, is afraid to drive, and suffers from periods of deep depression. Her marriage is failing.

I don't know what became of him. I do know he didn't go to jail and it frightens me to think he may still be out there on the highway.

I didn't like him. I don't even know if I took care of him very well. And worse, I don't even know if I care.


The cold wave continued. A weak low pressure system worked its way into the Carolinas and the local weatherman reported that we might get some form of precipitation in the next twenty-four hours. What we got at seven o'clock the following evening was a sudden and severe ice storm.

I switched on the outside light and opened the door. Already there was about an inch of ice on the porch railing. I shivered and closed the door.

"I would rather have ten inches of snow than this ice," I commented to David. I sat down beside him on the sofa to watch the evening news. Jennifer was asleep and the boys were perched in front of the radio downstairs, hoping to hear an announcement of school closing.

The tones went off.

"It's going to be a wreck," I said.

101

"Mmm," David nodded, his attention focused on Peter Jennings. "Probably."

It was.

I heard the location, Route 3 east, and listened for the duty crew to respond. It took them twice as long as the average four minutes. They had just started en route to the scene when the tones went off again, for another wreck, this one further east on Route 3.

"Do you mind if I go on the second call?" I asked. "It's another wreck."

"If you think it's safe."

"Oh, I'll be okay," I assured him.

He shrugged. "Go ahead, but take it slow."

I took David's advice and took it slowly, so slowly that the ambulance pulled away several minutes before I got to the building. No problem, I thought to myself. I'll just drive to the scene of the second call.

I turned right east onto Route 3. The lights of the ambulance disappeared around the curve ahead of me. I looked down at the speedometer, forty-six, too fast with the ice on the road beneath me. I stepped on the brake, knowing in that split second that it was a mistake.

My car veered suddenly to the left. I tried steering in the same direction, but it was too late. The car spun out of control, then came dangerously close to going off the right side of the road, where the shoulder dipped sharply. Instead, it balanced the edge like a tightrope walker, then eased slowly to a stop.

My hands gripped the steering wheel. My heart pounded, my thoughts raced . . . I had almost wrecked . . . almost rolled the car . . . what kept me on the road . . . if I'd wrecked would there have been anyone left to come for me . . . would I have hung upside down in my overturned car, suspended by my seat belt until . . . until . . . if I spun out, then another car could . . . and hit me . . . I had to get out . . .

I opened the door and stepped out onto the ice, the ground was so slippery I had to hold onto the car to get around it.

I would have to walk back and wanted to get as far off the road as I could. Another car might spin on the ice and instead of coming to rest on the grass, it could easily come to rest on me. I moved as quickly as I could toward the line of evergreens well away from any oncoming traffic.

I wore jeans, a sweatshirt, tennis shoes, and my rescue jacket, which was not designed for a night such as this. I had no gloves, no hat, no boots.

The ice continued to fall. Under different circumstances, I would have been able to appreciate the beauty of such a winter wonderland. Even in the darkness I saw that everything around me sparkled, the grass, the pines, and the cedars.

I stood for a moment trying to decide whether to stay parallel to the road or to go beyond the trees and cut across the golf course. I could see no traffic in either direction, but was still nervous about staying near the road. I knew too well how quickly something could happen, so I turned to go deeper into the grove of trees surrounding the golf course.

I had, however, forgotten about the fence. It was a simple rail fence, well camouflaged by the trees. It, too, was ice-covered, but lacked the glitter of the grass and evergreens. Actually, I forgot about the fence until I walked into it.

I felt for the bottom rail and placed my right foot on it, stepped up and started to swing my left leg over the top.

Except for the fact that the fence was not moving, it was a great deal like falling off a horse.

I lay on my back perfectly still for a moment, then slowly straightened my right leg, which had twisted when I fell. My knee hurt. I knew I should feel the knee and compare it with the left one, to make sure there was no deformity, but wasn't sure I had any feeling left in my fingers.

I lay on the ground staring upward into the trees and wondered aloud, "Is this really what I want to be doing with my life?"

I left my family and my warm house with logs blazing in the fireplace for this?

I sat up, then cautiously stood, hoping my knee wouldn't buckle. It was sore, but stable. I felt my way through the trees and out onto the golf course. I was in the open. Without branches above me for protection, I took the full brunt of the falling ice.

It stuck to my hair. It hit me in the face. It fell into my pockets where my hands were burrowed.

About 50 yards ahead I saw a lighted house and headed for it. I walked carefully up the ice-covered steps and knocked on the door.

The door opened.

"Pat!"

"Betty!"

"What are you doing over here?"

"It's a long story," I told her. She opened the door and welcomed me inside.

I had stumbled onto the home of Betty and Dick Ferguson. He was one of our firemen. She fixed me a cup of tea, and then I reluctantly called David. He and John Beery went to get the car, then David came to get me.

"You hadn't even turned off the ignition," David scowled on our way home. "The lights were on. Everything was on."

"Well, it was nice and warm for you," I said.

"That was really stupid, Pat."

"Maybe it was," I conceded. "Did you all have any trouble getting there?"

"No, not really."

"I guess I need more practice."

"You want to drive now?" he asked me as we turned onto our street.

"No, thanks. No more tonight."

The next day Joyce told me that it took them an hour to get to the hospital. She and Bob transported the three patients from both wrecks and sent the second ambulance back in case there was another call.

"We went off the road twice," she said. "None of our patients was seriously hurt, but they were really scared. So was I," she admitted. "When we got to Fredericksburg, we pulled behind a sand truck and he made a path for us to the hospital."

"That was lucky."

"It sure was," she nodded. "Just be glad you weren't out in it."

"Well," I began . . .

Even from a distance it was terrifying.

And I was unprepared.

How can one make ready? How could I have been primed, rehearsed for this? The sight of a fully involved structure fire, the acrid odor of smoke so thick that it coats the tongue, the sudden impact of oppressive heat, and the knowledge, the awful knowledge, that there are children trapped inside.

They were sisters, aged two and five. They had been up at dawn to find their baskets from the Easter bunny. It was a beautiful spring Sunday and they had spent most of the day outside. By 6:00 they were ready for bed. They climbed the stairs to their bedroom on the second floor of the old farmhouse. Their mother tucked them in bed and kissed them goodnight. By 6:15 they were sound asleep.

There was still some daylight left, so their father went back out into the field. Their mother carried the laundry basket outside and began taking the clothes off the line.

She had her younger daughter's pink-and-white socks in her hand when she saw the smoke drifting through the back porch screens. She yelled to her husband, then started for the house, but already the smoke had thickened.

He reached her side just as the heat shattered the kitchen window. Flames engulfed the back porch, spread rapidly through the downstairs and barricaded all entrances to the house. They would have to go to a neighbor's house to call for help.

As we moved down the long narrow road which led to the farmhouse, we could see the red glow in the sky. When we reached the clearing . . .

". . . Jesus Christ," John's voice, a whisper.

Suzanne involuntarily moved her foot from the gas pedal to the brake.

"There can't be children in that house," I said aloud, as if my words could make it so.

We continued. I radioed Bud Morley who was with the fire truck and asked him where he wanted us.

"Go to the end of the field," he told us. "The family's there."

We veered to the left and saw Larry Hurlock from Richardsville's Fire Department.

Suzanne stopped the ambulance.

"The parents are over there," Larry said, pointing behind him. "They've lost their kids. The mother's in bad shape. You better check on her."

John had taken his fire gear and joined the other firemen. Mine Run's engine was on the scene along with an engine and tanker from Orange. I went to the mother.

Friends had moved her to this area to keep her away from the fire. They felt she would be safer in the field. Near the house she had continued to break away from them in an attempt to get inside to her children.

She was kneeling on a blanket. Her husband sat behind her, softly caressing her back. One of her friends held her arm. Her face was turned toward the house and I could see the reflection of the fire in her eyes.

"My babies," she moaned. "I want my babies."

Her friend tightened the hold on her arm, but she pulled away suddenly and started to stand up.

"I've got to get my babies out," she cried.

Her husband turned away, to a neighbor who sat beside him. He could no longer absorb her grief along with his own.

I moved slowly toward her, reached out and placed my hand on her shoulder. I tried to take her hand but felt something there. I thought it was a handkerchief. Then I looked and saw that she was grasping the pink-and-white socks from the clothesline.

I knelt to the ground with my hand still on her shoulder. She came with me. I didn't say anything. I just put my arms around her, turning her until her back was to the fire and held her close to me.

She rested her head against mine. Holding her, I could feel her cries before I heard them. I felt as if my own heart were breaking.

I don't know how long we stayed that way. Suzanne returned to tell me that the Orange County Squad was going to take the parents to the hospital.

"We've got to get them out of here," Suzanne whispered to me, "before the firemen find the bodies."

I wrapped a blanket around her shoulders and helped her to her feet. I held her as we approached the ambulance. She walked trance-like until the doors were opened, then tried to pull away.

"No," she screamed. "I'm not leaving my babies."

We had to lift her into the ambulance.

Over the years since that Easter Sunday, I have journeyed thousands of miles in an ambulance. I have witnessed tragedies and experienced profound grief, but never felt the immeasurable helplessness of that night when I held her in my arms.

I walked back through the field toward the fire. Suzanne and I got the oxygen tanks and drinking water for the firemen. We helped them set up the lights.

The left side of the house collapsed. Sparks of fire crackled and fell. Voices echoed over the radio. Firemen moved, shimmering silhouettes drifting into and then away from the intense heat.

At 11:45, John told us we could return to the station.

At 12:30, they found the children's bodies.

At 1:15, our firemen came home.

# Chapter 12

SUNDAY, APRIL 24, dawned grey and rainy in Lake of the Woods. It was to be another spring day disguised as winter. The downpour of the previous night had added two and a half inches of rain to the already saturated earth and swollen lakes. The thermometer would not hit fifty.

Six miles away in Spotsylvania County's Lake Wilderness, a waterfront development much like Lake of the Woods, a real estate agent, Jo Ann Murphey, was showing property to Beth and Larry Williams. The Williamses, searching for a piece of land away from the frenzied life of northern Virginia, would soon find their lives dependent on the strength of a single steel guidepole and the combined efforts of five fire and rescue organizations.

The clubhouse at Lake Wilderness, situated atop a gently sloping hill overlooking the lake, is a drawing point and the Williamses were anxious to see it. Access to the clubhouse grounds is over a forty-foot concrete bridge which spans the water at the base of the lake's spillway. Water level on the bridge is not usually a hazard. On that Sunday, however, local flooding had turned the spillway, angled at forty-five degrees, into a surging waterfall.

Mrs. Murphey hesitated at the water's edge. "I think I can make it across," she told the Williamses. She drove cautiously onto the bridge. As they advanced, the water continued to rise.

Halfway across, the engine stalled. The Volkswagen Rabbit was caught in the turbulent waters.

Keeping a firm grip on the car roof, Mrs. Murphey eased out of the car. The Williamses, first Larry, then Beth, followed.

"I'll walk across and get help," Mrs. Murphey yelled above the noise of the rushing water. "Open the doors so the car won't go over." The water's force had thrust the Rabbit against one of the five guidepoles lining the bridge.

With her briefcase in hand and her purse strap around her neck, Mrs. Murphey stepped away from the car. The rushing water immediately caught her and swept her off the bridge and thirty feet downstream, then threw her to her knees on the bank. The force of the water had pulled off her slacks. Unable to swim, Mrs. Murphey had miraculously survived.

A resident whose home overlooked the spillway witnessed the near tragedy and called for help.

At 1:03 our tones sounded. "Attention Lake of the Woods Fire and Rescue members. You have a call at Lake Wilderness. People are trapped on a bridge in high water."

Lake of the Woods also has a spillway bridge.

Fire and rescue members responding from the west side of the Lake property must cross it. Our bridge had been closed several times in April because of high water. When it was closed we had to detour out to Route 3 and from there back to the property of the fire and rescue building. The detour slowed our response time.

The bridge was closed again that day.

As I approached the hill leading to the spillway, I saw the warning sign: BRIDGE CLOSED, DETOUR. To save time I decided to try to make it across anyway. The sawhorses blocking the roadway left just enough room to squeeze through. However, the driver of the car in front of me, seeing my emergency flashers, pulled over to allow me to pass. In doing so, he cut me off from the narrow passageway to the bridge and forced me to take the detour. I thought of this later. I was driving a Volkswagen Rabbit.

Linda, Ed, Jean and I were in the ambulance which arrived on the scene at 1:27. Buzzy O'Toole came behind us, driving the crash truck and towing the water rescue boat. Chancellor's Chief, Nat Harefield, arrived. He would assume the responsibility of scene commander. He radioed the Spotsylvania dispatcher and requested assistance from the Fredericksburg dive team, the Chancellor brush truck, and the 100-foot aerial ladder truck from Orange. He wanted all options open, all equipment available. Our squad was responsible for caring for Mrs. Murphey and the Williamses.

On the bridge the Williamses stood close to the stalled car, both of them gripping the door's frame. He stood behind her, his arms encircling her, trying to protect her from the brunt of the water. They shared the knowledge that she, like Mrs. Murphey, could not swim.

Eight fire and rescue members from the responding companies formed a human chain across the footbridge forty feet downstream from the concrete bridge. If the Williamses fell into the water, the people on the footbridge would be in position to attempt a rescue.

Mrs. Murphey stood on the lake bank, wrapped in a blanket given her by one of the Lake Wilderness residents. Her eyes were fixed on the Williamses. She was shivering from the cold. I wrapped another blanket around her. My presence did not divert her attention from the Williamses.

"We'd better get you in out of the cold," I told her.

"No!" she insisted. "I'm staying here. Can't someone help them?" she asked. "When are you going to help them?"

The options open to Nat were limited. He considered driving one of the brush trucks onto the bridge alongside the Williamses, but the possibility of the truck's losing traction and dislodging the car made this plan too dangerous. It also did not seem feasible to work our heavy rescue boat out to them. The rising water could sweep it against the car.

The greatest potential for disaster lay in the fact that the bridge guidepoles were not close enough together to hold the car if it were hit.

Above the roar of the water Mr. Williams called to us. "Please hurry. Please!"

Hearing his call for help heightened our sense of urgency and anxiety.

Mrs. Murphey began to cry. I laid my hand on her arm.

"Let me go," she said, pulling away. "It's my fault. I've got to help them." She started toward the water.

Linda stepped in front of her. "Mrs. Murphey," she said, "these people are trained in water rescues. It always takes a little time to get the equipment ready. If you will sit in this truck, you'll still be able to see them and you'll be warm."

Finally she looked at us. "I'm so scared," she cried. "I'm so tired." She no longer pulled away. Instead, she allowed us to lead her to the brush truck.

Meanwhile, Nat decided to attempt a foot rescue. John Harkness volunteered for the job. A professional fireman for the City of Richmond, John, twenty-five, is also a volunteer on our rescue squad and our fire department. He is skilled and dependable. I like running calls with John.

The first step was to secure a rope across the spillway bridge. On our side, rescue workers wrapped the rope around the bumper of the Chancellor brush truck and knotted it tightly. John carried the coil of rope, easing it out as he crossed the footbridge to the other side of the spillway. He walked the rope up the lake bank until it ran parallel to the spillway bridge, then pulled it taut and tied it to a pickup parked at the end of the spillway bridge. He crossed back over the footbridge to our side. Rescue workers attached a lifeline to the rope and secured the line around John's waist.

We watched him step out into the water. The Williamses watched too, their eyes following him as he inched along carefully, holding tightly to the rope. As he entered the more turbulent water near the car, it was apparent he was having difficulty keeping his footing. Twice he almost fell but finally he reached the Rabbit. We could see him talking to the Williamses.

On shore, we relaxed. For the first time, Mrs. Murphey smiled. The waiting was almost over.

No, Nat decided. It was too dangerous. It had been difficult enough for John to cross the water. The Williamses had been on the bridge for over an hour and had weakened under the strain of withstanding the unremitting assault of the frigid water. John would have to practically carry them across. What if he slipped or if they lost their hold? We also now had the information that Mrs. Williams could not swim.

We saw John speak once again to the Williamses. Then he returned to the bank alone.

Frustration mounted. Once more Mr. Williams called to us, "Please hurry!"

It was now apparent that the need for the aerial truck was crucial. Contact with Orange County was reestablished. Nat's message was "Expedite!" Orange's dispatcher informed him that the truck was five miles away. We moved all vehicles from the immediate area so the aerial truck could get as close to the water as possible.

Its arrival made us feel hope again. It slowly maneuvered into position. Three times the firemen extended the ladder before proper placement was attained. The top of the ladder came just above the top of the car.

John Harkness began his second rescue attempt.

He edged across the rungs of the ladder stretching horizontally across the water. There was stillness throughout the entire group of rescue workers and onlookers watching him from the bank. In a crouched position he walked across, rung after rung, taking with him life jackets for the Williamses.

John reached the car and let himself down beside the Williamses. An audible sigh of relief rose from the crowd. He helped Mrs. Williams into a life jacket.

Across the ladder now came Scott Clements, an Orange County fireman. Cautiously, John eased Beth Williams onto the roof of the car and then onto the ladder. With great care, Scott assisted her as she slowly crossed the rungs toward safety.

They were halfway across the ladder when our worst fear almost became reality. The car, held precariously by the guide-pole, began to move ever so slightly. John's weight and movement had caused it to shift. With Scott and Mrs. Williams only halfway across, John knew the ladder, in its horizontal position, could not support any additional weight.

"Hurry!" he called to Scott.

Scott hurried. As soon as Mrs. Williams was safely on the firetruck, he immediately returned to the car. It had stabilized for the moment, but they needed to be off it quickly in case it started moving again.

We were there with blankets when Beth Williams was lifted down from the firetruck. We helped her into the ambulance, where Linda and Jean removed her clothes and piled blankets on her.

I left the ambulance to await Larry Williams. John had positioned him on the car, then helped him step onto the ladder. As soon as Scott and Mr. Williams reached land, John followed.

It was over.

Nat's leadership, combined with the joint cooperative efforts of the five fire and rescue companies, had paid off. The Williamses had been saved.

In September 1983, at Virginia Beach, during the annual convention of the Virginia Association of Fire and Rescue Squads (241 squads with 7,500 members), Lake of the Woods Fire and Rescue Squad received the award for RESCUE CALL OF THE YEAR.

John Harkness was the recipient of the Harlan Sanger Award, "for the most heroic deed, above and beyond the call of duty, performed by an individual in the saving of a human life."

Jo Ann Murphey and both the Williamses attended the awards presentation in a ceremony at Lake of the Woods.

It was an emotional moment for John. His reaction, revealed in the wording of his brief acceptance, was typical of him.

"Scott Clements deserves this award as much as I do," John said. "I thank you. This is a real honor."

# Chapter 13

WHEN WE REACH the eleventh hour of our twelve-hour day shift, we feel it's pretty much over. It doesn't matter how often we have been proved wrong. We still tend to do it.

It was a little after five. I put the roast in the oven. Dave and Matt had friends over and were playing downstairs. Tammy, one of my regular sitters, was watching TV with Jennifer. She came home from school with her on my duty days in case I got a call. Of course, by the eleventh hour . . .

. . . the tones went off.

The call was for a diabetic. We found the young woman unconscious on her living room floor. She was in insulin shock. Suzanne tried to start an IV in order to administer a heavy dose of dextrose, but the woman's veins were too delicate. We quickly transported her to the hospital. She would recover, but it was not an easy call.

I got home at 7:30.

The roast was black. Dave and Matt and their friends had teased Tammy to the point that she locked herself in Jennifer's room and came out only when David got home from work at six. He had attempted to fix bacon and eggs and had scorched the eggs.

I was met with angry stares, a heavy aroma of burned food and a full account of what had transpired since my departure.

"I don't think it's too much to ask," I told Dave and Matt. "Just leave Jennifer and Tammy alone."

"They were yelling at us," Matt argued.

"I don't care who started it," I said. "I want it stopped!"

"Well, it was sure a mess when I got home from work," David said. "What good is a babysitter if she's sitting in a locked room crying?"

"Jennifer was in the locked room with her, wasn't she?" I asked him.

"If that was supposed to be funny, I fail to see the humor. And," he added, "why didn't you set the timer on the oven? Maybe someone would have heard the buzzer, even above the crying and yelling."

"I was going to," I told him, "but the tones went off right after I put the roast in."

"The tones went off!" David said. "Maybe we should set some tones off around here when we want something!"

"I don't think you're being fair," I told him. "I'm on duty every four days. That's less than twice a week. It's not like I'm never here. Besides," I said, smiling, "I've burned meals standing right in front of the stove. I don't need an excuse."

"You're right about that. Okay," he shrugged, "I've had a long day."

Jennifer crawled up into my lap. "Daddy's eggs were yucky, Mom. Will you fix me something else to eat?"

"Sure," I told her. "How about a hot dog? We can't ruin that, can we?"

"Mom," Dave said, just as I thought the discussion was finished, "if you go off duty at six, how come you just got home?"

I looked at him sitting cross-legged on the floor, "I'm on duty until six o'clock. If there's a call at one minute before six I have to go. If that means . . . oh, what difference does it make? Look," I said to him, to each of them, "you all have things that are important to you. Well, this is important to me." I eased Jennifer off my lap and got up to go into the kitchen. "Now, who wants a hot dog?"

Four hands shot into the air.

I understood how they felt. Until the day I joined the rescue squad, I had been only wife and mother, Cub Scout leader, nursery school aide, elementary school volunteer, PTA member, chauffeur and cheerleader for swim meets and soccer games, and David's crew on the sailboat. All of them saw me as an extension of themselves, not a separate entity.

When I joined the rescue squad, my goal had not been to affirm my individuality. Yet somehow I was becoming more my own person. Myself. My self.

Gradually, my family's resentment diminished. I even saw in them a growing sense of pride in what I was doing.

"My Mom saves lives," I heard Jennifer tell a friend of hers one day. On one of her first grade papers, written in her painstaking beginner's handwriting, was: "My Mom is on the Lake of the Woods Rescue Squad. My Mom goes on rescue calls. She helps people who have been in wrecks. She helps people who are very sick. She takes them to the hospital. Because my Mom is an EMT and I am going to be one too."

On Mother's Day of that year, Dave gave me a poem he had written, entitled "My Mother." It included these lines:

> Another thing about my Mom . . .
> She has determination.
> It took a lot of time and patience,
> But she finally made this proclamation:
> "I'm an official EMT and a darn good one too!"
> I'm proud of her, but not surprised,
> Because this, with her kindness,
> I knew she could do.

Matt drew a picture of an ambulance and Jennifer colored it. David gave me my own stethoscope and blood pressure cuff.

I hadn't realized how sweet the icing on the cake could be.

That summer my family joined my parents for our traditional week's vacation at Topsail Beach, North Carolina. As always, we loved every minute of it, fishing, swimming, shelling, relaxing.

It was also nice to come home, however. The boys headed for the park. David went to his office for a few hours, taking Jennifer with him. As I sorted through the suitcases, it occurred

116

to me that it was my duty day. Suzanne had covered for me during my absence, but as long as I was back I decided I might as well put in three hours of duty. I called Suzanne and relieved her.

Dave and Matt came in, switched on the TV and plopped down on the living room floor. I carried the basket of dirty clothes downstairs and was putting them in the washer when . . .

"Did the tones go off?" I called up to the boys. My pager was in its charger in the living room.

"I don't think so," Dave answered.

I walked upstairs to check and heard Orange dispatching Mine Run for a 10-50. Their tones were similar to ours.

"You were right, Dave," I said on my way back downstairs.

Moments later he yelled to me, "Hey, Mom. Now they are."

I heard them. I ran up the steps and grabbed my pager, then back to the bedroom to find my jumpsuit. I had no way of knowing when I pulled out of the driveway that it would be nine hours before I returned home.

Our call was to assist Mine Run on the 10-50.

The delivery truck's brakes had failed. The driver lost control and the truck swerved off the road, hit a tree, and immediately burst into flames.

By the time we arrived on the scene, Mine Run's fire department had extinguished the blaze. Battlefield's rescue squad members had bandaged the men's burned arms and were pouring water over them.

Orange notified us that the Burn Unit at the University of Virginia Hospital in Charlottesville could handle only one patient. The driver was in critical condition with second- and third-degree burns over 80 percent of his body. Battlefield would transport him to Charlottesville.

Our patient, with severe burns over 60 percent of his body, was fully conscious. It would have been better had he not been.

His name was Walt.

We moved him from the ground onto our ambulance. Ed drove. Jean and Lou and I were in the back.

"Please," he moaned, holding up his bandaged arms. "More water."

We poured container after container of fluids over his arms, legs and chest, but his relief was short-lived. All his hair was singed on his head, in his nose and on his chest, and his eyebrows and lashes were burned away. Patches of burns covered his body and face, some blistered crimson, others charred black.

"Oh, God," he cried.

I wanted to reach out to him but his burns were so widespread there was no place to rest my hand. I was afraid even the light touch of my fingertips would intensify his pain.

"Walt," I said softly.

He looked at me. His eyes were sea blue and their beauty startling against the contrast of his burned and blistered face. With our eyes, we made our only contact.

I sponged his parched lips. Jean poured water over his arms. "Earl," he said. "Where's Earl?" His voice was dry, raspy.

I leaned closer to him. "The man with you?"

"He didn't die," he said, not a question, a plea.

"No, Walt, he didn't die," I told him. "Another ambulance took him to Charlottesville, to the hospital there."

"I tried," he said. "I tried so hard."

"What do you mean?" I asked him.

"I got out," he said. "So much fire. I had to get Earl out . . . had to go back for Earl." His breaths were shallow, labored. I moistened his lips again. "I ran to a stream," he continued, "to put out the fire on me. I carried water in my hands for Earl." He started to cry. "The fire was still on Earl."

We learned later that he had received most of the severe burns on his arms and face when he pulled his friend Earl from the truck.

"Walt," Lou said, "I'm going to give you a shot for the pain." She had talked to the hospital. With Walt's arms so badly burned and covered with bandages, she would not attempt an IV, but instead would administer the morphine intramuscularly. She injected it into his thigh.

He continued to cry.

We reached Mary Washington Hospital and rushed him into

118

My first Team 3. Left to right, Woody Fox, Jean Lodge, Pat Ivey, Buzzy O'Toole.

My second Team 3. Left to right, Joe Broderick, Pat Ivey, Jean Lodge.

The men of Station 52.

Scene of the accident in Chapter 16.

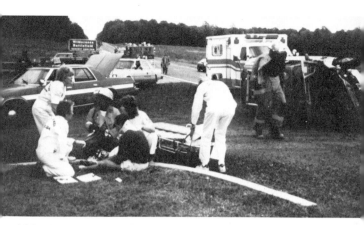

ACCIDENT SCENE. Left to right, Pat Ivey, Millie Droste, Marcus Wallace, Mara Bueng, Joe Broderick.

MOTORCYCLE ACCIDENT. Squad members, left to right, are Jean Lodge (standing), Buzzy O'Toole, Joe Broderick, Kathy Gates, Pat Ivey.

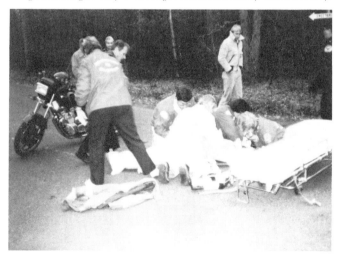

PEGASUS

Easter Sunday fire in which two small children died.

WATER RESCUE. John Harkness moves the Hilliards to safety and is later presented the award for heroism.

Joe Broderick comforts child following minor accident.

SCENE OF WRECK at which Lake of the Woods fireman, Harry Haas, suffered heart attack. Harry is second from the right, facing forward, in this picture which was taken minutes before he went into cardiac arrest.

the trauma room. "We're going to stabilize him," the doctor told us. "That's all we can do. You'll have to take him to the burn unit at MCV."

"Take the pillow out from under his head," a nurse told me. "then rinse his arms again."

I slowly pulled the pillow away. Walt's hair came with it. The stench of burned hair and flesh was overwhelming. I gasped.

"Breathe through your mouth," the nurse told me.

The saliva was rising in my throat. "I . . ."

"Do it!" she ordered.

I dropped the pillow on the floor and rinsed his arms, all the time taking quick breaths through my mouth. It helped. I didn't vomit, but the feeling of nausea stayed.

The doctor uncovered enough of Walt's arms to start an IV of Lactated Ringers to prevent him from going into shock. With the IV established, the morphine could be injected into his veins, a much faster route, and he began to relax.

It was a long trip to Richmond. Walt moaned most of the way. Although Lou gave him the maximum permissible amount of morphine, there was no possibility of taking all the pain away.

At the Medical College of Virginia hospital, we followed the labyrinth of hallways to the burn unit: a bleak and melancholy place. There were no pictures or decorations on the institutional green walls. But what could be done to brighten this place of unremitting pain, this place where survival was often out of the question?

We wheeled Walt down the hallway past room after room of burn victims. Some were bandaged and sedated. One man had lost both ears. Another had severe facial scars and only a slit for a mouth. Many strained to see us, to get a look at Walt, perhaps wondering if he was in worse shape than they were.

He would be a member of this brotherhood, this tightly-knit group whose bonds were pain and disfigurement.

We left him there. Leaving was difficult because we had been with him for so long and because we knew that, for him, the worst was yet to come.

Walt and Earl were in the hospital for months, but they survived. They were both scarred and would carry those scars with them, but they were alive.

We later learned that they had been boyhood friends. They'd gone through school together and afterwards, found jobs with the same food delivery service.

They took turns driving the truck. That day had been Earl's turn at the wheel. Had it been Walt's, Earl would have done the same for him.

We never saw either of them again, but we will always remember Walt. We remember him as a hero. Walt, I'm sure, would not agree.

Our next training session was for the benefit of our cardiac technicians: John, Mark, Lou, Suzanne, and Bob Luckett. CTs are encouraged to start four IVs a month. When the number of advanced life support calls has been less than usual, they must find a way of honing their skills.

Lou had all the supplies out, angiocaths, tourniquets, alcohol swabs, tape, bags of D5W, lines, and three-way stopcocks. Throughout the room, sleeves were pushed up, veins inspected.

Bob Luckett grabbed my arm.

Bob had joined the squad a year earlier when he and his wife, Karen, moved to Lake of the Woods. He worked on an ambulance in the city of Alexandria.

We had some "professionals" on our rescue squad and in the fire department. They were all good at what they did and we were eager to have their help, but now and again there would be problems. Perhaps they would be too pushy or perhaps we would be too defensive.

Bob was pushy. He was opinionated and pompous. He could be vulgar and he was always loud. He had all the characteristics I dislike, but I still liked him.

He was smart and confident. He had a greater understanding of emergency medicine than any squad member I've known because he made the effort not just to know what physiological changes occurred with illness and injury, but why those changes occurred. He was someone I liked having beside me on a call.

He told me I could be more and I believed him.

I looked at his hand on my arm. "You're after my veins, aren't you?"

"No," he said, letting go. "I get enough practice at work. Pull up a chair. You're going to practice on me."

"I can't, Bob," I told him. "I'm not a CT."

"Sit down," he said. I sat. He walked over to the IV box, carried the items over to me and dropped them in my lap. "Do you know what all this is?"

"I know what it is," I said. "But I can't do it."

He picked up the angiocath, pulled the wrapper off and handed it to me. "You can do it."

"Bob," I started to object.

He held up his hand. "No, don't say it. I've been thinking," he told me, "and I've decided you'd be a good CT."

I smiled, shaking my head.

"What's so funny?"

"Oh, just shades of Lou and John," I said. "You people deciding what I should do."

"You make the decisions," he told me. "We just help you along a little."

"That's how it works, huh? Suppose I don't like the idea?"

He shrugged. "I don't give up easily." He held the angiocath closer to me. "Now, stick me."

"Bob, I really don't want to."

"I don't have all night," he said.

I sighed. "Where did you put the tourniquet?"

He handed it to me and I tied it tightly around his upper arm. He placed my hand on the vein at the bend of his elbow. "I'm a fat boy so you can't see it. You've just got to feel for it."

"Feel for it?"

"Yep. It'll be good for you. There are a lot of fat people out there."

I wiped the site with an alcohol swab and removed the cap from the angiocath. Again I felt for the vein, then placed the needle against his arm. My hand was shaking.

"I can't do it," I said.

"Yes, you can."

I pushed the needle into his skin and slanted it toward the

vein. His blood filled the chamber. "Okay, kiddo," he grinned. "You've got flashback."

"I did it, Bob!"

"Of course you did. Now, take the needle out."

In an actual emergency, as soon as the needle's withdrawn, the line is attached to the catheter still in the vein. We had no line here and when I withdrew the needle I forgot to apply pressure on the vein just above the entry site, to prevent his blood from flowing from the catheter.

"I can't believe I really did it!" I exclaimed.

"You did it, all right," Bob said as we both looked down to see his blood streaming down his arm. He applied pressure with his fingers and the bleeding stopped. "Take the catheter out and give me a band-aid," he said, "before you have to give me a transfusion."

"I'm sorry," I said, putting the band-aid on his arm. "Other than that, how was it?"

"It was good," he said. "Class starts in January."

"What class?"

"Cardiac technician class."

"I'll think about it," I told him.

"Here's something else to think about," he said. "We have what's called a ride-along program at work. You could come to Alexandria for a day and run calls with me."

"In the city?" I asked.

He laughed. "Where do you think we run our calls?"

"I just meant . . . I don't know. It would be so different."

"That's the point," he said.

"It does sound interesting," I admitted.

"Believe me, it is."

"I'll think about it."

"Good," he nodded. "I'll give you a call."

Ed went off the squad that fall. He'd had problems with his back for a long time and his doctor finally told him he'd have to give up the squad.

"I'm really going to miss you," I said to him. "You were so good with me, and so patient."

He smiled at me. "You didn't take much patience, Pat," he said. "We had some good ones, didn't we? Remember our call for the brushfire and we got lost and had to ask the little boys which way the fire trucks went?"

"I remember them all, Ed," I told him.

"You're the team leader now," Lou said to me.

"I am?"

"You'll be fine," she said. "You're ready."

"I hope so," I told her. "Who else will be on my crew, besides Jean?"

"Buzzy and Woody."

"What a crew," I said.

And what a crew we were.

If Bob Grim was our somewhat mirthless Winnie-the-Pooh, then Buzzy was our bouncy Tigger. Always smiling, forever enthusiastic and full of energy, even on 6:10 A.M. calls. He was thirty-two years old, the baby of our team, but he was big and strong and he guarded over us. He was our paladin.

His mother was terminally ill. I believe most of his inner strength came from his relationship with her and the other members of that closely knit family. They owned and operated a local real estate agency. Even in the final weeks before her death, she sat at her desk still in charge. She was a fighter, and she was always smiling. When she died, Jean and Woody and I were there for Buzzy.

After our calls, Buzzy would buy us breakfast or lunch. If we weren't hungry for a meal, he'd get us a Coke or ice cream or a candy bar.

"What'll it be?" he'd ask, reaching for his wallet.

When he went on vacations, he'd return with gifts for the three of us.

"Buzzy, this is too much," we'd tell him.

"But you're my second family," he'd say.

"I shudder to think of Buzzy leaving us," Woody said one day. "We'd all have to go out and get real jobs."

Woody Fox was our humor.

We were a strange mix. In many ways we were so different. Jean was rigid. The rest of us weren't. They were Republicans.

I was the only Democrat. For two years in a row, our duty fell on election day. We went together to vote. "You might as well stay home," Woody told me.

Woody's hair is white; Jean's, gray; Buzzy's black, and mine is blonde. They towered over me. Buzzy would prop his elbow on my head. "Just resting," he'd say.

Given our choice, we may never have picked one another. What a loss that would have been, but Lou put us together and we were together for almost two years.

One of our first calls together was for Gladys. We've all had our turns with her. When the tones go off for a call at Gladys's, we groan. We don't drive quite as fast getting there.

"It's Gladys again," someone always mutters.

John once suggested that our EMT patches be withheld until we get a call for Gladys. "That's our real graduation," he grinned.

My "real graduation" was a memorable one. I'd heard a lot about her, that she was hostile and vulgar when she was drunk and no one had ever seen her when she wasn't. You never knew what you'd find when you went to Gladys's.

Maybe this time would be different, I thought to myself as we rounded the turn out of Lake of the Woods onto Route 3. I was up front with Buzzy. Jean and Woody were in back.

"We'll give her a lot of tender loving care," I told them. They laughed.

"We can try," I insisted.

"You're such a dreamer," Jean said to me.

Gladys was in bed. One of her sons walked with us into the tiny trailer bedroom. Her back was to us.

"I gotta go wait for the deputy," he said, turning to leave.

"The deputy's coming?" Buzzy asked. "For this?"

"No," he grinned, exposing yellow teeth. "Not for this."

For what, I wondered.

I sat down on the bed next to her and began to gently rub her back. "Gladys," I said softly, "can you tell me what happened?"

"No," she barked, squirming away from me.

Woody picked up an empty glass next to her bed and smelled it. "Whew," he whispered.

"What have you had to drink?" I asked her.

"Nothing." Her back was still to us. "I've just got this pain in my gut."

"Well, turn over and let us take a look."

"No!"

"Come on, sweetie," I said.

She did, quickly, with fists flying. She landed one on my arm. I stood up. Buzzy stepped forward.

"Get your damn hands off me," she yelled, "and don't give me any of that sweetie shit. I ain't no baby."

I stood next to her bed, looking down at her. "I'm not giving you any shit," I told her. "If you want to get better then get up and let's go to the hospital."

Buzzy's mouth opened.

Jean snickered.

"So much for TLC," Woody said.

"That's right," I snapped. I couldn't believe I had actually talked to a patient like that.

It did get her attention though. She let us help her onto the gurney and we carried her to the ambulance. We walked past her son. He was still waiting for the deputy.

"Give 'em hell, Mom," he laughed.

"You're a big help," Jean said to him.

There really was something about Gladys's place that just brought out the worst in us. After that first experience, our calls to Gladys's took much less time. I skipped the backrub and the "sweetie shit" and got quickly to the point.

We headed toward Mary Washington Hospital. Gladys lay quietly on the gurney, her hands folded across her chest, her bloodshot eyes staring at the ceiling. Jean, Buzzy, and I watched her closely.

Suddenly she shifted her gaze to us. "What the hell you looking at?" she said.

"Nothing," Jean answered.

Somehow I knew that was the wrong answer.

"What the hell you mean, 'nothing'?" she said, raising her fists again. "I oughta hit you."

"If you hit me," Jean told her, "I will hit you back."

"Jean!" I said.

"I mean it," Jean said to me.

Gladys's eyes closed and her fists relaxed. She lay still on the gurney.

"I'm going to wash her mouth out, too," Jean continued.

I bent over to look at Gladys. "I don't think she's breathing."

I tilted her head back, opened her mouth and put my cheek right next to her face. I smelled the sour odor of whiskey and felt her breath against my cheek.

"Good lord," I said. "I thought she'd died on us. Get her pulse."

"Gladys," Buzzy said, shaking her. I rubbed her sternum with my fist, then pinched the fleshy underside of her arm. She didn't respond to either pain stimulus.

"Her pulse is 82," Jean said. "She's alive."

"Okay." I relaxed. "I guess she just passed out."

"Can I wash her mouth out now?" Jean asked me.

We got her into the emergency room where she came to again, screaming and fighting and as foul-mouthed as ever.

"Thanks a lot," one of the ER nurses grumbled.

"Well," Woody smiled as we headed for home, "another save."

"To what avail?" Jean said.

"I don't even want to talk about it," I told them.

When Buzzy reached for his wallet and asked, "What'll it be?" I told him.

"I just want to go home."


Her name was Bea Oertel. David and I met her several months after we moved to Lake of the Woods. Politics was our common bond. She had worked for Vice-President Humphrey during the Johnson era. She served with David on the LOW Board of Directors. Bea and her husband, Joe, were childless and our family helped to fill that void in their life.

She was a spunky lady. There was no middle of the road for

Bea. She was never without a cause. She was also loving. Her friends were not the only ones who found her homemade breads and cakes on their doorsteps. If she heard of any neighbor who was going through difficult times, she was there for them, too.

She gave her time and talents to civic organizations and to our rescue squad, donating her popular baked goods and quilts to our fund-raisers. In 1981, she was awarded the Lake of the Woods Public Service Award.

My crew was on duty the day the call came in. I heard the tones and "Attention Lake of the Woods Rescue Squad members. You have a rescue call at the Oertel residence."

Lou came with us and when we arrived on the scene, we found her bedroom filled with friends and other rescue squad members.

She smiled when she saw me. I went to her and took her hand. "Hi, love," she said. Her breathing was labored. I took her blood pressure. It was a little low. Buzzy put oxygen on her and Lou placed the electrodes on her chest to monitor her heart.

"I'm just a little tired," Bea said. "I was up all night working on a quilt."

Lou started an IV on her. She was so good with Bea, smiling and calm, but I sensed that something was not right. Was it something in the tone of her voice, an expression on her face when she looked at the monitor? I don't know how I knew, but I knew.

As we carried Bea to the ambulance she was shouting orders to Joe, what phone calls needed to be made and who was to get the carrot cakes. "And don't forget my sewing box and quilt when you come to the hospital," were her last words to him.

The ambulance doors were closed.

"I'm sure it's just my ulcer acting up," she said to me as we drove toward Culpeper Memorial Hospital.

Her electrocardiogram said it was something else.

I stayed close to Bea. I was with her, but my eyes were on Lou. I didn't know what she saw on the monitor. To me, it was nothing more than squiggly lines.

Lou called the hospital and received orders for Lidocaine

which she immediately administered. She continued to watch the monitor.

We left Bea in the emergency room. She blew me a kiss. "I'll be home soon," she called to me. I wanted to believe her.

She died that night.

David was a pallbearer at her funeral. It rained that morning, but by afternoon the skies had cleared. We stood at her gravesite and listened to the minister read from Matthew:

"You have my Father's blessing: come, enter and possess the Kingdom that had been made ready for you since the world was made. For when I was hungry, you gave me food: when thirsty, you gave me drink: when I was a stranger you took me into your home, when naked you clothed me: when I was ill you came to my help, when in prison you visited me."

When I was ill you came to my help.

I had done that for Bea.

I wanted to be able to do more, to know what the squiggly lines meant. I didn't want to have to read a patient's medical prognosis from someone's facial expressions.

It was too late for Bea, but there would be others.

Several weeks later, Bob called me. "You ready to go to work in the big time?"

"I'm not sure," I told him.

"Come on," he insisted. "No guts, no glory."

"I'm not after glory."

"You'll see things you've never seen here," he said.

"That's what worries me."

"Come on, Pat."

"I said I'd think about it, Bob."

"Thinking time's over. I talked with the Chief and he said it would be fine. How about in two weeks, on a Wednesday or Thursday?"

I looked at my calendar. "Well . . . ."

"I knew you'd go," he said.

"That's not what I said. I'm thinking. I'm looking at my calendar and thinking. Don't be so pushy."

"I can't help it," he laughed.

"I know. Look, I'll have to get a babysitter and talk it over with David. What time would we leave that morning? And when would we get back?"

"We'd leave about 5:30."

"Gosh, that's early."

"It's the big time," he said. "We'll get home around 8:00 that night. My shift is from 7:00 to 7:00. Sometimes we can leave a little early if the night shift rolls in by 6:30."

"Okay," I told him. "I'll let you know for sure by next week."

"Sounds good," he said.

"Bob."

"Yeah?"

"I'm going to take the CT course."

He wasn't the least bit surprised.

# Chapter 14

WE PULLED ONTO U.S. 95 heading toward Washington. It was 5:15, still dark and already muggy. It would be even more oppressive in the city. I sipped my coffee. Bob talked.

"Our last ride-along came from Covington. That was the time we got the dude on PCP," he said, chuckling. "I told the cop I wasn't putting him in my ambulance so the cop shoves him in his car. Halfway to the hospital, cop pulls over and starts yelling at me that this guy's gone berserk. So we handcuff him. You ever see anybody on that stuff?" he asked.

"No," I said.

"Well, you wouldn't believe how strong it makes 'em. Took me and my partner and the cop to wrestle him down. The ride-along just stood there. His eyes were as big as saucers." Bob laughed. "Bet he went back to Covington and stayed there."

I failed to see the humor. I took another sip of coffee. It had cooled.

"Can just anybody be a ride-along?" I asked.

"Sure they can." He grinned. "Otherwise, you think you'd be going?"

"Bob."

"Nah, not just anybody," he conceded.

"Well, who can?"

"The guy from Covington was on a volunteer squad there. He was somebody's cousin, I think. We take some cops, some reporters. It just has to be okayed by the chief."

"I think it's really neat," I told him.

He glanced at me. "Let me hear you say that in twelve hours."

He switched off the headlights. I watched out the window when we reached Alexandria.

"That's where we used to live," I said, pointing to a row of townhouses clustered on a hill. In that area between Duke and Beauregard Streets the various apartment complexes were squeezed together so tightly it was difficult to tell where one ended and the next began. "I couldn't live like that again."

"Didn't like it much, huh?"

"No, not at all." I shook my head. "I'd never lived in a city and the two years there were enough. We bought our lot in the Lake shortly after four people were killed in the Roy Rogers restaurant which was a block away from us."

"Yeah, I remember that," he said. "Gruesome."

"Yes," I agreed, "it was. Indiscriminate killing. It's so frightening."

Bob nodded.

"Last night," I told him, "when I was getting my stuff together for today, Dave came in my room. He just stood there for a minute and then he said, 'Mom, please be careful when you go to Alexandria.' It surprised me because I hadn't really talked a lot about this and I didn't know it was on his mind. I gave him a hug and assured him I would be fine, but knew then that he had remembered. His concern almost made me change my mind, but I thought that if I did I would be saying that he does have something to worry about." I turned to Bob. "I don't want him to be afraid of the world."

"It can be pretty frightening though," he said.

"I know it can, but we can't let fear hold us back from living," I responded.

I felt his eyes on me, briefly, and knew he was smiling. It might have been his familiar mocking smile. I didn't return his look so I couldn't know for sure. It could have been that rare warm smile of his which I saw so seldom. He knew my history, not all of it, but enough to know that my comment to him was significant.

We turned into the section of the city which Station 22 serves. We rode several blocks before Bob pulled into a parking lot.

"This is the place," he announced. He got out of the car, locked his door and started toward the station.

"Could you wait, please?" I asked him, gathering my textbooks, my bag with my stethoscope and BP cuff, and my purse. I got out and kicked the car door closed.

He had stopped. "Didn't you lock it?"

"In case you didn't notice, my arms are full," I told him.

He returned to the car, locked my door, and started back across the parking lot. I tried to keep up with him. He waited for me at the entrance and we walked into the bay area together.

There were two ambulances, a tanker, and a hazardous materials truck.

Bob pointed to the bathroom. "When you go in there, close and lock the door. Otherwise somebody's gonna walk in on you." Then he showed me a filing cabinet. "If you've got any money, lock it up or it'll get stolen."

I stood there looking at him.

He opened a drawer of the cabinet, then grinned at me. "Welcome to the big time."

I put my purse inside.

"You'll need four dollars for your meals here," he reminded me.

I took a five dollar bill from my purse and stuck it in the back pocket of my jeans. Carrying my books and bag, I followed him up the three steps to the door to the living room.

"Guys, this is Pat Ivey, our tick for the day."

There were five of them and they all found Bob's introduction humorous. He never made it easy. I had no idea what he meant, but somehow knew this wasn't the time to ask.

"This is Danny, our Chief, and Ted, Bill, Jim, and Carl," Bob said with a wave of his hand.

And that was that. They went back to what they were doing. Danny, Carl, and Ted, Bob's partner for the day, were getting information off the computer. Bill and Jim were reading the morning paper.

I sat down at the table.

"Bad night?" Bob asked Danny.

"Nah," Danny answered. "Just five calls."

Bob took a sheet of paper from Danny's desk and put it in front of me. "Pat, you gotta fill this out," he said.

I took out my pen and looked down at the paper. It was a form for ride-alongs, explaining the procedures, requesting that a low profile be kept during any domestic violence calls (no problem there) and requiring my signature releasing the city from liability in case I was injured.

There was also a space for the reason why I was there as a ride-along. I simply put that I felt it would help me in my cardiac technician course. I didn't put that I also wanted to see the difference between rural and urban squads and between volunteers and paid professionals. If I wrote that down and any of them read it, they might look at me differently.

They might look at me.

So far they hadn't really, any more than they might glance at an extra chair.

I wondered again what a "tick" was.

It was almost time to begin our shift. Bob went upstairs to change into his uniform: blue slacks and a blue tee shirt with "Alexandria Paramedic" on it. I put the form on Danny's desk.

Bob poked his head in the doorway. "I gotta go get a blood test," he told me. "Part of our yearly checkup. I'll be back in about an hour."

"What if we get a call?" I asked him.

He shrugged. "Another station'll get it."

And he was gone.

The rest of the gang filed out shortly. They had their morning work detail, safety checks, and public service calls.

"Hey, Pat," Danny said to me, "can you hold down the fort for a while?"

"What am I supposed to do?" I asked him.

"Nothin'," he grinned. "One of us'll be right outside." He opened the door to leave. "Make yourself at home," he told me.

"Thanks, Danny."

I walked into the kitchen. The men were required to keep it

133

neat, and it was. Still, its appearance revealed its caretakers. Nothing sparkled. I found the dishcloth hanging from the sink spigot and wiped the counters, cleaning under and behind the coffee maker, scrubbing dust and crumbs from hidden corners. I rinsed the cloth and replaced it.

I found a cup, poured myself some coffee and spooned sugar into it. I opened the refrigerator for milk. On the top shelf stood a bottle of ketchup, a box of Arm & Hammer baking soda, and a half gallon of milk. Three bottles of salad dressing, a can of tuna fish, and a jar of mayonnaise completed the inventory.

I wondered what my four dollars was going to get me when mealtime came.

I carried my coffee into the living room and set it on a long wooden coffee table in front of one of the two sofas. A cabinet across from me held a TV, which could be turned on only during the lunch hour, from 12:00 to 1:00, and later for the evening news. Day crews were not allowed to stretch out on the sofas. For night crews, regulations were more relaxed, but nine-to-five was nine-to-five: the work hours. The men vacuumed the floors and after the breakfast dishes were washed, mopped the kitchen. They polished the vehicles and swept the floors of the bays.

I settled down on the sofa and opened the morning paper. I couldn't concentrate. The ceiling fan hummed above me and the speaker on the wall burped out a cacophony of beeps and buzzes and faraway voices. It occurred to me that I wouldn't know even if we did get a call. I didn't know what the station tones sounded like.

I set my paper aside and got up from the sofa. On the wall, pictures hung haphazardly, pictures of old fire companies. There was also a plaque commemorating Smokey the firedog, who died in a structure fire in 1965. I was attempting to straighten them when I heard the door open and turned to see Danny come in, two bags of groceries in his arms. He kicked the door closed. I glanced at the pictures and wondered why I had bothered.

"You need some help?" I called. He was in the kitchen and I could hear cabinet doors opening and closing.

"Nope," he called back. "I got it."

I was finding it difficult to remain seated while a man did the chores which were so much a part of my life.

Danny returned to his desk and sat down. "How long you been on the squad, Pat?" he asked me.

"Two and a half years."

"You get any bad ones down there?"

I nodded. "We get our share."

"Yeah, well," he said, "I guess people get sick and hurt whether they live in the city or the country."

"We don't get as many calls as you all do," I told him, "and we don't have a lot of violent calls, involving shootings and stabbings."

He leaned back in his chair. "You're not missing much," he said.

"I know. But," I added, "I guess you all don't get many farming accidents."

He grinned. "I can honestly say we've never had one!"

The other firemen burst in like boys from recess, boisterous, complaining, joking. Bill was stocky, dark, with a full moustache and black curly hair. Twice married, he had a five-year-old girl and a six-month-old boy. Jim had coloring similar to Bill's, but he was taller and more slender. He was separated from his wife.

Carl, the quietest and the youngest, looking not much older than Dave, had two children, aged two and five.

Sitting around the table, they continued their lively discussion of the people now coming into the department, people not really wanting to be firemen, but coming in for the paycheck.

"Snoops and crybabies," one of them said, "looking to move up the ladder by using politics."

"It sure wouldn't be by their performance on the job," another added.

Bill seemed to sum up the feelings of the group when he said, "When I'm inside a burning building I want the man behind me to care about me and my ass."

There was a unanimous nod.

The box on the wall beeped several times. They all came to their feet. Automatically, I stood up too.

"What is it?" I asked.

"Automobile fire," Bill said as he ran out. The door slammed. The pictures drooped.

I heard the sirens as they pulled away from the station. If I were at home, I thought, I'd be going on this call. I glanced at my watch: 9:30.

The door opened. "Come on, Pat," Bob barked at me. "Let's go."

I got up and started toward him. "To the fire?"

"Hell, no. To the garage."

I stopped. "The garage? What garage?"

"Just come on."

I followed him out into the bay area.

"You take the one that needs to be checked," Bob said to Ted. "Pat and I'll follow you in this one."

I got on the ambulance with Bob.

"You can ride up here with me now," he told me. "But when we go on a call you ride in the back."

"I don't think we're ever going to go on a call."

I buckled my seat belt as we pulled out of the bay. At the garage, Bob introduced me to the mechanics, then suggested we go by the dispatching center while they were working on the ambulance. Ted got up front. "You get in back," Bob said to me.

I tried the handle to the side door. It wouldn't open.

"Is this locked?" I asked Bob.

"Damn right it's locked," he said, reaching through the front door window to unlatch it from inside. "Somebody could get our drugs and be gone and all we'd see would be shirt-tails flapping in the wind."

I was in the city.

The dispatching center was filled to capacity with switchboards, phones, and maps. Two people were on duty at all times. There was no sound of activity now; I wondered if that quiet was an indication of how the rest of the day would go.

The second unit was ready when we returned to the garage. "Are we on duty now?" I asked Bob as we traveled back to the station.

"Not until we've parked one of these babies."

"Then will we be on duty for the rest of the day?"

"Yes, Pat. Yes!"

Ted backed in first, then Bob. I opened my door to get out. The radio beeped three times.

"Get back in," Bob said.

"Why?" I asked. "Where do we have to go now?"

"On a call, dummy."

"Really?"

I listened to the radio. "Medic 22, respond to 427 G Bradley Road. Person unconscious."

Ted moved past me and got in the front.

"Get in the back, Pat," Bob yelled.

I used his through-the-window maneuver, got the door open and jumped on. Bob switched on the emergency lights. The siren screamed as we pulled out into the street. We were on our way.

Bob moved the ambulance through heavy traffic with a proficiency which amazed me. We rounded a corner onto a narrow street.

"This is it," Ted said.

Bob switched off the ignition.

"Can I carry anything?" I asked Bob and Ted. Their arms were full.

"No. Just come on."

I got out and pushed the door, but it wouldn't close. I turned the handle; it was stuck. I glanced behind me and saw them entering an apartment building.

"Damn," I muttered. I'd waited all morning for a call and now I was going to end up standing in the street guarding the ambulance from thieves. I reached through the window of the open door and turned the handle from the inside. It clicked. I pushed the door again. It closed.

I turned and ran to the apartment entrance. No one was on the first floor. I climbed the flight of steps, saw a door ajar. I looked inside.

Bob and Ted were kneeling in front of a woman. Bob wiped her face with a towel. I walked in.

The room was small, hot, and stuffy. An old man sat in a rocking chair across the room. He quietly rocked and watched. The door opened wider and the firemen entered. Bob had told me that in the city firemen also respond to life-threatening emergencies. But I was still surprised to see them there in full turnout gear. The room was filling up fast.

The woman's eyelids fluttered.

"Did you vomit?" Bob asked her, wiping white sputum from her lips.

She was unresponsive.

"How old are you?"

She mumbled, "Ninety."

Bob turned to the man. "How old is she?"

"Seventy-six," the man answered apparently unsurprised by her response.

"Did she lose consciousness?"

The man nodded and Bob's questions continued. "How long ago?" "For how long?" "Does she have a heart problem?"

The man shook his head.

"A respiratory problem?"

He nodded. "Emphysema."

"Where's her medicine?"

"In the kitchen." He pointed to the room behind me. "On the refrigerator."

"Pat," Bob said. "Get the medicine."

I walked into the kitchen and gathered the medications from the top of the refrigerator. I sorted the prescription drugs from the vitamin pills and aspirin and returned to the living room. I knelt beside Ted and held the bottles so he could read the labels.

I felt a foot kick mine and turned around. Danny was standing behind me.

"Well," he grinned. "What do you think?"

I smiled back. About what, I wondered.

Ted opened the IV kit and placed everything neatly on the floor beside him: catheters, tape, tourniquet, two-by-twos, and alcohol swabs. Bob contacted the hospital and handed me a small paper bag. "Get that stuff," he said. I picked up the IV equipment from the floor and put it in the bag while Ted listened to the woman's breath sounds. I set the bag down beside him.

"Hospital wants us to start a line," Bob said.

Ted reached toward the floor, then looked around. "Where's the IV stuff?"

"I put it in the bag," I told him.

Bob chuckled.

Ted reached for the bag and dumped it all back out on the floor, then handed the bag back to me.

"The medicine goes in here," he said.

I reached for the medicine on the table where Ted had set it and started putting the bottles in the bag. Again Danny kicked my foot. I turned to face him.

"Well," he was still grinning. "What do you think?"

I couldn't return his smile this time.

I was off to a great start. I knew the next ride-along would not be initiated with the story of the poor fellow from Covington, but would hear instead about the dumb blonde from Lake of the Woods.

Ted started the IV in the woman's hand. He also administered terbutaline. By the time the firemen carried in the chair stretcher, the woman was breathing easier.

I glanced at the old man as the firemen carried the woman out of the apartment. He was still quietly rocking, his eyes fixed on the chair where the woman had been sitting.

"Sir," I spoke to him. "Are you coming with us?"

He slowly turned his gaze in my direction and shook his head. I left the apartment, closing the door behind me.

As the firemen started down the stairs with the woman, Bob said to me, "Get the outside door." An easy job, except that a mailman stood in the way and became a little hostile when I asked him to move.

En route to the hospital I watched Ted take the patient's blood pressure and listen again to breath sounds. I felt strange, just sitting there. I wasn't used to being inactive on an ambulance.

We took her to Alexandria Hospital's Emergency Room. I had never been in the ER of a metropolitan hospital. This one was impressive in both size and equipment. Equally impressive was the attitude of the staff there toward Bob and Ted. They listened attentively to all the information on our patient. They read the chart carefully and advised the doctor as to the medications Ted had given her and the change in her condition.

We gathered our supplies and started back to the station.

"They really listened to you in there," I said to Bob and Ted from my seat in the back of the ambulance. "Sometimes I feel like my crew gathers all that information and then nobody listens. How come it's so different here?" I asked.

Ted looked at Bob. I saw them smile. Then Bob raised his right hand from the wheel and rubbed his thumb back and forth across his fingers.

"Money?"

He nodded.

"I don't understand," I told him.

"Money talks," he said.

"What money?"

"The money we're paid and you're not."

I leaned forward. "You mean because we're volunteers?"

"Yep," he nodded, "and we're professionals."

"No," I responded. "You're a paid professional. We are unpaid professionals. I can't believe that is what makes the difference in attitude."

"Believe it or not, it's true."

"I'm on a volunteer squad too, Pat," Ted said to me. "And I can see the difference."

"Because we don't draw a paycheck doesn't mean we're not as good," I told him.

"Of course it doesn't," he agreed. "And not all ER personnel treat you differently, right?"

"Right. But there are always a few."

He turned to me and smiled. "Don't let it bother you," he said.

We pulled into the bay. When I got off the ambulance, I was met by the aroma of vegetable soup.

"Good timing," I said.

"Yeah," Ted laughed. "We plan our calls this way. As soon as we eat we'll get another one so we'll miss the dishwashing."

"I'm going to the ladies' room," I told them. "And then I'll be right in."

"Lock the door," Bob said.

Once again the sound of three beeps, our tones. We all stopped to listen. "Medic 22, respond. Sickness. 2700 Randolph."

We were off again.

"So much for lunch," Bob said.

"And for the bathroom," I added.

The call took us to a duplex in another section of Station 22's area. This time I didn't even touch the side door. I exited from the back.

Bob knocked, then eased open the front door of the duplex and called out, "Rescue squad."

"Upstairs," a woman answered.

Ted walked in and I stepped aside to let Bob go next, but he motioned for me to go ahead. The living room was dark and sparsely furnished. Ted started up the steps. I followed him. As the three of us climbed the stairs, I realized that Bob was keeping me between them.

"Mama's dying!" the woman cried. She was perched at the top of the stairs, waiting for us. Her blue sleeveless dress was torn at the neck. A red bandana covered her hair. "Hurry up! She's dying!"

"Where is she?" Ted asked.

"She's in there." The woman pointed. Ted disappeared into the bedroom.

"Hurry! Please hurry!" the woman sobbed.

"Lady, you're gonna have to calm down," Bob said. "Tell us just what happened, so we can help your mother."

Bob's tone of voice had a calming effect on her hysteria. "She's got low sugar," she told us, crying more softly now. "She keeps falling out, and she won't stop crying."

She stepped back for Bob and me to enter the room. Her mother was seated on a bare mattress on the floor, her head resting on her knees. She wept quietly. Ted was preparing to do a dextrose stick test.

He took her hand. "You had much to drink today?" he asked.

"A little bit." Her speech was sluggish.

"I've got to stick your finger," Ted told her. "Hold still." She didn't flinch. The test revealed a critically low blood sugar level. She was a diabetic—and worse, a drinking diabetic—and had eaten nothing all day. She was in danger of going into insulin shock.

We carried her out in the chair stretcher. "I'll call Frankie and we'll come along, Mama," the daughter called to her from the porch.

In the ambulance Bob started an IV of D5W. Into the IV port he injected D50, dextrose, which went directly into her bloodstream.

The change in her condition was almost immediate. It was incredible. She stopped crying, glanced around, then looked at me and smiled.

"How are you today?" she asked.

"I'm fine," I told her. I reached out and took her hand. "How are you feeling?"

"Pretty good," she responded. "I be feeling pretty good, now."

"I'm glad to hear that," I said. She continued talking, telling me about her children and grandchildren. At the hospital she thanked us over and over again.

"That was really amazing," I said to Bob on the way back to the station.

"Hey," he shrugged. "I'm a miracle worker."

The firemen had saved us some tuna salad, enough soup for three, and a sink full of soapy water to wash our dishes. I volunteered and Bob and Ted immediately accepted. At least they were letting me help, even if it was just to wash dishes.

We had four more calls that day. The first came at the hospital, while Ted was filling out papers on our diabetic patient. "Medic 22," came over the portable radio. "Respond to an injury."

Bob was leaning on the desk in the nurses' station, the radio in his back pocket. I looked at him, then at Ted, who continued writing.

"We have another call," I told them.

Ted didn't even look up. "Another station'll get it," he said.

142

"But if we hurry, we can get it. Are you almost through?"

"Pat," Ted answered, "we haven't even signed back on yet. Station 54 has it."

Bob only laughed and shook his head.

Twenty minutes later we returned to the station. The firemen glanced up when we walked in.

"Well," I said, smiling, "we had two calls and we could have had another one if Ted hadn't been so slow at the hospital."

They just looked at me, and they weren't smiling.

A while later there was a call for an automobile accident. It was in our area but another Med unit, already out and closer to the location, took it. Then we were dispatched to a fire on the other side of the city because the Med unit in that area was on another call. Halfway to the fire we received a message to return to our station. We weren't needed.

One daily requirement at Station 22 is training. On this day we watched a documentary film on forty-eight hours in an emergency room. I had seen it. None of the guys had. Watching it with these men I saw it not through my eyes, as before, but through theirs. Several people in the film had deeply stirred my sympathy. These same people aroused different emotions in the men of Station 22.

The Vietnam veteran in the film lived on the street. He was brought to the emergency room because he had had a seizure. There he talked about his war injuries, about his wife who left him, about his children he never saw. Later I learned that one of the men in Station 22 was also a Vietnam veteran. Although wounded, he had continued to lead his men to safety. Yet, he never talked about his Vietnam experiences or the decoration for valor he had received. As he watched the film that day, he made no comment, but his eyes were narrowed, dark.

When a young doctor spoke of his need to go home after his shift and talk to his wife about the situations he had faced and the emotions he had experienced during his long hours in the emergency room, I heard mumbles of "shit" and "like hell."

I then remembered some of my worst calls: the baby who died, the two small children killed in a house fire, and their young mother who I held in my arms. I thought of the emptiness after those calls, my feeling that there should be an interim between the scenes of pain and death and the familiar tasks and routines of my home.

I see life change tragically for people and have never gotten over the feeling that time should momentarily pause for the sharing of grief. Yet, my life continues as before. I know it is unfair to expect my family and friends to understand that I need a quiet respite, if not physically, then emotionally. So I return home, fix supper, remind the children to brush their teeth, tuck them in for the night, and go to bed with my husband.

At 3:30 our last call came, to the twelve hundred block of Duke Street for a patient with chest pains. I was the first one on the ambulance. I really wanted to see them run a cardiac call.

"I know that area," Bob said. "They better check this one out."

A policeman soon radioed us that the call originated from a phone booth. He was investigating it.

"Somebody called from a phone booth?" I asked. "Maybe it was a motorist."

"More likely a wino," Bob said.

Several minutes later, the policeman reported back that he was at the phone booth and the only other person there was a wino.

I leaned forward from my seat in the back. "Ask him if the wino has chest pains."

Both Bob and Ted groaned. Bob made a quick U-turn and we drove in silence back to the station.

The rest of the day passed uneventfully. The men couldn't lie down on the sofas, but at 5:00 they could slump a little. The news was switched on with reports from San Francisco and the upcoming Democratic Convention. Listening to their remarks I silently conceded that I was not only the one woman there, I was the one Democrat. On the day Mondale announced his choice for vice president, I thought about the men in Station 22.

At 5:45 we sat down to supper. Danny had fixed meat loaf, potatoes, and corn. His meat loaf was the best I'd ever tasted, but I missed my family's constant chattering, which was an integral part of our every meal. That evening, except for the clinking of silverware on dishes, the stillness was unbroken. The squad ate with the urgency of starving men who at any moment might have their plates yanked away.

Afterwards, I washed dishes, but not before asking if it was okay. The affirmative response was unanimous, so I washed, and four of them dried, and we had it done in no time.

I no longer felt like a stranger.

At 6:45 Bob said it was time to go home. "It's been fun," I said to the crew.

They nodded and waved and Danny said, "Yeah, Pat, you come back."

"Can I?" I asked him.

"Sure," he said. "A ride-along can have two shifts."

"Okay," I smiled. "I'll be back."

I walked out to the bay, got my purse from the filing cabinet and joined Bob in the parking lot.

"All right," I said to him when I got in the car. "I've been waiting all day to ask you this. What is a tick?"

He laughed. "It's a little insect that gets on you and sucks your blood." He was still laughing when we headed out of the city.

"Why did you call me a tick when you introduced me to the guys this morning?" I asked him.

He glanced over at me. "A tick is a volunteer."

"A volunteer? Why?"

"Because you take all the patients away from us pros. You suck our blood dry."

"Bob, that's the dumbest thing I've ever heard. How could we take patients away?"

"Pat, it's just a joke. It's the way we razz volunteers."

We turned onto U.S. 95.

"Why would you want to razz us?"

Bob rolled his window down. I lowered mine. Away from the city the air was cooler.

"I joke," he said, speaking louder now above the blast of air. "I joke a lot and sometimes it seems I don't care, but I do."

"I know you do," I told him. "I never said you didn't care."

"I may joke on the way to a call," he said, "and on the way

back to the station. But while I'm with a patient no one cares more than I do. Understand?''

"Yeah," I said, facing him now so he would hear me. "Like *M*A*S*H*?"

"Exactly!"

"I didn't like *M*A*S*H* when I first saw it," I admitted. "I thought they were insensitive to all the pain."

"That's what I mean," he said. "You've got to learn to lighten up some. You're really good at what you do. I love making calls with your crew because of the way you treat your patients. You practically love 'em to death. That's great." He paused and then added, "But joking is okay too."

"Maybe I would have found this tick thing amusing if you hadn't said that about the money earlier."

"Nothing anybody says can make you less than what you are," he said. "You know that."

"I know," I agreed. "I guess I still have a long way to go."

"Yeah," he said, smiling, "but for a tick, you're really something."

# Chapter 15

THE PREREQUISITES FOR enrolling in the cardiac technician class were active membership on the squad for two years and approval by my squad captain. I had served the mandatory time and Lou put her signature on my application. "I'm so glad you're going to do this," she told me.

"The final step," I said.

Class was held at Mary Washington Hospital. Our primary instructor was Dr. Bob Kravetz, Medical Director for the Rappahannock Emergency Medical Services Council and an established anesthesiologist at Mary Washington. His dedication to emergency prehospital care was his prime motivation.

"You people will save lives," he told us that first night, "using the skills you'll learn in this class. You will be the difference between a patient's living or dying."

Sixty-three of us were there that first night. Thirty-seven took the final exam.

We studied the body systems and patient assessment as we had in EMT class. Then we moved on to the areas of advanced life support, IV infusion, pharmacology, and cardiac arrhythmias. I studied page after page of EKGs. Now they were much more than squiggly lines on a monitor.

We would cover the entire text *Emergency Care in the Streets*, by Nancy Caroline, which began, "The role of the paramedic entails new prestige, but it also imposes new responsibilities.

Paramedics are entrusted with the lives of other human beings, and there is no more awesome or sacred responsibility than that. Your education as a paramedic must not stop with this text. You must continue to read and study and ask questions, to refine your knowledge and skills that you may give to each patient the best of which you are capable. You must learn to conduct yourself with humility, to accept criticism, to learn from mistakes as well as triumphs, and to demand of yourself and your colleagues nothing less than the best. For only then will the title of paramedic signify what it is meant to, a commitment to other human beings."

Our Rescue Squad Standing Operating Procedures govern our actions. They cover everything from general requirements and personal standards to infection control and helicopter protocol. They are clear and to the point.

Concerning acts of violence, it reads, "If a call is dispatched indicating a shooting, stabbing or any act of violence, request a police officer, sheriff or deputy to respond to the scene immediately. When you have word that a law officer is on the scene, schedule your arrival. DO NOT ENTER UNTIL THE LAW OFFICER TELLS YOU THAT YOU MAY ENTER."

Clear and to the point.

The tones woke me. I opened my eyes and looked at the clock, 4:30. I still had an hour and a half to go before my Saturday morning shift began. The night crew would answer that one. I rolled over, snuggled up next to David and went back to sleep.

At 5:45 the tones went off again, this time for "a shooting." The night crew was still out. This one was ours.

"A shooting," the dispatcher repeated. A shooting, I thought to myself. I moved quickly out of bed and put my jumpsuit on, glanced at David and held the pager close to me to muffle it. A shooting. If he heard that, he'd bar the door.

Bob Luckett and Buzzy were already there when I arrived at the building. I climbed in the back. "Let's go," Bob said.

"It's a shooting," I reminded him.

"I know that," he said. Buzzy announced to the dispatcher that we were en route and asked for further directions.

"We're supposed to wait," I insisted.

Bob looked back at me. "The deputy's on his way," he said.

"How do you know?"

"The call came from Orange, from the Sheriff's Department. They're on their way."

I sighed and sat back.

"LOW to Medic 29," our dispatcher called. "Take Route 3 West to the second house on the left before you get to Germanna Community College."

Bob asked for an ETA on the deputy and all our dispatcher could tell us was that he was on the way.

"Is that all they know?" I asked. "He could be anywhere between here and Orange." I looked up at Bob and Buzzy. Together they probably weighed at least 500 pounds. "If I budge from this ambulance," I told them, "you two people are going to be in front of me."

They laughed.

"I'm serious," I told them.

We turned west onto Route 3. Bob drove at non-emergency speed.

I moved up and knelt between them. "I think the directions are wrong," I said.

"You got any suggestions?" Bob asked me.

"Well, my first suggestion is that we pull over and wait. But you won't do that," I told him. "I don't remember any houses on the left toward Germanna. I think it might be down 601."

"Okay," he said, pulling over in the left lane, "we'll try that."

Buzzy radioed our dispatcher as we turned onto 601. "Any word on the deputy yet?" he asked.

"Negative."

We moved slowly down 601 without lights or sirens. We came to the first house on the left and passed it. The second was just around the next curve.

We rounded it and saw a man standing in the road waving his arms.

"You were right, Pat," Bob said. "I guess this is the place."

"I don't think we should do this," I told him.

"Well, what do you think we should do?" he asked, as he drove toward the man. "We'll just stay in here until we check it out."

He stopped. "What happened here, man?" Bob questioned.

"Bastard broke into my house and I shot him."

Clear and to the point, just like our SOP.

It's a good thing Jean's not here, I thought to myself. She'd wash his mouth out.

"Where is he?" Bob asked.

"Lying in the yard back there."

"Where's your gun?"

"It's in the house."

"Where's the deputy?" I mumbled.

"You're not screwing with me, are you?" Bob asked him.

I thought of Jean again.

"No, man, being straight with you."

"Okay," Bob told him. "You walk toward the guy and we'll follow you."

The man walked away from us and into his yard. Bob eased the ambulance forward, slowly. Buzzy radioed our dispatcher and told him we were on the scene.

"LOW to Medic 29," the dispatcher called back. "Could you give us some directions? The deputy's having trouble finding it."

Bob laughed as Buzzy gave the directions.

"Your sense of humor remains a mystery to me," I said to Bob.

"Get the trauma box, Pat," he said. "I'll leave the engine running."

Bob and Buzzy got out. I walked behind them.

We found our patient lying face down on the ground. He looked to be in his late teens. He had been shot in the back with a 12-gauge shotgun.

"You sure did a job on him," Bob said to the man.

"He shouldn't have broke into my house."

Bob rolled the young man over. He was barely conscious.

"Don't let me die," he moaned.

"We're not going to let you die," I said.

He had nine entry wounds and six exit wounds. Three of the shots were still inside him. His pulse was rapid and weak, his blood pressure was dangerously low. We bandaged his wounds and put MAST trousers on him and Bob started a line of Lactated Ringers. We were moving him into the ambulance when the deputy arrived.

"Boy," the deputy said, "I had a hell of a time finding you all."

Bob glanced at me and grinned. "Perfect timing," he said. "Right, Pat?"

We transported the boy to Culpeper Memorial Hospital. Buzzy drove; Bob and I rode in the back with our patient. His pulse and blood pressure were more stable. He was fully conscious now and in a great deal of pain.

"I'm not going to die, am I?" he continued to ask me.

And I continued to tell him, "No."

The emergency room doctor asked us if we wanted to stay to watch the surgery. Bob did. Buzzy and I had to return because we were part of the duty crew.

"We'll go back and get covers," I told Buzzy on our way back to the Lake. "And then we can come back for the surgery."

We had it so well planned. What we had not anticipated was an encounter at the fire and rescue building.

Bob Grim was our assistant captain. We saw him leaning up against the building when we pulled into the driveway.

"Uh, oh," I said to Buzzy.

"Here it comes," Buzzy sighed.

And it did.

"Would it help our case," I asked Bob, "if we told you we stumbled on it?"

It wouldn't.

"Well, he would have died if we had waited on the deputy," was my final argument.

"It was dangerous," Bob said. "If you get a call like that again, don't leave this building until the deputy is on the scene."

Buzzy and I nodded.

As it turned out, Bob Grim's lecture was the lesser of the two I received that day. The second and more severe one would come when I got home.

Buzzy and I got others to cover for us and drove back to the hospital just as the surgery was completed. Bob did give me the surgical shirt he wore in the operating room.

"They had to take out ten inches of his intestines," he told us. "He was really lucky. All the shots missed his kidneys, and his arteries, too. It was really something," he said. "You should have been there."

"We would have been," I told him, "but Bob Grim was waiting for us. You should have been *there*," I added.

"My fearful leader," Buzzy said.

"What?" I asked him.

"You," he smiled. "My fearful leader."

"You got it." I laughed with them. "That's me."

The boy survived. I visited him twice in the hospital. "Things can be different," I told him, "if you want them to be."

I never knew what happened to him afterwards, whether things were different or not.


I once told David, shortly after I joined the squad, that there were two incidents I really dreaded. One was the death of a child. The other was a school bus accident.

"I don't even know if I could respond," I remember saying to him.

I could, of course, and did.

Still, it is always frightening.

"ATTENTION LAKE OF THE WOODS FIRE AND RESCUE MEMBERS," our dispatcher announced. "You have a 10-50 PI. School bus involved."

It was 7:30 A.M. I had driven Jennifer to the bus stop and was standing with her as she waited for her bus. When the tones went off, I hurriedly kissed her good-bye, got in my car and headed for the fire and rescue building.

"Directions," Buzzy requested of the dispatcher.

"Turn left on Route 3. It's two miles west."

Two miles west on Route 3.

"Oh, no," I said.

I knew which bus it was. If the directions were correct, it was Jenny's bus. Jennifer's closest friend since nursery school, since before the night their brothers were lost in the woods. Jenny.

"School bus involved . . . " Then that grey area between the time the tones sound and the time we arrive on the scene, that time of not knowing, when our minds are filled with awful imaginings.

It was a long two miles.

The bus was upright. That, in itself, was a relief.

We pulled up close to it and I got off.

In the back window I saw Jenny's face pressed against the glass. She was waving to me and was smiling.

Thank God, I thought. She was all right.

But there were seventeen other children.

A pickup truck had hit the bus broadside. Woody went to the truck driver, whose injuries were minor. Jean, Buzzy, and I got on the bus. I took a quick look to assess injuries. The children all seemed to be okay. I questioned each of them and found only one child who was hurt, complaining of neck pain. I sat down with her to further check her. Jenny crawled into my lap.

We transported the child and the truck driver to Mary Washington Hospital. Another bus came to pick up the other children and take them to school. Before we left, I kissed Jenny good-bye.

"I'm so glad you're okay," I said, holding her in my arms.

Many of our patients are strangers to us, but when the tones go off, we are equally as likely to encounter someone we know. We found Greg, one of my former Cub Scouts, now Dave's age, in a ditch. He'd been thrown through the front window when his car hit a tree.

Our neighbor across the street had a heart attack, a friend's child fell down the stairs, and the grandfather of Matt's best friend died.

The list is long and it grows longer.

It is good that we are there for those we know, but sometimes that can be extremely painful.

Again, a call during that last hour.

In the darkness we traveled south on Route 20.

The call is for a man unconscious in a car, which is not what we will find.

"I think," Woody said, "that day teams should go off duty when it gets dark. Day means light. Night means dark," he mumbled, looking out the front window.

I smiled at him. "Did Marge have supper ready?"

"Yep," he nodded.

We found the car on a narrow country road. There was no one in it. Buzzy checked with the dispatcher. We were sent further down the road to a residence, where a deputy was waiting for us in the driveway.

"This is getting very interesting," Jean said.

"I don't like it to get too interesting," I told her.

"That's my fearful leader," Buzzy smiled.

"What is this all about?" Woody asked.

"Let's go find out," I said.

I got off the ambulance. "We were dispatched to this residence," I told the deputy. "What's the situation here?"

"There's a man out in the woods," he said. "Probable DOA."

"How long has he been there?" I asked.

"Quite a while, I think."

I was somewhat bewildered. "Well," I said, "what do you want us to do?"

"Tell us if he's dead."

"Tell you if he's dead?"

He nodded.

"Okay. Where is he?"

"Follow me," the deputy said.

I got back on the ambulance.

"Well?" Woody asked.

"You were right," I told him. "We should go off duty when the sun goes down."

Buzzy turned to me from the driver's seat. "What are we supposed to do?"

"Follow the deputy. There's a man in the woods up there and they think he's dead."

"But what do they want us to do?" Jean asked.

"Tell them if he is."

Buzzy started the ambulance and we moved down the narrow trail into the woods. "I can't go much farther," Buzzy said. "We'll never get out."

"Okay," I told him. "Park it here and we'll walk."

Woody and I got out the back. I had the jump bag. He walked in front of me with the flashlight, Jean and Buzzy behind us. A pickup truck was parked to the right of the trail. Woody shined the light inside. The truck was empty.

"Up here," the deputy called to us. He was pointing in front of the truck.

The man lay face down on the ground.

"Don't move him any more than you need to," the deputy said, stepping back from us.

We didn't have to move him at all to know he was dead. I took my stethoscope from the jump bag and listened. No sound. I raised his eyelids to check his pupils. Fixed and dilated. His skin was cold to my touch. I had to push his eyelid back down.

I stood up. "No pulse. Pupils fixed and dilated," I told the deputy.

"Thank you," he said.

It was eerie. A tight circle of deputies and spectators had formed around the man, Woody, and me, so that when I stood up all I could see were flashlights and featureless faces.

Lights were handed to Woody and me. "Hold these," another deputy told us, "so we can take pictures."

We held them.

"A little lower," they said. "We've got to get his face."

Flashbulbs exploded around us. The medical examiner arrived on the scene. Then the sheriff. Then Clyde, from the funeral home.

"Do you suspect foul play in this?" Buzzy asked a deputy.

"Just a precaution," the deputy shrugged. "He probably had a heart attack."

They finished taking pictures. We returned their flashlights. Clyde stepped forward from the back of the circle.

"Hello, Clyde," I said.

"Pat," he nodded.

I wondered how he did it. We handle death but we also deal with the living. Clyde's world has only one dimension.

"I still don't know what that was all about," Jean said as we walked out of the woods back to the ambulance.

Buzzy shook his head. "Frankly, I don't either."

We returned to the squad building and finished the paperwork. Woody and I were the last to leave. I switched off the light and walked outside.

"Well," he said, "another save."

I stopped. "Woody! He was dead."

"Not him," he said. "The unconscious man in the car."

I smiled at him. "There wasn't any unconscious man in the car."

"That's what I mean," he told me. "Another save."


Once again I carried study cards with me everywhere I went. I bought or borrowed books on cardiovascular drugs and on EKG interpretation. I did set aside Sunday afternoons for sailing with David, however, and we began our third summer of racing. We still had not beaten John and Yvonne across the finish line.

That summer John quit the rescue squad.

"Why?" I asked him.

"I have to," he said, looking tired, drawn. "I've got to travel more with my job. I just don't have the time I used to."

"I'm sorry, John."

"Yeah," he sighed. "Me, too."

We stood inside the bay together. He reached out and rested

his hand on the side of the ambulance. He didn't look at me when he spoke.

"Pat," he said, "I don't care anymore. The tones go off and I simply don't give a shit."

# Chapter 16

I PASS THAT stretch of road often. The skid marks are gone now, but I never travel that way that I don't remember.

It was a Saturday in August.

Jean, Buzzy, Woody, and I were on duty. The four of us along with the Saturday night crew had the usual weekend cleanup detail. Jean and I checked supplies and cleaned the interior of one of the Med units while the night crew cleaned the second.

"Orange County's Sheriff's Office to Lake of the Woods," our pagers echoed inside the ambulance. "We've just received a report of a 10-50 PI two miles up Route 20 from the Route 3 intersection. Can you dispatch a unit?"

We heard the familiar notes of our tones and our dispatcher's voice repeating the message.

We pulled away from the squad building. It was a clear day. The sky looked like October: deep blue with tiny wisps of clouds, sunny and peaceful and not at all indicative of what lay ahead.

We turned off Route 3 onto Route 20. Just beyond the crest of the first hill I saw a pickup truck off the road on the shoulder. Relieved, I said, "It's not bad."

But Buzzy didn't stop.

"Wasn't that it?" I asked him.

"It couldn't have been," he said. "We haven't gone two miles from the intersection yet."

We approached the crest of the second hill, reached it and crossed over. Then I saw it.

"Oh, God," I whispered.

Newspaper accounts would later report that the woman driving the car had passed a truck, then pulled back too sharply into the right lane, causing her to lose control and swerve back into the path of an oncoming pickup.

Recollections of my first impression of the scene are blurred. A cloud of steam hung over the wreckage so that it looked like a misty illusion. As we drew closer, the images cleared. Sketchy outlines took on form and substance.

"The woman in front is dead," the off-duty policeman from Washington, D.C., said to me as I stepped down from the ambulance. He had arrived on the scene shortly after the accident occurred. "There were three people in the pickup and two more in the car," he informed us.

I turned to Buzzy. "Call for assistance."

Jean grabbed the trauma kit and she and the policeman headed for the truck. Woody and I went to the car.

The young woman was sitting in all that remained of the front seat, her forehead resting against the crushed hood which, through the force of the impact, had been driven through the shattered windshield. Dried blood caked the lacerations that crisscrossed her face. Her left arm lay against the steering wheel, her hand open, outstretched, as if she had fallen asleep waiting for change and would awaken at the touch of cold coins on her palm.

I held her limp hand, feeling for a radial pulse, then felt her neck for a carotid and finally used my stethoscope to listen for heart sounds. Nothing. Her head and left side had been spared. But that was all. The rest of her body had been crushed on impact.

I looked past her and all around. A young boy lay on the ground not far from the car. Beyond him, one of the passengers from the truck sat alone. Blood covered his face and chest. He was staring at his hands, slowly flexing and extending his fingers.

I was in charge of this accident scene. There was triage to do and much more, so much more. There were four of us and five of them, the boy, three men from the truck, and still another man, in the back seat of the car, trapped by crushed metal.

I leaned inside the car. The man was conscious, though he had a head laceration and a severely angulated left leg. Bandaging the laceration, I spoke to him. "Your right leg is caught between the seat and the door. We're going to remove the door and get you out." He looked around him in bewilderment, as if just becoming aware of his environment. I put my hand on his. "We're going to get you out," I repeated. This time he nodded.

I had asked Woody to do an assessment of the boy and he was still with him. One passenger remained in the truck. He had head lacerations, both his ankles were broken, and complained he had difficulty breathing. Jean stayed with him while Buzzy returned to the ambulance for oxygen.

Just as I approached the man sitting on the ground, the policeman walked the third passenger from the truck toward me. "How did he get out of the truck?" I asked, concerned about possible spinal injuries.

"He was out when I stopped," the policeman told me. "He was just wandering around."

He, too, had head lacerations. He also had a gaping hole in his right arm, between the elbow and shoulder. Tissue, muscle and bone were exposed. I asked him to sit down. He wouldn't. I asked the policeman to stand with him while I bandaged his wounds, to try to keep him from moving around anymore.

Next, I knelt in front of the man on the ground. He was shaking. I took his hands in mine. "You're going to be all right," I told him. I bandaged a jagged laceration which had gone through to his mouth and gums. I looked at his chest. No injuries. The blood there had come from his face.

I moved quickly from patient to patient checking airway, breathing, circulation. That was all. There wasn't time for a secondary assessment. I didn't even have any call sheets. There wasn't time.

I left the policeman with the two men who were now sitting side by side on the ground next to the road. I had bandaged their wounds. That was all I had time to do.

I walked back toward the vehicles. Our firemen were hosing

down the area while Jean and Buzzy removed the man from the truck, sliding him gently onto the backboard. A sheet was draped over the driver's side of the car, covering the young woman.

"Pat, come here," Woody called. I hurried toward him, then knelt beside him while he continued his assessment on the boy. I felt spray from the firehose spatter on my back. Rivulets of water muddled the area. In the distance I heard sirens.

"His vitals are okay," Woody told me, "but he's got severe pain in his abdomen."

I felt the boy's chest, checked the symmetry, moved my hand down to his abdomen. It was rigid, but not extremely so. I pulled my stethoscope from my pocket and listened for bowel sounds. They were there, but he winced each time I touched his abdomen.

"I'll get Buzzy over here and we'll move him to the ambulance," I told Woody in a low voice. "There is possible internal bleeding. Stay with him."

I saw our second unit arrive and walked toward Lou and Al and Suzanne, pointing out the patients ready for transport, the three men from the truck. "You'll have to complete the assessments on each one in the ambulance," I told them after briefly describing the men's injuries. When the second unit left, Lou stayed with us on the scene, and in a few minutes Bob Grim arrived to help.

In retrospect I realized I should have put the boy on the first ambulance that left. At the time I had thought it better to transport the father and son together. It was a mistake, but I am thankful it wasn't a costly one.

After Buzzy and Woody moved the boy to our ambulance, I returned to his father. The firemen were pulling the extrication equipment off the truck. The left rear door of the car was open. The boy must have been sitting here, I thought, as I crawled inside. This was the only undamaged part. The man turned toward me. "Try not to move your head," I told him, taking his hand.

"What happened?" he asked me. "I was asleep. Do you know what happened?"

"No." I replied, "I don't know what caused the accident.

161

But you'll be out of here very soon. They're going to cut the door away now.''

He looked at me, his eyes clouded with fear and pain.

"Where's my baby?'' he asked.

Briefly, my mind drew a blank. I felt frozen in time and space, then my thoughts rushed back with all the clarity of the bright August sky. Baby? What baby? Did he mean the boy? Dear God, let him mean the boy!

"My baby,'' he said again. "With my wife.''

Then I knew he didn't mean the boy. I wondered if he could see what was there, the dash and the hood where the front seat had been.

I took his hand again in both of mine. "I'll go see about your baby,'' I told him. I was trying to give him comfort, but to me my words sounded hollow.

I got out of the car and saw John Harkness and Dick Ferguson approaching with the extrication tools. I waited until we were together before I told them.

"I think there's a child in the front seat.''

John looked at the car and wearily shook his head. "Okay,'' he sighed softly. "We'll find out.''

I watched while they started the generator that fired the jaws and then began to cut away at the door. They had placed a tarp over the man to protect him from glass and metal.

I went back to the ambulance to check again on the boy. Jean had gone aboard ahead of me to stay with him until we could get his father out of the car and in the ambulance with him.

The boy was thirteen years old, my son Matt's age. He looked up at me as I wrapped the blood pressure cuff around his arm.

"I want my mama,'' he said.

I told him the truth, but not all of it. "Someone else is with her while we take care of you,'' I said, hoping my voice wouldn't betray me.

His vital signs were stable and I left Jean there with him, holding his hand, speaking softly to him, letting him hear a woman's voice, feel a woman's touch, hoping these memories might help to ease the shock of the void in his life, a void still unknown to him.

Later, when the father again asked for his baby and his wife, we gave him the same half truth. It was all we could say then. They had fears. We had truths. If we could modify these truths, at least for a while, perhaps we could somehow bandage a greater wound.

The door had now been cut away from the car. We eased the father onto the backboard. While Bob and Lou applied MAST trousers, the firemen continued to shear open the mangled front of the car.

My gaze drifted to the road. The two lanes had been reduced to one and traffic was moving slowly. As the cars went past me, I saw expressions of horror, of pity, of "it could have been me," and of relief and gratitude that it wasn't.

I heard the sound of metal snapping and turned back to the car. I saw a fragment of green shorts, a shred of striped shirt. Almost concealed by the crushed metal was the body of a small child.

John put down the extrication tool and slid his hand between the gnarled metal and the child's leg to feel for a femoral pulse. I moved beside him and also searched for a sign of life. But like his mother, the five-year-old boy had been killed instantly.

John looked at me and I met his gaze. "We'll go now," I said.

I glanced back several times as we drove past the long line of clogged traffic. The firemen would be on the scene longer. The generator would continue to fire the Hurst tool. The roof would have to be peeled back before removal of the bodies of the mother and child could begin.

In the ambulance en route to Mary Washington Hospital, Jean remained beside the boy, still holding his hand. I added information to the call sheets, the time the IV was started on the father, the latest vitals on him, and on the boy. I handed them to Lou who was in contact with the hospital's emergency room. I asked Woody to check the MAST, then knelt beside the father. I looked at his face. His eyes were closed. I reached under the blanket covering him and took his hand. His pulse was strong.

They had been so close to their destination, to grandparents who surely must now be looking at the clock and glancing anxiously out the window. This man's world had been cut in half and all our medical knowledge and shiny equipment couldn't alter that fact.

We reached the hospital and moved the two of them into the trauma room. I lingered at the door a while before leaving.

We were quiet as we returned home. Lou sensed our feelings. Loving and caring, she supported us. "All of you did a fine job," she told us, knowing we now felt very inadequate. "You really worked as a team." She was right. During that time at the scene we had seen each other only briefly. Yet, we had never worked more closely together.

We pulled into the driveway of the squad building. The firemen had just returned. John, sitting on the front of the firetruck, watched me get off the ambulance. I knew what I looked like. My jumpsuit was smeared with blood, and I felt as if great weights were suspended from my body, so that each step I took required all of my strength. John, too, seemed weighed down with grief.

After we cleaned and restocked the ambulance, I went home and changed clothes. Blood had soaked through to my underwear. I put it and my jumpsuit into the tub and filled it with cold water, then found my winter uniform, just in case.

The house was quiet. I found a note from David in the kitchen. They had all gone to the pool. I cleaned up the living room and kitchen, washed out cereal bowls and scrubbed dried egg from the frying pan. I folded the clothes from the dryer. Then I sat down and cried.

We had three more calls that day: a child who'd fallen and hurt her knee; a fire; another 10-50, this one minor with one patient, one small laceration. None of these calls took us back to Mary Washington Hospital.

Between the fire and the second 10-50, I went to the pool to find my family. For a few minutes before going in, I watched them from outside the fence, playing and swimming, thinking of how much I loved them, and how thankful I was for their lives.

David sat at a poolside table, reading. I walked over to him and sat down. "Hi," I said.

"Hi," he smiled at me. "It's been a really bad day, hasn't it?" he asked, then added, "We saw the wreck. The firemen were still there when Jennifer and I went to get Dave from football practice."

Jennifer's wet arms circled me from behind. "Mama!"

I turned and picked her up and sat her on my lap.

"I'm so wet!" she squealed.

"I don't care," I told her, pulling her close.

"We saw the wreck," she said, her eyes wide and serious. "The car was all mashed."

"I know."

"Were you there, Mama?"

"Yes," I nodded. "I was there."

"A man told Daddy that a little boy was killed, a little boy and his mama. Did you see them get killed?"

I shook my head. "No."

"Did you put bandages on them?"

David reached out for her. "Come here, hot shot."

"It's all right," I told him and turned back to Jennifer. "They were killed before I got there, honey. But I put bandages on the daddy and we took good care of the other boy."

I smoothed down her hair, wet from the pool. "Mama," she said softly, "it was kind of scary."

"I know it was, Jennifer. It was scary for me too."

Evening came and our duty ended. I fixed supper, then took my jumpsuit out of soaking. The bloodstains came out in the wash. I hung it up, fresh and white from the dryer. Fresh and white, as if the day's events had never happened.

Later, I read Jennifer a book and tucked her into bed, talked with the boys a while before telling them goodnight, then joined David in the living room. The phone rang. It was Lou. She called all four of us that night to see how we were feeling, to express her love for us, her pride in us, her understanding.

"You okay?" David asked when I sat down again, this time with my journal in my hands.

"I will be," I smiled at him.

I opened my journal and dated the page, but the words wouldn't come. I couldn't focus. My only recollections were peripheral ones: the spray of the firehose, the lights of the second unit approaching, the white sheet draped over the car. I closed the journal.

The following Wednesday my crew met to discuss the call. We talked about what we had done, what we might have done differently, and then about the feelings each of us had experienced. The emptiness was still there. We called the hospital to check on the conditions of the father and son. They were recovering. They had been unable to attend the funeral of the mother and other child, so a memorial service had been held for them in the hospital chapel. They shared a room until the boy was released, about a week after the accident.

I passed the scene often, each time slowing down. One day I stopped. The ground was still dark with stains of oil and gasoline. Scattered about were strips of gauze, alcohol swabs, and soiled bandages. As I walked slowly through the area I saw socks, a shoe, and a rearview mirror. I got a plastic bag from my car and put it all in there and threw it away.

On my way home, I stopped at the fire and rescue building to pick up my September schedule. Bob Luckett was there. He looked at my face for a moment, then knowing me well, said, "Pat, what's the matter?"

As we sat over coffee, I tried to explain to him what I was feeling. It wasn't easy because even I didn't really understand,

He frowned at me. "You know, if you can't let it go, it will kill you too."

"That's a little severe, isn't it?" I asked.

"No. It'll start eating away at you," he explained. "You've got to keep it in perspective."

"Don't be too tough with me on this one," I said. "It was our worst one, you know."

"Of course I know," he acknowledged. "I do this for a living and I've never had one that bad." He was quiet for a moment, then said, "Pat, did you do everything you could do?"

"Yes," I answered.

"Well," he asked, "what more do you want?"

"I don't know," I told him.

My first day of work in Mary Washington Hospital, to fulfill the requirement for my cardiac technician class, was with the IV technician. She wasn't in her office so I stopped at the nurses' station to ask where I could find her. They told me and I thanked them and turned to go, then stopped.

I knew the father was still here and on this floor. I asked for his room number, then slowly walked down the hall to the last room on the right. The TV was turned on to "Leave it to Beaver." I knocked and heard "Come on in."

A white curtain was drawn, separating us. I walked around the curtain and barely recognized him. He looked so different— freshly shaven, his eyes bright and clear. He looked at me, and I knew he didn't remember. He thought I worked there.

"Good morning," he smiled.

"Good morning," I returned his greeting. "How are you feeling?"

"Pretty good," he nodded.

"And your son?" I asked.

"He's back in school," he said. "He's staying with my folks until I get home."

"When do you think that will be?"

He patted his leg which hung in traction. "As soon as this old leg can get me out of here," he smiled.

I smiled back at him, then glanced at my watch. I was five minutes late. "I'd better get to work," I told him. "I'm really glad to see you're doing so well."

He held his hand out to me and I took it. "Thanks for coming by," he said. "It's good to see a new face."

I left his room. A new face. I was a new face to him. He didn't remember that mine was one of the first he'd seen after the accident. I felt it was better that he hadn't remembered. I didn't want to bring back the memories. I just wanted to know that he was all right.

I went back for short visits, taking him checkers and backgammon. We talked about ordinary things: the weather, fishing, sports. Neither of us spoke of his wife, or of his little son.

It was two weeks later that I walked the short flight up to the second floor during my break from emergency room work. When I sat down, I asked him what he'd been doing to drive his roommates away. He'd had four since my first visit. We laughed. He ate his lunch as we talked. After a while I rose to leave. "Got to get back to the emergency room," I told him.

"Is that where you work?" Before I could answer him, he went on, "Were you there the day they brought me in?"

This wasn't supposed to happen, I thought. Before long he would have gone home and I would have been just another visitor. Yet, I had known since the first day I entered his room and reentered his life that this moment might come. I wasn't going to tell him any more half truths.

So I said, "I brought you in . . . my rescue crew brought you in."

I waited, perhaps for anger, for I have seen the faces of those who have called us, the eyes that say, "You are here. Everything will be all right because you can make it so." They think that we can because we come with sirens and flashing lights, because we wear white and carry stethoscopes and use words they don't understand, but we can't always make it right. There are some things we cannot make right.

"You brought me in that day?" His voice was low, subdued.

I met his stare and nodded and waited. The anger never came, nor the bitterness or desolation.

"We were going to take the smaller car," he said finally. "If we had, we would all have been killed."

He talked, his words hesitant at first, then faster, cresting and overflowing, as if he'd been waiting for some link with that day. He told me stories of his family, his wife, the son he had lost, the son who lived.

I sat back down and stayed while he talked, until he was exhausted from talking. When, at last, he laid his head back against the pillow, he was still remembering and he was smiling.

His question had freed us both. His words had to come and perhaps better within the sterile walls of confinement, of safety, than later when he would be faced with daily reminders of his loss.

His words had given back to me something I had lost that day in August. I had needed to see that he was healing, to see him

168

smile, to know that he was beginning to fit the pieces of his life back together again.

I had needed to believe that I could at last let go.

The next day he returned to his home in Pennsylvania. I didn't get to see him again, but that day in his room had been our good-bye. He and his son would go on with their lives. It wouldn't be easy, but then letting go never is.

# Chapter 17

"GOOD MORNING," I greeted the men of Station 22.

I didn't feel that over a year had passed since I'd seen them. There is a timelessness in that room where seconds can be longer than minutes and an hour can fly by or stretch into tomorrow.

"The tick is back," I said, smiling.

"You all remember Pat," Bob said, gesturing toward me as if I were a worn piece of luggage he had dropped in the doorway on his way to the kitchen for coffee. He was my security in this place, but he already knew I would be able to keep a greater distance from him this time.

Jim, sitting at a table leafing through a magazine, looked up and smiled.

Danny turned from his desk. "Hey, Pat, good to see you."

Carl, quiet Carl, sat fixed at the computer. Bill was no longer there.

"We've got problems this morning," Danny said when Bob returned from the kitchen. "Both units are out." I sat down at the table across from Jim to complete my ride-along form. "Pete's checking one out now, but I think it's going to have to go to the garage."

It did.

"How long is this going to take?" I asked from my seat in the back of the ambulance.

"How am I supposed to know?" Bob yelled back at me.

I knelt down, looking through the window at the streets ahead, wondering if every workday here started with a trip to the garage.

Pete drove. He was Bob's partner for the day. We'd met when we climbed into the ambulance together. He was taller than Bob, blonde, with cold blue eyes. He was quiet, but unlike Carl, his quietness did not reflect shyness. Pete was remote, aloof. His silence was self-imposed.

The garage mechanic opened the hood, sighed deeply and glanced at Pete. "What the hell do you do to these things?" he asked. "This is the third adapter I've had to replace this month."

Pete shrugged. "I can't control the thermostat in this city."

I heard voices on Bob's portable radio. Station 22 was being dispatched for a call.

"That's us," I said.

"Fifty-five will take it," Bob responded. "It's just a sick call."

"Some bimbo wants a free ride out of nowhere," Pete said, unwrapping a cigar.

The three of us sat in the small office adjoining the garage. I thumbed through the book of code numbers.

"You have to give a code number for every place you respond to?" I asked Bob. "Homes, schools, businesses—it's even broken down into the type of business."

"Yep," he nodded, leaning back in his chair, his eyes closed. Pete stood, slowly drawing on his cigar.

"This is really something," I said. "You've got code numbers for every imaginable place. There are pages of this stuff."

Bob opened his eyes and glanced at Pete, "She gets excited over little things," he said. "And wait until we get a call," he grinned. "She's a hand holder."

"Only you could make compassion sound distasteful," I told him.

"You should see her," Bob continued. "We had this thief who got shot and she not only holds his damn hand, she visits him six times in the hospital."

"I went to see him twice," I cut short his exaggeration. "We were at the hospital on calls. I just wanted to talk to him. Sometimes it can make a difference."

171

"Shit."

I looked at Bob and smiled. He closed his eyes again and leaned back further in his chair.

His outbursts never surprised me.

Pete's, however, did.

"I don't want you holding any hands up here," he said, pointing his cigar at me. Bob's eyes opened, mine widened, Pete's narrowed. "You're not to hold any hands when you're with me," he repeated. "Not one!"

"Why not?" I asked him.

"I'll tell you why not," he said, taking a step toward me. "Because you'll hold their hands and then you'll go home, back to your little volunteer rescue squad. And when you're gone they'll expect me to hold their hands and I'll be goddamned if I'm going to."

"All right," I conceded. "It's your territory. I won't hold any hands, here. I can wait until I get back to my . . . what was it . . . my little volunteer squad."

"You're damn right you won't!" He took a step back, puffing on his cigar, his cold eyes on me. I didn't look away.

"Ready to roll." The mechanic's voice, cheerful by comparison, reached into the small room. I closed the book of codes, got up and followed Bob and Pete to the ambulance.

I thought Pete drove too fast on the way back to Station 22.

John Wayne loomed across the television screen in the lounge. His heavy drawl was another audible irritant in that room.

"I didn't think you could watch TV during the day," I said to Bob.

"On Sunday things are looser."

He and Pete and I shared the *Washington Post*. Bob got the sports page. I took the front section and Book World. Pete read *Parade*. Jim and Danny were doing John Wayne impressions.

A city policeman wandered in and sat on the sofa. After asking which John Wayne movie they were watching, he announced the movie's ending and rose to leave. "Busy day," he said. "Last call we got was for a dead cat in the road." Then he was gone.

The men at Station 22 were immune to comings and goings.

172

The bells sounded. Danny and Jim rushed out of the room. I looked at Bob. He was still reading.

"What was that for?" I asked. I heard the sirens of the fire trucks.

"Just a car on fire," he answered me, his attention still on the newspaper.

He looked up from the paper. "No, Pat, remember we don't go."

At 11:30 the bells sounded again.

"That's us," Bob said.

The call was for a twenty-seven-year-old woman with chest pains. I followed them into the residence: sparsely furnished, but neat and clean. After a quick assessment, they decided it was not cardiac-related, but was hyperventilation.

"We've been here before," Bob told me while the woman was upstairs getting her purse. Pete was returning the jump bag and monitor to the ambulance. "Boyfriend must have walked out on her again," he said. "She does this, hoping it'll get him to come back."

His gaze drifted around the living room. "Well, well, what have we here?" he said, walking over to a small table next to the stairs. I followed him to see.

"Grass, my dear." He pointed to the brown leaf particles sealed in a plastic bag.

"Let me see it." I reached for the bag.

"Don't touch it!"

I jerked back my hand and looked at him.

"Don't ever touch anything. Especially somebody's drugs. You don't touch it. You don't even see it. Understand?"

"I don't see anything," I said to him.

"Good girl."


"Wonder how long it'll take him to come back this time," Pete remarked as we traveled back to the station from the hospital.

The trip there had been uneventful. The woman had kept her head turned away from us the entire time.

"A couple of days, probably," Bob said. "Then it'll happen all over again."

I thought it was sad.

"Damn bimbos," Pete muttered.


There was little talk at lunchtime. The men gulped their soup and sandwiches, belched and left the table. It was Jim's turn to wash the dishes. I helped him stack them and carry them to the kitchen. I did no more than that.

Bob had returned to the sports page. Pete had gone upstairs to take a nap. Danny and Carl watched television. I opened the door and walked into the bay.

I really wanted to go outside the building, to walk around, get some fresh air and stretch my legs, but Bob had told me not to.

"You don't just wander around the streets up here," he had said. "This isn't Wilderness, don't forget."

How could I?

I sat down on the cool cement steps which led down from the lounge to the bay area.

I suddenly just wanted to go home.

I heard the bells and got up. Bob met me at the door.

"That's us," he said.

I opened the back door of the ambulance and got in. Bob got in the driver's seat. Pete was yawning as he stepped aboard.

"What have we got?" he asked Bob.

"Domestic," Bob replied. "Pat," he called back to me. "Don't try to do anything. Just stay with me."

"Okay." The paper I'd signed had informed me to keep a low profile on responses to calls for domestic violence. I didn't have to be reminded.

We entered the neighborhood, and I watched out the front window as Bob pulled into the parking lot of an apartment building.

"Are the cops here yet?" Pete asked.

"Yeah, I see them," Bob said. "They're waiting for us."

The ambulance stopped. Bob glanced back at me. "Would you rather stay in here?"

I shook my head. "No way. I'm coming with you." I didn't really want to go into the building, but did not want to stay by myself either.

I opened the side door slowly and stepped out, then closed the door tightly behind me. Bob was waiting for me. I glanced up at the building.

"Just walk," he said. "Don't look around."

I stayed in step with him down a narrow crumbling sidewalk which led to the end building. Two policemen waited at the foot of the steps.

"Go ahead," they said to Pete.

"After you," Pete responded.

They gave him an angry look and started up the stairs. We followed them into the building. The inside stairway smelled of urine. I kept my hands off the railing as we climbed to the second floor and approached the door of the apartment. Pete, Bob, and I stood there with the two policemen.

"Police," one of the two yelled at the closed door. I took a step back. My mouth was dry. The door remained closed.

"Paramedics," Bob yelled.

The knob turned slowly from the inside. The policemen had their hands on their holstered revolvers.

The door opened slightly.

"Don't need no paramedics," a man's voice came from inside the apartment.

Bob eased the door open wider with his foot, then stepped inside. The policemen followed, then Pete. I was last.

In the living room, chairs and a coffee table were overturned. Slivers of glass were scattered over the linoleum floor.

A man sat at the kitchen table, holding a towel to his cheek. The towel was soaked with blood.

"Anybody else here?" Bob asked him.

"No."

The policemen checked the bedroom and bath and found both empty.

"What happened to your face?" Bob asked.

"Son of a bitch cut me." The towel muffled his words. "Cuts me, then he goes out and cuts my tires."

"You know him?"

"Sure I know him. My wife's bastard son." He looked at the policemen. "Get him, why don't you?" he told them.

He took the towel from his face and I saw the laceration. It was at least two inches long and had surely gone through his cheek.

"You want us to take you to the hospital?" Bob asked.

"Hell, no!" the man shouted.

"How much you had to drink, buddy?"

He looked at Bob. I noticed his eyes were swelling.

"Two beers."

"Two beers," Pete echoed. "I swear to God," he said, shaking his head. "I've never seen a drunk who's had more than two beers."

The man glared at Pete.

"Let me put a bandage on that cut for you," Bob said.

"Just get the hell out of here and leave me alone."

Bob pulled out a paper form. "Sign here and we're gone." He handed the man a pen.

He printed his name on the refusal of treatment/transport form. Pete had already started out the door. I waited for Bob.

We retraced our steps out the building and out to the sidewalk.

"Hey!" came a voice behind us.

Bob kept walking. I stopped and turned around.

"Pat," Bob growled at me.

The man approaching us wore a spiked collar. "Hey," he said. "Did that guy take a human man-assed beating or what?"

"He's okay," Bob told him, stepping slightly in front of me.

Pete, already on the ambulance, moved into the driver's seat and drove closer to where we were standing.

The man stiffened. "Well, I'll go see for myself." He looked from Bob to me. "You better not have left him hurt."

Bob turned slowly and took my arm, and we walked the short distance to the ambulance.

He didn't let go of my arm until he had opened the side door for me. "Get in," he said.

I did.

Pete moved over and Bob drove. As we eased through the

parking lot, I looked out the back of the ambulance. I saw broken windows stuffed with newspapers. Scraps of toys and beer cans littered the tiny squares of dried grass between the cracked sidewalks.

Before we rounded the corner I saw, on a top floor window ledge, a row of potted plants secured with torn sheets. Behind the window, a child was waving.

I waved back.

"Pat!" Bob yelled.

I knew it was coming.

I moved up closer to him. "You don't have to say anything," I told him. "I know."

He looked at me in the rearview mirror. "What do you know?" he asked.

"I shouldn't have stopped."

"You have no street sense at all," he said, shaking his head.

Pete laughed. "To say the least," he added.

The bells sounded no more that day.

At 4:15, we ate supper, Danny's famous "buck-buck," fried chicken and the trimmings. It was almost as good as his meat loaf. Afterwards Pete beat us all at Trivial Pursuit. At 6:30, the night crew started coming in.

I began gathering my things for the trip home.

"You come back any time, Pat," Danny told me.

"I thought we could do this only twice," I said.

"Well," he grinned, "that's up to the Chief, and I say you can come back any time."

"Thanks, Danny," I smiled.

It would, however, be my last day at Station 22.


Bob was quiet as we traveled out of the city and down U.S. 95. I let him have his silence, knowing he needed it. The sun was setting as we turned onto Route 3.

"You see," he finally spoke, "why it's worth the long drive?"

"Yes."

"I love the country," he said, an affirmation made less to me than to himself. "I couldn't live in that city. I couldn't live in any city."

I agreed, but said nothing. He didn't want conversation. He just wanted to talk.

"Some nights I take two, three showers. I wash and wash and still don't feel clean." He sighed, paused a moment, then continued. "It's not the dead ones we pick up—the babies, the children, people killed by each other, old people dying alone—it's not the ones we take away, it's the ones we have to leave behind."

I thought of the child waving to us from the window.

"I think I understand," I told him.

He looked at me and smiled. "Yeah."

It was not long after that that Bob left Station 22. He returned to school to become a fire marshal for the city of Alexandria. Shortly after that, he resigned from our rescue squad.

He still lives less than three miles away, but I rarely see him. When I do, it's different. What continues to be an important part of my life is a thing of his past.

He made the good times better, the bad times bearable.

I miss him.

# Chapter 18

Each Thursday evening Bob and Joyce and Phyllis and I traveled together to Mary Washington Hospital for CT class. Just to the left of the sidewalk which led to the hospital's main entrance stood a young oak tree. I watched it grow and change with the seasons.

In January its limbs were bare. In early spring, buds sprouted from its slender branches. By summer it was thick with leaves, its foliage a shimmering green in the late afternoon sunlight. In autumn a bouquet of iridescent hues.

It was that autumn, in late October, that we took our final exam. It had been a long ten months. On our EMT exam, three years earlier, we had to score 70 to pass. For this exam, the requirement was 80. We wouldn't know until the next day that we had all scored in the 90s.

My telephone rang at 9:35 the next morning. It was Suzanne.

"Hi, CT," she greeted me.

We partied that night.

Jean baked me a cake. "It's from all of us," she told me." On top it read:

CONGRATULATIONS
FEARFUL LEADER
PAT I.V.
LOVE, TEAM THREE

Our seasoned CTs, Lou and Mark and Suzanne, assured us they would try to run our calls with us until we felt comfortable with our new responsibilities.

I waited for an ALS call.

And waited.

We had calls for stomach pains and cut hands and one for a broken leg. We had several minor automobile accidents and three calls for patients who had the flu.

"I'm going to forget everything before I can use it," I told my crew.

"Just don't practice on us," Woody said.

Twenty-one days after my exam, I ran my first advanced life-support call.

I heard the tones go off. "An unconscious male." It was 3:45 A.M., during Mark's shift. I went back to sleep. At 4:30, the tones again awakened me. I got up to listen. Mark was requesting another CT.

I thought for a moment. Al and Lou were out of town, so were Bob and Joyce. Suzanne couldn't leave her son, Eric, alone for nighttime calls, and Phyllis didn't respond to calls after midnight.

That left me.

I called the dispatcher for directions and told him I was on my way. As I pulled out of the driveway, I heard him announce, "CT Pat Ivey is en route to the location."

The lights of the ambulance marked the scene for me. I entered the house and climbed the stairs to the bedroom. Buzzy and Paul were doing CPR on the patient.

"Pat," Mark said, "I've got to go to work. Can you take over from here?"

I looked at the monitor. The rhythm was agonal, the sign of a dying heart.

"We're working a full code," he told me. "I've given one round of everything. I just gave the second round of Epi."

"Do you have to go now?" I asked him.

He looked at me. "Okay, rookie, I guess I can be late."

I worked my first code with him beside me. I administered the second and third rounds of drugs en route to the hospital.

"Stop CPR," Mark said to Paul and Buzzy. We looked at the monitor. There was a little more rhythm, but it was still primarily agonal.

"Defibrillate, Pat," Mark said.

I picked up the paddles, turned them on and charged them to 300 joules. I leaned across the man.

"Everybody clear," I told them. I glanced around to make sure no one was in contact with the man or the gurney, then pushed the paddles hard against his chest and fired.

His body jumped.

"Once more at 380," he said.

I recharged the paddles and fired again. On the monitor nothing more appeared than what we'd seen after the first firing: straight line and then the return to agonal.

Mark shook his head. "Continue CPR," he said.

Five minutes after we arrived at Mary Washington Hospital, the doctor pronounced him dead.

"Your first code," Mark said to me on our way home.

"Yes," I responded. "My first."

"Don't be discouraged," he told me. "That's the way most of them end and it's tough. But we've brought a few back and those are the ones you remember. There's nothing," he continued, "like seeing someone up and well and walking around after suffering cardiac arrest with no pulse, no respiration, and we brought them back. Those are the ones that keep us here. So," he said, "stick around long enough and you'll get your 'save.'"

"I plan on sticking around a while," I told him, "and speaking of sticking around, thanks for staying with me."

"Well, I couldn't just throw you out of the nest. Not yet anyway."

Several nights later the tones went off for a "possible heart attack." The location was one block from my house.

"That's the Hammels," I said to David. "I'd better go."

I drove the short distance to their home. His wife met me at the door. "I'm really worried about him, Pat." Alan was pale

181

and diaphoretic and was complaining of a heavy feeling in his chest. I took his pulse. It was rapid. His blood pressure was a little low.

The Med unit arrived with Mark and Phyllis and Norm. Norm put oxygen on Alan. Mark placed electrodes on his chest and attached them to the monitor cable. Phyllis unlocked the IV box and took out the supplies she would need to start a line. I watched her closely. I had not yet started an IV on a call. The only ones I'd done were in class and during my hospital work.

"A few PVCs," Mark said. PVCs are premature ventricular contractions: the ventricles firing on their own. If there were more than a few contractions and they were left untreated, they could progress into ventricular tachycardia, then ventricular fibrillation, which meant cardiac arrest. "I'll run a strip to the hospital," he told us. "They may want us to give Lidocaine."

The oxygen was helping our patient. There were fewer PVCs. The hospital ordered nitroglycerine for his pain. Mark placed a tablet under Alan's tongue.

"I feel a little better," he said.

"That's what we like to hear," I told him.

Phyllis had the tourniquet around his arm and was inserting the angiocath. "Flashback," she announced and Mark handed her the line. She attached it and started taping the line to Alan's arm.

Norm was holding the bag of D5W. "It's not dripping," he said.

Phyllis checked the IV site. The fluid had infiltrated. She untaped the line and withdrew the catheter.

"I don't know what happened," she said, then turned to me. "You want to try?" she asked.

"Sure," I answered her, sounding as if I'd done it a hundred times before.

I tied the tourniquet around his upper arm, then reached into the IV box for an angiocath and alcohol swabs. I found an accessible vein and uncapped the catheter.

"That's the first time I've blown an IV," Phyllis remarked to Mark.

Alan looked up at her.

"You're going to feel a stick," I told him.

"Well," Alan said to Phyllis, "at least it's not the first time you've done one."

"Flashback," I announced.

Alan smiled at me. "Good job, neighbor."

"Thank you," I told him.

"Hook it up," Mark said.

I did. "Does the hospital want Lidocaine?" I asked Mark, as I taped the line to Alan's arm.

"No, not if we don't see any more PVCs."

I checked the chamber of the administration set. The fluid was dripping. "Looks good," Mark told me. "You coming with us?"

"No, I have to go home." I turned to Alan's wife. "Let me know how he's doing."

"I will," she said. "Thank you."

I helped move him to the gurney and to the ambulance.

"That was a good IV," Phyllis said as I started to leave.

"That was my first one in the field, Phyllis," I told her.

"Your first!"

"Shhh," I said. "Don't let Alan hear you. He'll never let me forget it."

Several months later I told him myself. Sure enough, he hasn't let me forget it.

I had been a cardiac technician for over two months. I had always had another CT with me on our ALS calls as I started lines, administered drugs, and defibrillated.

I knew my days as a fledgling were numbered. They were nudging me out of the nest and turning me loose.

The tones went off for "a man unconscious in a car."

"Another one?" Jean asked.

"I hope it's not the same guy," Buzzy said.

"Can't be," Woody added. "We saved him."

Buzzy drove. Jean, Woody, and I were in the back. Woody cleaned his nails. Jean, sitting on the bench with her feet resting on the gurney, unwrapped a Hershey bar.

I sat in the seat opposite them, scanning the protocol book. I didn't have Mark with me this time, or Lou, or Suzanne. This was my first one alone. They had turned me loose.

"Unconscious," I said to myself. "Could be heart, diabetes, stroke . . ."

"Could be drunk," Woody interrupted me.

I glanced up at them. "How can you eat?" I asked Jean.

"Energy," she said. "You want a bite?"

"No."

"What's the matter?" she asked me. "Are you nervous?"

"A little," I admitted. "Aren't you?"

"Why should I be?" she shrugged. "You're with us."

I smiled at her. "Eat your Hershey bar."

I heard Buzzy mark us on the scene and leaned forward to look out the front window.

"What's going on?" I asked him.

There were two deputies' cars and a small group of onlookers. One of the deputies was holding a man up against a car.

"They're not going to send us into the woods again, are they?" Woody asked.

"I don't think so," I told him.

I stepped off the ambulance. As I walked toward them, I saw the man collapse. The deputy caught him before he hit the ground.

"Keeps passing out," he said. "We found him in his car. When he comes to, he gets violent. We better get him in your ambulance."

Buzzy helped the deputy carry him and put him inside.

"How violent does he get?" I asked.

"Oh, he cusses and swings his arms a little. He's too drunk to do anything else."

"What'd I tell you?" Woody said.

The man lay still on the gurney. "Let's get his pulse and blood pressure," I told them. "I'll hook him up to the monitor."

His EKG showed sinus tachycardia. "Pulse is 110," Jean said.

"Yeah, that's what I get on the monitor," I told her.

"Blood pressure's low," Woody reported. "100/60."

I reported our information to the hospital. The nurse told me to start a line of Lactated Ringers.

"He's still out," Buzzy said, as I unlocked the cabinet to the IV and drug boxes, "but the deputy's hanging around, just in case."

"That's good," I told him.

I handed Jean the bag of Ringers and the administration set. "Get this ready, please." I took from the box everything I would need and placed it beside me. I extended the man's arm and laid it across my lap.

"Look at this tattoo," I said to them.

"It's certainly graphic," Woody said.

Buzzy whistled. "Be careful where you stick that needle."

"Disgusting," Jean added.

I tied the tourniquet and rubbed the site with an alcohol swab. Buzzy stepped outside to talk to the deputy. Jean and Woody were draining the IV line. I leaned over his arm to insert the angiocath.

Then I felt his fingers move across my breast.

I sat back, staring at him. He looked unconscious. His eyes were closed. So again, I leaned forward. And again, I felt the pressure of his hand on me.

I looked up at Jean and Woody.

"The line's drained," Woody said. "You ready for it?"

"Almost."

I leaned to my right. An awkward position for inserting the angiocath, but it kept my chest out of his reach.

Jean stared at me. "What are you doing?" she asked.

"I'm starting the IV." Quickly. "Flashback," I said. "Give me the line." I hooked it up. "Tape." I taped it.

"Boy," Jean said. "That was fast."

"Uh-huh."

He lay quietly with his eyes closed all the way to the hospital, but I never took my eyes off him.

"Fine one to turn me loose on," I told Lou that evening.

"Hey," she said, "I read the call sheet. You did great."

I laughed.

"Well, what happened?" she asked me.

"I'll tell you about it some day."

* * *

I responded to the tone-out for a CT. Paul Lewis was waiting with Kathy Gates, who had recently joined the squad. I pulled into the lot just before Bob.

"Take it," he called to me. "I'll go back to bed."

"You sure?"

"Yeah," he said. "It's probably not much." He waved good-bye, turned his car around and headed home.

I got in the back of the ambulance.

"Hi," I greeted them. "What have we got?"

Paul would drive. Kathy moved into the back with me. "Sixty-three-year-old man. Weak and dizzy," she said. "It's a long way out, too."

We piled everything we might need on the gurney—jump bag, monitor, IV and drug boxes and oxygen, and sat back down. We still had a twenty minute drive.

Kathy and I talked. She was from New York and had recently moved to Lake of the Woods with her three children. A practical nurse, she worked for our family doctor at a nearby medical center. I liked Kathy.

"You're a Shock-Trauma, aren't you?" I asked her.

She glanced at the patch on her jacket. "Yeah," she said. "That's right."

I laughed. "Can't you remember?"

"I just need a few minutes to wake up," she smiled.

"I know," I told her. "One of the things I don't like about night calls is that you're sound asleep one minute and the next minute you're in your car out on the road."

She nodded. "And trying to think clearly. Can you go back to sleep when you get home from a call?"

"Depends on the call," I answered.

"We just turned off 692," Paul called back to us. "Shouldn't be much farther."

Our patient was sitting on the sofa in his living room. He looked pale to me when we entered the house, but he said he was feeling better.

"Did you lose consciousness?" I asked him.

"Just for a moment," his wife responded.

"Are you having any chest pain?"

186

He shook his head.

We went through our series of questions concerning symptoms, medications, allergies, and past medical history. He suffered from high blood pressure, but said his medicine kept it under control.

"I was outside working on my tractor most of the day," he told us. "I think I just got too tired. I'm all right."

"We're going to take a look at your heart," I told him, as I placed the electrodes on his chest. "Just to make sure."

"I think you're going to a lot of trouble for nothing." he said.

His blood pressure was somewhat elevated, considering he was on medication. His pulse was 72. An occasional PVC crossed the monitor screen. I called the hospital with the information.

"What is your ETA?" the nurse asked.

"About forty minutes," I told her.

"Start a line of D5W," she said. "If there are any problems, let us know."

We left the residence ten minutes later. We had him on four liters of oxygen and I'd started the line. He was resting comfortably. Kathy sat close to him, talking quietly with him and listening attentively when he spoke to her.

I kept a close eye on the monitor. I spotted one PVC, then another, and leaned forward to run off a paper strip of the reading. Then I saw another.

I placed my hand on his arm. "How are you feeling, sir?" I asked him.

"Oh, pretty good," he answered me.

"No discomfort?"

He raised his hand and rubbed his chest.

"Not really," he said. "Just a little tightness."

I saw an episode of bigeminy on the monitor, a normal ventricular response, then a PVC, then a repeat of both. He was close to ventricular tachycardia.

"Kathy, turn the oxygen up to six liters."

I lifted the receiver and pressed the call button. We had problems. "Lake of the Woods Medic 29 to Mary Washington Hospital."

I called the hospital six times. There was no response.

The runs of bigeminy continued.

"It's probably just indigestion," he said to Kathy.

I tried the hospital once more, then reached for the protocol book and heard . . .

"LAKE OF THE WOODS MEDIC 29, THIS IS MEDCOM. DO YOU COPY?"

Kathy looked up. "Who is MEDCOM?" she asked.

I shrugged and reached for the receiver. "MEDCOM, this is Lake of the Woods Medic 29. We copy."

"Can I be of assistance?"

"Yes!" I told him. "Can you relay information to Mary Washington Hospital for us?"

"Ten-four. Be glad to."

I gave him the most recent information on our patient's condition, emphasizing the PVCs and the continuing episodes of bigeminy. "We are requesting orders for Lidocaine," I said.

"Stand by, Medic 29."

I sighed, then smiled at Kathy. "Out of the blue," I said.

She looked pensive. "Actually, I think they may be out of Charlottesville."

At that moment I wanted to just reach out and hug her. There was something endearing about her, so caring, so genuine. She was good medicine. I nodded at her. "Kathy, I think you're right."

"MEDCOM to Medic 29."

"This is 29. Go ahead, MEDCOM."

"Mary Washington Hospital wants you to administer 75 mg of Lidocaine bolus and start a 4-to-1 drip."

I repeated the order. He verified it. "And," he added, "they want an update after you give the Lidocaine. I'll stand by."

"Ten-four. Thank you."

I glanced at the monitor as I opened the drug box. "Run a strip off," I told Kathy. I could see the continuous bigeminy on the screen before the printout was ejected from the monitor.

I removed the bag of Lidocaine mixture and the additional

line we would need to connect it to the existing one. "Set this up, please," I said, handing it to her.

I took the Lidocaine for the bolus out of the drug box and injected it into the IV port. Kathy had the line ready. I connected it and calculated the flow rate.

I watched the monitor. Within minutes the bigeminy had vanished. The PVCs were gone. The monitor showed normal sinus rhythm.

It was a beautiful sight.

MEDCOM stayed with us until we arrived at Mary Washington Hospital. "Thanks so much for your assistance," I said to him during our final transmission.

"My pleasure, Medic 29. Glad we could help. MEDCOM clear."

"That's what it's all about," Dr. Kravetz told me later, smiling broadly. "Prehospital care," he said. "That's where we save them. That's how we save them."

I thought back, remembering our CT graduation banquet. Dr. Kravetz presented to us our Cardiac Technician certificates, issued by the Commonwealth of Virginia Department of Health, Office of Emergency Medical Services.

"Could I have a wall for this?" I whispered to David.

"If you don't stare the lettering off before we get home," he said.

The speaker that night was W. Sidney Armstrong, Vice Mayor of Fredericksburg. He had notes before him and he spoke from them. "You people provide an invaluable service," he told us. "To volunteer your time and your energies in such an endeavor is truly a gift of love and commitment." He looked closely at his audience, divided equally between men and women. "And it was a proud day," he said, "a proud day for rescue squads, the day they opened their doors to women." That remark received a round of applause.

His speech was good, with equal proportions of inspiration and humor. As he drew to a close, he pushed his notes aside and looked out at us.

"You know," he began, seriously, thoughtfully, "to be able

to save a life, to actually save a human life, well,'' he said, ''that must be the most wonderful feeling.''

It is.

# Chapter 19

Squad membership was at its ebb. The days of the four-person crew were past. Lou did not seek reelection and Bob Grim took over as captain. He took Buzzy and Woody off Team 3 and put them on Team 1.

"It won't be the same," Woody said.

"You'll still get free meals, Woody," Jean told him.

"Yeah," he sighed, "but it won't be the same."

It wasn't.

Crew members were shifted around over the months until membership increased enough for Bob to make permanent assignments. Joe Broderick was placed on our crew.

Joe owned the local hardware store. He was fifty-three years old, tall and thin with blue eyes and flaxen hair. He wore gold-rimmed glasses and a smile as warm as sunshine.

Jean and I knew Joe and we liked him. He had been on Joyce's crew, but had covered several times on ours for Buzzy.

"Whoever covers for Buzzy treats," Woody had told him.

He bought us milk shakes.

Joe was with us on the call for the motorcycle accident. The young cyclist had sustained only minor injuries, but he was drunk and belligerent and became extremely agitated on the way to the hospital. Joe calmed him, talking quietly to him until we reached the emergency room.

On another occasion, Joe and I had transported a cancer patient from her home in Lake of the Woods to a nursing home in

Fredericksburg. I'd been on several earlier calls for her, as had Joe, but it was apparent that the trip we took that day would be her last.

"You know," she said, turning to me, "I still have my driver's license." She reached into the pocket of her robe, took it out and held it up for me to see. "I don't know why," she said. "Maybe it's the expiration date. It keeps me going." She held the license tightly in her hand. "You know the poem," she asked, "by Dylan Thomas?"

I knew which poem she meant. "Do Not Go Gentle Into That Good Night" I told her.

She nodded. " 'Rage, rage against the dying of the light,' " she said. "That's the important part." She returned the license to her pocket.

"Got to make a quick stop," Joe called back to me.

"Are we here already?" she asked.

"No, we're just stopping for a minute," I told her, wondering why we'd stopped at a 7-11 store.

Moments later he opened the back door of the ambulance and got in with us. In his hand was a single rose, bright pink and fragrant. "For you," he said, "from us." He handed it to her, then leaned over and kissed her softly on the cheek.

When I handed her a tissue to wipe the tears from her eyes, I took one for myself, too.

Jean and I welcomed Joe to Team 3.


That summer we were requested to send an ambulance to Caroline County's Fort A.P. Hill for the National Boy Scout Jamboree. Joe and Mara Bueng and I volunteered to help cover the final events of the Jamboree.

Leroy Gardner, Director of the Rappahannock Emergency Medical Services, was in charge of assigning ambulance positions for the day's activities, which were expected to draw close to a quarter of a million people. We stood in the group of area personnel awaiting our assignment.

"Lake of the Woods." Leroy called us. We stepped forward. "Okay," he said, pointing to a map of the area. "I've got you over here to the left of the stage. "Now, when Nancy Reagan's helicopter lands, if anything should happen to her, God forbid, you all would respond first.''

I glanced at Joe and Mara.

Mara's eyes widened.

"Some assignment," Joe said.

I imagined the three of us in the Rose Garden receiving medals and warm handshakes from our grateful President.

The temperature that day soared to 102 degrees. We treated fourteen patients, both scouts and visitors, the majority of them during the afternoon for heat-related problems.

Nancy Reagan's appearance was scheduled for five o'clock. We searched the skies for the helicopter and finally saw it approaching in the distance. We were hers. We were ready.

Our eyes remained fixed on her as she stepped off the helicopter onto the red carpet. On stage, she spoke briefly, praising the Boy Scout organization, its leadership, and the boys themselves. We watched her every move. She finished her speech and walked, flanked by security, back to the helicopter.

"Do you suppose she might twist her ankle?" I asked them. "Just a tiny sprain?"

"Or," Mara suggested, "maybe a cut finger. Nothing that would need stitches, just a band-aid."

"We could splint a cut finger," Joe added. "I mean, if the cut is on a joint, it would heal better if we splinted it."

We waved to the helicopter as it flew over us.

"Oh, well," I sighed.

That evening the Oak Ridge Boys performed against the backdrop of the American flag, and the night's finale was the most spectacular fireworks display I've ever seen.

"What an experience," I said as we drove home late that night. "Everyone in America should have an experience like that. It just makes you feel so proud and so thankful."

"Yeah," Joe nodded, "but Nancy Reagan sure missed the opportunity of a lifetime."

In August, Captain Joe Maiden died.

We draped black crepe across the front of the fire and rescue building. We mourned. His funeral was in Fredericksburg, but he was to be buried in a nearby cemetery. Jean, Joe, and I were on duty and couldn't attend the funeral service, but we stood by at the entrance to the cemetery awaiting the procession.

We saw the police car approaching, followed by our second Medic unit, and then the hearse. Joe switched on the ambulance lights and the three of us stood together beside it. We stood erect in our white uniforms looking, as Captain Joe demanded, professional.

"I never thought you'd amount to anything," he'd said to me with that wry smile of his, "but I'm beginning to think I was wrong."

It was the first time in six days that the sun had broken through the clouds. It was a gorgeous autumn day, a clear crisp morning which eased up into a delightfully warm afternoon. The sparrows and chickadees sang. Small children frolicked in the fallen leaves.

On a narrow dead end road a two-and-a-half-year-old girl played in the front yard of her home. Her playmate was a small dog which ran ahead of her, darting left and right. The girl's mother stepped inside for a few minutes with a younger child. The dog turned, spotted a rabbit, and ran after it into the deep woods which surrounded the yard. The girl followed.

Our tones went off shortly after 1:30. "Attention Lake of the Woods fire and rescue members. You are needed to assist in the search for a small child."

Several neighborhood women stood in the yard with their own small children, holding them closer than usual. They had helped in the initial search, walking in the woods and down the open road, calling the child's name.

A county deputy was inside with the mother. I walked toward the house as they emerged. There was something I wanted to say to her.

We stood face to face.

"Please find her," she pleaded.

"We will," I told her. I laid my hand on her shoulder. "My child was lost once," I told her and our eyes met in a moment of understanding, "and these people found him."

194

I didn't tell her that he was eight, not two. I didn't tell her that he was lost all night. She didn't need facts. She needed hope. She needed someone to say to her, "I understand," from someone who really did.

Linda was there with her search dog, a German shepherd, named Happy. She handed me the portable radio and we walked into the woods together, the dog just ahead of us.

"I know what she's going through," I said.

"I know you do. I remember. This is how you and I met," she said to me. "Less than two miles from here."

"I was just thinking of that," I told her. "I guess we've come full circle."

We walked down a narrow trail. "She would have followed the path of least resistance," Linda said. We continued on until the trail ended at a small gully, normally dry but now swollen with the past week's rainfall.

The German shepherd waded through the water. Linda and I found a place where the stream narrowed and jumped across.

"Find her, girl," Linda called to the dog.

"Do you think she could have crossed here?" I asked Linda.

"I don't know," she said. "Happy's after something."

Over the portable radio, we heard our tones set again for additional help. A deputy on the trail behind us asked if we would call the dispatcher and ask him to tone out Mine Run also.

"We're going to need more help," he said. "These woods are awful."

We walked to the crest of the hill and met a neighbor who told us he had covered the territory beyond the hill. Linda whistled for Happy and we headed back to search the area from the house down to the end of the road.

We found nothing and returned to the house.

Additional personnel had responded to the second tone out. We were divided into groups with designated areas. One of our firemen, Bud Morley, instructed our group—Cliff Wolff, Dick Ferguson, Bill Belt, Woody, Joe, and me—to form a straight line with six yards between each of us. We were to make a complete circle of the woods surrounding the house.

I glanced at my watch. We had perhaps two and a half hours of daylight remaining.

"They're sending us into the woods again," Woody said. "Pat, I'm getting too old for this."

I smiled at him. "Never, Woody."

We stopped only to check the neighboring structures, then reformed our line and continued. The woods were thick with evergreens and underbrush. Vines pulled at our feet. Sharp briars cut through our clothes and into our skin. I was in the middle of the group and could very seldom see the people at either end.

We emerged from the woods at 4:00. We had covered the entire area and had found no trace of the child.

We heard the helicopters in the distance. They took shape above us and we watched as they descended, hovering over one area, then moving on to another.

There were soft drinks for us. We clustered in small groups, resting on the tailgates of the pickup trucks, talking, occasionally glancing up at the helicopters, listening to the alternating static and voices coming from the police radios.

"We're going down to 614," a man from one of the search parties said to us," and cut through the back way. You all want to go with us?"

I looked at Joe and Woody.

"How about if we start from this side and meet you?" Joe suggested.

"Okay," the man agreed.

How I wish I'd gone with them.

I don't know who said it first or from which direction it came, "They found her!"

"Who?"

"The guys who just went over to 614."

"Where?"

"About a mile and a half from here. Near that old abandoned building."

"Is she all right?"

"She seems to be."

The sound of her crying had alerted the search party to her.

She was wet from her shoes to her waist. She had crossed the creek.

The girl's mother and father stood on the porch of their home. From there, they couldn't have heard the news on our radios. I watched the deputy walk toward the house. I couldn't see his face, but I hoped he was smiling so they would know the news was good. Oh, the news was so good.

We watched them as they listened to the deputy. The man put his arm around his wife. She leaned on him, crying, her head against his chest. Those of us who had come to this place together glanced at each other and smiled.

We stood back to give the mother and father and child time and space for their reunion. There was a stillness in the crowd. Then, one by one, we approached them. We all wanted to be close to her.

I touched her blonde hair, then slipped my fingers into her small hand. She squeezed them and smiled shyly at me.

"Now I know how you felt," her mother said to me, holding the girl tightly, "when they found your child."

I baked a cherry pie for dessert that night and piled vanilla ice cream on top of each piece.

Matt grinned at me. "My favorite dessert, Mom," he said.

"I know," I told him.

"What are we celebrating?" David asked me.

I could think of no answer other than, "Matt."


On a quiet street in our neighborhood, a fifty-eight-year-old man hanged himself from the attic rafters of his new home. He planned it well. There was little room for error or for a sudden change of mind. He left behind his wedding band and a note to his wife.

It happened on a beautiful summer day. Jennifer and I were playing at one of the Lake's beaches. I heard the call for a "possible hanging" while standing at the water's edge. Thinking I had misunderstood our dispatcher, I retrieved my pager from my beach bag. As I watched Jennifer play, I listened to the truth of it and thought about life's inconsistencies.

I heard the siren's wail as our ambulance traveled toward the scene. I thought of Bob and Joyce and Jay Broderick, Joe's son, who, as the schedule happened to fall, had duty that day.

Several months earlier my crew had responded to a call for this same man. His pickup had gone off the road and hit a tree. He told us a deer had crossed in front of him. Later, I wondered.

We treated his minor injuries, bandaging the lacerations on his face and hands. He refused to let us take him to the hospital.

"I'm all right," he insisted.

He wasn't, of course.

I thought back on it after that second call, that final call for him. I wondered if we could have said something more that day. I wondered if we had looked deeper into his eyes, could we have seen something there, some indication of what was to come and been able to help him through and out of whatever darkness he found inescapable.

Once, within a forty-eight-hour period, we had two calls for suicide attempts. A twenty-seven-year-old woman downed sixty-two pills with a half gallon of wine. Fortunately, the pills were non-prescription and non-lethal. At the hospital, the ER doctor examined her, then transferred her to the psychiatric ward.

We then found a forty-five-year-old man in the garage of his home, locked in his car with the engine running. We coaxed him out of the car and into the house and talked with him for over two hours. Finally, we suggested he come with us to the hospital or let the county deputy take him to the mental health clinic. He chose the latter.

We were toned out, "nature unknown." I don't like those calls. We followed the directions our dispatcher had given us. The night was cloudy. Joe switched on the floodlights so we could see the house numbers. Up ahead we saw a woman waving a flashlight. I picked up the radio. "Med 29 is on the scene," I announced.

I heard our dispatcher. "Ten-four, Med 29, on the scene at 2240 hours."

I rolled down the window as we pulled up beside the woman. "Can you give us any information on the patient?" I asked her. Bob stepped out the side door of the ambulance.

"Well, we don't know," the woman said. "He knocked on our door and said he lived down the street and had a gun . . ."

Joe interrupted her. "He has a gun?"

"No, he had a gun at his house and said he was going to kill himself," she told us.

Bob called our dispatcher and asked for a deputy. "Stay outside until the deputy gets here," he said.

The woman turned toward him. "Oh, no," she said. "He's not going to hurt you. My husband is in our house with him now. He came and knocked on our door and asked us to call for help."

"Has he done this before?" I asked her. "Threatened to kill himself?"

She shrugged. "I don't know. We don't know him."

"You don't know him?" Joe asked.

"No, we just moved here last week."

"You're sure he doesn't have the gun?" Joe asked her.

"I'm sure," she said. "The gun's at his house."

I sighed. "Okay, let's go."

We approached the house, walked up onto the porch and into the kitchen. I saw the older man first, sitting at the end of the kitchen table. Beside him sat a younger, darkhaired man. I couldn't see his face. His hands covered it. I sat down and pulled my chair close to him.

"What's your name?" I asked him.

He lowered his hands and looked at me. "Allen."

I smiled at him. "Allen, my name is Pat. We're here to help you."

He turned suddenly toward me. I braced myself in the chair. He slipped his arms around my neck, clasping his hands together, pulling me toward him. Joe stepped forward. But just as he did, Allen relaxed his grip on me and leaning his head on my shoulder, he began to cry. "Don't let me kill myself," he said. "Please don't let me do it."

"We're not going to let you," I told him.

"Oh, God," he sobbed. "I had the gun loaded." Abruptly he straightened and stared at me. His eyes were brown, unblinking, the pupils enlarged. There was a desperate, an almost savage look in them. His right hand and fingers moved into the shape of a gun that touched my forehead. Slowly, his eyes still on mine, he shifted his hand until his forefinger rested against his temple. "I had it this close," he said. His body slumped. "This close."

He clung to me as we walked toward the ambulance. Joe had hold of his right arm, but his left arm was still tight around my neck. We eased him down on the gurney and took him to the dispatcher's office. Bob decided it would be safer that way since the deputy was still fifteen minutes away. I agreed.

We walked him into the office. I sat on the sofa and he lay down, his head in my lap, one hand gripping my wrist. Bob was on the phone to the sheriff's office. Joe sat at the opposite end of the sofa.

With his other hand, Allen reached up and touched my face. "You won't let them hurt me, will you, Pat?" he asked. His hand was damp.

"No," I told him.

He closed his eyes.

Joe rested his arm on the back of the sofa. Bob, still on the phone, kept his eyes on me. I felt helpless. I took shallow breaths so Allen, his head pressed against my stomach, couldn't feel me move.

"Five minutes, Pat," Bob said, hanging up the phone.

Allen opened his eyes. "They're not going to take me to jail, are they?" he asked.

"No, they're not," I said. "They're going to take you to the hospital."

Bob moved toward the sofa. We all knew Allen was volatile. We had looked into his eyes. "Okay, Allen," Joe said, "Deputy's almost here. Let's sit up and get ready to go."

Allen now gripped my wrist with both hands. For a long moment he stared at me, his grip steadily tightening. My wrist ached. "Will you go with me, Pat?"

I glanced at Bob. "I'm going with you," he told Allen.

Allen's gaze shifted to Bob. His body tensed. Then he released my wrist, once more touched my cheek, and sat up.

"Can I kiss you good-bye, Pat?" he asked. I didn't look at

him. I leaned slightly toward him and felt his lips touch my cheek. "Thank you, Pat," he said. "You've been so kind."

Then they took him away.

I remained on the sofa. So did Joe. Finally, I looked at him. "I was really scared," I admitted.

"I know," he said. "You shouldn't rush in like you did. You shouldn't take chances like that. He was a strong young man; his strength was probably even greater because of his panic. You were good with him, but you should have let Bob or me sit beside him."

"How about those people who took him in?" I asked. "They took a chance."

"I guess you're right," Joe said.

"We take chances, Joe. Every time the tones go off, every time we get in the ambulance, we take a chance."

He held up his hand. "Stop," he said, smiling at me. "Or you're going to scare me right off the squad."


"I really want to deliver a baby," I told Jean over and over. "I think that would be so wonderful."

Joe shuddered. "Count me out," he said.

"Somebody's got to boil the water," Jean teased him.

"No." He shook his head. "All we need for an OB call is a tank full of gas and the cravats."

"Why would we need cravats?" I asked him. We used cravats, long pieces of cloth, for wrapping splints and securing patients to backboards.

"To tie her legs together," he said.

We had come very close to delivering twins. As soon as we reached the emergency room, the nurse rushed her into the delivery room. Six minutes later she gave birth to the first of two boys.

"I'll never get to deliver a baby as long as a man is driving the ambulance," I said to Jean.

"Well, honey, just forget it then. On an OB call, they're always going to push us aside to get to the steering wheel."

At 2:30 one morning the tones went off. It was a call for "a woman in labor." I jumped out of bed, switched on the light, glanced at David sleeping soundly and grabbed my uniform. I paused by the door just long enough to put it on. I carried my shoes to the car and drove barefoot to the building. Bill Werber was already there. Mark pulled in behind me.

"Can I go?" I asked them, slipping on my shoes.

"You bet," Bill said. "Get on."

This was the woman's fifth child. Her contractions were a minute apart when we arrived. I examined her and found a large amount of bloody discharge.

"Has your water broken?" I asked her.

She moaned deeply, then answered me, "Yes."

"Well," Mark said, "if you don't need me on this one, I'll just go on back." Mark had left the classroom the night we watched the film on childbirth.

"Mark," I told him, "it's going to take two of us in the back. One for the mom and one for the baby."

He smiled weakly.

"There's no traffic this time of night," Bill said. "We can make good time."

We did. Mark could have stayed home.

We took her straight to labor and delivery. I helped the nurse move her onto the bed in the delivery room. Bill and Mark returned to the emergency room to change the sheets on the gurney.

The doctor came in and examined her. "Won't be long," he told her.

I looked at the nurse. "Do you mind if I stay?" I asked her.

"Not a bit," she said. "Just put on a gown."

"Thank you."

I stood at the foot of the bed, waiting. Every few minutes the doctor would come in and check the woman. Each time the door opened, I saw Bill and Mark standing in the hallway. They would glance at me. I would look back at them and then the door would close. I wasn't budging.

The woman moaned deeply during her contractions. The nurse, big and loving and encouraging, would pat her hand and moisten her lips with a sponge. Between contractions the woman lay with her gaze fixed on the ceiling.

I'd seen her house and the four small children she left behind to have this baby. She had no husband. I wondered what she was thinking, what future she was seeing as she stared at that one spot above her head.

She was having another contraction. The nurse lifted her off the pillow. "Push," she told her. "Push."

The doctor came back in. "Looks like this is it," he said, slipping on his gloves.

With her next contraction, the baby's head appeared. With the next one, it emerged. The doctor quickly suctioned the baby's mouth and nose. Her next contraction fully delivered the little boy. His entrance into the world was a noisy one.

"Oh, look at him," I exclaimed. My eyes were damp with joy. "Just look at him."

The doctor smiled at me. The nurse wrapped the baby in a blue blanket and then held him out to me.

"Do you mind?" I asked his mother.

She shook her head. "No."

I took him in my arms and held him close to me. He quieted.

"Looks like you've had some experience," the doctor said.

"Three times," I told him. "Is there anything more precious?"

"Well, Mama," he said to the woman, "you think we're going to have to pry your baby away from her?"

"You might have to," I said to him. I carried the baby to her bed and laid him down beside her. "He's beautiful," I told her.

"Thank you." She looked at the baby a moment, then back at me. "He is beautiful, isn't he," she said.

"Is Pat ever going to stop talking?" Bill said to Mark on our drive back.

"No," he answered, yawning. "Probably not."

It was a harsh winter. In Virginia the snow fell in record amounts. We answered calls following the tracks of snow plows. We slipped and we fell.

"It's my back," Jean said.

She lay in the snow drift. I dropped the jump bag and clipboard and reached down to help her. She struggled to her feet.

"Jean, are you all right?"

She straightened her back, slowly. "Yes," she said, "but I can't make it through this snow."

I took her arm. "I'll help you back to the ambulance," I told her. "Joe and I can get our patient."

Joe had eased the ambulance as far off the road as possible without sinking the tires into the snow. He was getting off as we approached him.

"What's wrong?" he asked.

"She fell," I told him and we helped her into the ambulance.

The woman who'd called us had a urinary tract infection. Her husband didn't want to drive in the snow and I didn't blame him. She walked to the ambulance and lay down on the gurney. Joe and I tightened the straps across her. I took her pulse and blood pressure and recorded the information on the call sheet. She was feverish and kept her eyes closed for most of the ride to Culpeper.

I sat on the bench. Jean sat in the seat opposite me. It was a rough trip. The chains on the tires seemed to grind into the snow and the patches of clear pavement beneath us. The ambulance shook. I could see the pain in Jean's face and knew that we had lost her.

When we returned, Joe and I helped her into her car. "If you need anything," I told her, "call me."

She called me that night.

"I have to go off," she said to me.

Even now, when I respond to a call, I still expect to see her there, I miss her. I miss her dry sense of humor, the Hershey wrappers I'd find in the back of the ambulance, when we have a patient with a foul mouth, and I especially miss her company.

Many of those who were there with me in the beginning are gone. John. Ed. Ellen resigned after her accident. Howie is gone. So are Ken and Carmie. Suzanne left for a new job and to remarry. Lou and Al left because of family and business responsibilities.

"I still miss the squad," Lou said to me. "I hope someday I can come back."

"I hope you can, too," I told her.

And Captain Joe died.

Of those who joined after me—and now are gone—Bob Luckett was promoted to Fire Marshal in Alexandria, Buzzy moved to northern Virginia to sell real estate, and Woody resigned to get a real job. He's the accountant at Joe's hardware store. And Jean is gone.

We still have Joe and his son, Jay. John, our hero, is still on the squad, and Norm and Cliff and Kathi and Jack, Mara and Kathy, Marcus, Millie and Pia.

There are those who have been with me all the way: Linda, Bob and Joyce, Phyllis, Paul, Mac and Joanie.

"You're my second family," Buzzy had said to Jean and Woody and me.

He was right. We were a family. We are all a family, with family loyalties, family problems, and even family roots. We are a squad, a small group of people working together.

The call for "difficulty breathing" had come late in the afternoon.

The small green-and-white trailer sat back off the road. A woman waved to us from the front porch. Joe pulled into the driveway.

We could hear the man's labored breathing before we entered the back room of the trailer. His bed took up most of the space in the tiny room. He lay on his back. His eyes, half closed, were dull, filmy, his pupils slow to react. He did not respond when I spoke his name.

"How long has he been this way?" I asked as I placed the electrodes on his chest.

"He's had this bad cold," the woman told me. "He was watching television this afternoon and said he didn't feel good. Then he came back here and lay down. My little girl checked on him," she continued, gesturing toward the door, "and found him like this. That's when we called the rescue squad."

I saw the child standing in the doorway. Her eyes were fixed on the man, and she was crying.

The electrocardiogram showed sinus tachycardia. Joe placed an oxygen mask on our patient's face. I took out my stethoscope and listened to his lungs. I heard rales, the popping sound of fluid in the lungs.

"Any history of asthma, bronchitis, or emphysema?" I asked.

The woman shook her head.

"Turn the oxygen up to five liters, Joe."

Linda took his blood pressure, 90 over 60, very low, and his pulse, 138.

"I'm going to the ambulance to call the hospital," I told them. I took the call sheet from Linda and left the room.

"I always bring him his coffee in the morning," I heard the child say. She was following me.

I stopped and turned. "Do you want to walk out to the ambulance with me?" I asked her.

She nodded. I took her hand in mine.

She watched me while I talked to the nurse at Mary Washington Hospital and listened attentively as I reported the information on the call sheet on the man's condition: respiratory distress, low blood pressure, rapid pulse, and a Glascow Coma rating of three, the lowest possible scoring of a person's state of consciousness. The nurse told me to start an IV of D5W and to give her an update en route to the hospital. I switched off the radio and turned back to the child.

"Is he going to die?" she asked me.

I wanted time to talk to her, but I couldn't afford it. Her grandfather couldn't wait.

"He is very sick," I told her. As we walked back to the trailer together, I once more took her hand. "We're here to help him and we'll do all we can. The doctors and nurses at the hospital will try to help him too."

I glanced at her. Her face was sad, pensive.

"You've taken good care of him," I said, "bringing him his morning coffee."

She stood beside the bed while I started the IV.

"Does the needle hurt him?" she asked Linda, who had just checked his blood pressure again.

Linda smiled at her. "No, it doesn't hurt him at all."

Joe gently touched her shoulder, then picked her grandfather up from the bed and carried his thin frail body to the gurney in the narrow hallway. From there we moved him to the ambulance. This time the girl did not follow. She stayed inside by the window. As we pulled down the driveway, I looked back. Her face was pressed against the glass, her hand raised in farewell.

An ambulance had taken my grandfather away.

I knew he was dying. He had told me so. He sat in his favorite chair, holding me on his lap. "I want to tell you something, Patricia. A secret," he said. He kissed me on the cheek. "I'm not going to live much longer, but I want you to remember that I've lived a lot of years, a lot of happy years."

"You mean you're going to die, Granddaddy?" I had heard the word. It was what happened to Pudge, my cocker spaniel.

He pulled me closer. "Yes, Patricia."

"What is it like?" I asked him. "What happens when you die?"

"I will go away," he explained. "And after I go, I'll be able to see my parents and my sister and brother and," he smiled, "maybe even Pudge."

"Pudge? You'll see Pudge?" Dying didn't sound so bad if it meant seeing our dog that I missed so much. Dying sounded more like a family reunion. Still, something wasn't right. I picked at a thread on his sweater. "Granddaddy," I said, "when will you come back?"

He answered me softly, "You'll see me again. Someday."

Later I learned that I was the only one with whom he shared his knowledge of his coming death. I understand now that he did so out of love. He meant to help me cope with his dying, but I was not quite seven then and too young to understand.

I didn't ask my grandfather any more questions. I hadn't seen Pudge again. Pudge hadn't come back.

He reached out to switch on the radio so we could listen to the Brooklyn Dodgers game. We always did that, he and I. He would yell each time the Duke scored, and I would stay nestled in his lap until some time around the bottom of the third. That day he didn't yell once, but I stayed there with him through all nine innings.

An ambulance took him away; he did not come back.

"Is he going to die?" the child had asked me. A few minutes after we pulled away, her grandfather's condition worsened. I called the hospital for orders to administer Lasix, a diuretic. I injected 40 mg into the IV tubing and told Joe to expedite. Ten minutes after we reached the hospital, he went into respiratory arrest, then cardiac arrest. For twenty-five minutes we struggled to save his life. Finally, the ER doctor pronounced him dead.

I pictured her face against the glass and her small hand slowly waving good-bye. I hoped that whenever she looks back on the day an ambulance took away her grandfather, she will pause and remember Linda's smile, Joe's gentle touch on her shoulder and my hand holding hers. I hoped that she would know that along with the ambulance, the lights and the sirens, come people who help, people who care.

# Chapter 20

WE TAKE CHANCES.

There's always the risk of back injuries.

"Bend your knees," I say to my crew before we lift the gurney, but sometimes that's not enough. We lost Ed and Jean, and Norm continues to have problems.

We take chances when we enter the houses of strangers. A man in neighboring Spotsylvania County pulled a gun on a squad and fired at them six times. Fortunately, they were able to find cover, and he was too drunk to aim.

There's burnout: emotions becoming lethargic from too many bad calls, too much stress, too many losses, too much caring. If we're lucky we catch it before it begins to spread beyond our squad room and into our homes. John Beery was lucky.

Crisis Intervention teams are relatively new. Team members are doctors, nurses, psychologists, counselors, and peers, those who work in the same profession. A team was sent to Mexico following the earthquake and one traveled to the scene of the Amtrak disaster in Maryland. They minister to those who have cared for the hurt, the maimed, the dying, and the dead.

A team was recently sent from the University of Virginia Hospital to Mine Run to meet with firemen and rescue squad personnel who'd answered a call for a thirty-six-year-old woman and her eight-year-old daughter. It was a freak accident. Their car swerved off the road and hit a utility pole, knocking a transformer and live wires onto the car.

Their injuries were probably not serious, but when the woman stepped from the car she was electrocuted. Within seconds the car and the woman and child were engulfed in flames. There was nothing the rescuers could do. The firemen could not even turn their hoses on the car until the power had been shut off and by then the fire was already out.

You can't get the sights, the sounds, the smells out of your mind. The images are already recorded, so we must learn to live with the memories. Sometimes it's not easy and we often need help. In Salem, Virginia, the Lewis-Gale Hospital Employment Assistance Program provides fourteen volunteer rescue squads with confidential free services of crisis intervention and counseling.

I've been lucky. I've had family members who cared enough to listen, to give me space, and to give me comfort. I've also had those who truly understand the stress, the feelings of self-doubt, the anger, and the sorrow. I've had my friends on the squad: Lou, Ed, Jean, Buzzy, Bob, Woody, and Joe. They've kept me whole.

Pia Boot Van der Heiden is one of our newest EMTs. She is my age. She grew up in Holland. She loves to talk on the radio, and we love to listen to her. I am probably overprotective of her. Maybe it is that she reminds me of myself years ago.

Joe, Norm, Pia, and I responded to the call for a motorcycle accident. The seventeen-year-old boy had struck a guardrail and fallen twenty-five feet down an embankment.

He was conscious. He had cuts and abrasions on his neck and arms. His collarbone was broken. A long laceration on his left buttock was open to the bone. The flesh of his lower left leg was shredded. Fragments of bones were exposed.

Pia and I cut away his jeans and placed trauma dressings on the open fractures and then poured saline over them.

"Are you all right?" I quietly asked her, knowing this was her worst call so far.

She nodded.

"Pia," I said. "It's okay not to be all right."

"No," she insisted. "I'm fine."

She called me the next day. "I've been thinking about it so

much," she said. "Last night I couldn't think of anything but that."

"I know," I told her. "It was a terrible injury, Pia, an awful sight."

"It seemed worse afterward than when we were with him," she said.

"That's because we were working," I explained. "We weren't spectators. We were participants, thinking of what we had to do to take care of him. But we also were recording what we saw, and now we're looking at it. Like a picture after it's developed."

"You feel that way, too?" she asked.

"Of course," I said.

"But you've been on the squad for so long. I thought it would get better."

"It gets easier, Pia. The images are still there for me, but probably not as clear as they are for you. It's like your camera is newer than mine. Your pictures come out brighter."

"Pat," she said. "Did I do okay?"

"Pia, you were wonderful."


The National Association of EMTs publishes a report entitled "Accidental Deaths Occurring to Emergency Medical Personnel in the Line of Duty." The majority of these deaths are the result of traffic and helicopter accidents. There are other categories, such as the one which includes heart attacks.

"Don't become a statistic," we are told as early as the second week of our EMT class. As with everything else that hints of danger or tragedy, we think, "oh, that won't happen to me."

But we are not immune; we take chances.


It was another bad wreck on Route 20, another head-on collision. Jay and Linda went to the man in the first vehicle. Joe and I went to the couple in the second, a pickup truck. Both doors were jammed and the only way to reach our patients was through the side window. Glass fragments from the shattered window jutted out from its frame. I carefully pulled myself through.

The man was conscious and oriented. His face was covered with blood. I quickly found the source, a deep laceration at his hairline, and bandaged it.

"What's your name?" I asked him.

"Herb," he told me. "My head hurts," he said, "and my chest." He wasn't wearing a seat belt, and the sudden impact had thrown him against the steering wheel.

"How old are you?" I asked.

"Sixty-one."

"Do you have any heart problems?"

"No."

I asked John to get the monitor.

Herb turned toward his wife. Joe was leaning inside the passenger window talking to her. She, too, had a deep laceration on her forehead. Joe had bandaged it and was holding an ice pack against her forehead.

"Mary," Herb said. "Are you all right?"

"Yes," she answered him. "I'm all right."

I glanced at Joe.

"Other than her head and facial injuries," he said, "she's got some pain in her left side."

"Does it hurt you to breathe?" I asked her.

She nodded. "A little."

John passed the monitor through the window. "We've got to cut this door off, Pat," he told me as I placed the electrodes on Herb's chest.

I switched on the monitor. Normal sinus rhythm. Good. "How's the other man?" I asked John.

"Broken leg," he said. "Can we start on the door?"

"Just a minute," I told him. "Let us get a blood pressure." Once the generator was started we wouldn't be able to hear.

Herb's BP was fine. I waited while Joe took Mary's. I watched him pump the cuff again, for a second reading.

"Mary," I said to her. "How are you doing?" She slowly turned to me. She looked worse than she had when we arrived. She was pale. I took her hand. Her skin was moist.

"I hurt," she said. "Here." She pointed to her left side just above her waist.

Joe removed the stethoscope from his ears. "96 over 60," he said.

She was bleeding internally and sinking rapidly into shock. I moved the monitor, taking the leads off Herb, whose EKG was fine, and placed the electrodes on Mary's chest. Sinus tachycardia, another sign of shock.

John stuck his head in the window. "Ready, Pat?"

"How long is it going to take?" I asked him.

"I don't know," he said. "This door is really jammed."

"John, we're going to need Pegasus. Can you or Mark call them?"

"Right away," he said and stepped away from the truck.

I started a line of Lactated Ringers in her left arm and Fredericksburg CT Steve Elliott started another line in her right arm. She was still conscious, but wasn't communicating with us anymore. Her only responses were to shake or nod her head.

"Keep talking to her, Joe," I told him.

"Take care of her," Herb said. "Get her out of here."

I explained to him that the firemen were going to have to cut the door off the truck before we could get them out. I moved away from Mary and back across Herb so that during the extrication I could stay between him and the door.

Harry reached in with the tarp. "Here, Patrick," he said, handing it to me. Harry Haas, seventy-one, was the patriarch of our fire department. He was short and slender and always smiling. He called me Patrick.

"John wanted me to tell you," he said. "Pegasus is in the air."

"Thanks, Harry. You're a good man," I told him. I saw the other firemen: Bud, Bill, and John. Mark had arrived in our second unit, but put on his turnout gear to help with the extrication.

I moved away from the window and closer to Herb, pulling the tarp over our heads. I could hear Joe talking to Mary. "When they start the generator," I told Herb, "it's going to be loud."

"You've got to get us out of here," he said.

"It won't be long."

The generator was fired. I didn't say any more to him. He

couldn't have heard me anyway. I rested my head against his and pulled the tarp tighter around us. I could hear the Hearst tool against the metal of the door, scraping, grinding, and the harsh noise of the generator.

I thought about Mary. I wondered how long Pegasus had been in the air. I was getting hot under the heavy tarp and my legs were beginning to cramp.

The noise continued to explode around us. John had said the door was badly jammed.

Then, abruptly, there was silence.

But I hadn't heard the door pop.

Had the generator quit?

The voices from outside the car sounded strained, raised, distant and different.

"Can we get out now?" Herb asked.

"I don't know," I answered him.

I did know that something had gone wrong. I raised the tarp from my head. The door wasn't off. I moved towards it, pushing the tarp off me. I couldn't see through the window frame. A fireman was backed up against it and I couldn't see past his yellow turnout gear. I turned and looked out the front window.

Everyone was looking down.

Then I saw Linda's face.

"What's going on?" Joe asked me.

I leaned farther forward. Linda looked up at me. I mouthed the words, "What happened?"

Her mouth moved and I saw her say, "Harry."

I heard Mark's voice, "Everybody clear!" and closed my eyes for a moment and felt the warmth of tears against my lids.

"Joe," I said softly, "it's Harry."

"What?" he asked.

"Harry," I repeated. "Harry's down."

"Can we get out now?" Herb asked again, pushing against me. "How long is this going to take?"

I wanted to shout at him. I wanted to yell. "Harry's had a heart attack." I wanted to tell him I didn't want to be inside this pickup truck. I wanted to be out there with Harry.

Again I heard Mark, "Everybody clear!"

"Harry's down?" Joe said, still uncertain.

"We've got to get Mary out of here," Herb insisted.

I turned back toward him, so quickly that my sudden movement pulled the tarp off him. It crumpled onto the floorboard. He looked at me as I started to speak. Then I saw his eyes. I saw that his, like mine, were damp with tears. As much as I wanted to be with Harry, these people were my responsibility. Harry was one of ours, but I couldn't turn away from them.

"I know, Herb," I said to him. "We'll get her out. It won't be much longer."

I glanced at the monitor screen. Still sinus tachycardia. I heard the helicopter in the distance. "How is she, Joe?"

"Weak," he said. "Her respirations are really shallow."

"You sure it won't be much longer?" Herb asked me.

I simply nodded. I couldn't tell him why the door wasn't off.

"I'm not going to any damn hospital!"

Harry? Was that Harry's voice?

I heard Bud, "Oh yes, you are."

I turned back to the window. Linda was pushing the gurney toward the pickup and the firemen were moving back. From somewhere I heard laughter.

"I'm okay, I told you," I heard Harry say. I looked at Joe and smiled.

They wheeled Harry to our second Medic unit. I saw him, his head raised arrogantly and even though I couldn't hear him, I knew he was still arguing with them.

Within minutes the firemen popped the door and we moved Herb out of the truck and into the ambulance. We carried Mary to the helicopter in the open field across the highway. She would be in intensive care for several weeks. She had three fractured ribs, a severe lung contusion, and a ruptured spleen.

And Harry.

The firemen had been in the midst of extrication. The door was loose and ready to pop. Harry leaned against it to prevent it from springing back too fast.

"All of a sudden," Bud told us later, "Harry just slid down the side of the truck. I said to him, 'Come on, Harry. Get up.' "

Mark saw Harry go down. "Get the other lifepack," he

215

shouted to John. When Mark placed the paddles against Harry's chest for a quick look, he saw ventricular fibrillation, cardiac arrest, and immediately defibrillated. It was only after the second defibrillation that Harry's heart returned to normal sinus rhythm.

Then he opened his eyes and breathed.

"Welcome back, Harry," Mark said to him.

The doctors told Harry he couldn't have been in a better place to have a heart attack, surrounded by medical personnel with the abilities and equipment to save him.

What a save it was! Woody should have been there.

We take chances.

Our work is risky. There are always hazards.

Now there's AIDS.

"Where are your gloves?" the ER nurse asked me, staring at my hands.

I reached into my pocket and pulled them out. "I forgot to put them on."

"And you started a line?"

I nodded.

"Look at your hands."

I looked. I had to look closely, but it was there: specks of blood under two of my fingernails and around the cuticles.

"Those gloves won't do you a bit of good in your pocket," she said. "You know how I remember mine? I think of every patient who comes through those doors as having AIDS, because you never know." She held up her gloved hands in front of me. "This is my protection."

"You're right," I told her. "We've just got to get into the habit of wearing them."

"You bet you do," she said. "You should put them on as soon as you get on the ambulance. Wear them for trauma, for heart attacks, for everything. And," she continued, "remember this. You people on the rescue squad run a higher risk of coming in contact with an AIDS patient than we do. That is, you run a higher risk of coming in contact with them unprotected. So wear your gloves. Don't take chances."

Hers was the most impassioned plea I've heard regarding our

safety in the field and our protection against AIDS. We carry a box of surgical gloves on all our units. We try to remember to remind each other on every call: "Put your gloves on."

I keep a pair in the pocket of my jumpsuit and in the first aid bag in my car. Still, we are sometimes careless.

"Aren't you afraid you're going to offend some people," I was asked recently, "if you put gloves on before you touch them?"

"My dentist wears gloves," I responded. "That doesn't offend me. We've got to be careful."

Among the ranks of volunteer emergency medical personnel, there has not yet been a reported case of AIDS. If AIDS continues to spread as the Center for Disease Control predicts, however, there will be.

"You're not going to catch me without gloves on," Joyce told me. "My rescue squad work is really important," she said, "but it's not worth dying for."

# Chapter 21

I OPENED MY eyes in the half light of Christmas morning to see Jennifer standing beside me.

"Merry Christmas, sweetheart," I said to her.

"Look at my stocking," she squealed. "It's so full."

I reached out from under the covers and pulled her to me. "Santa brought you all that?"

"Yes, and Mama, come and look at all the presents. Nana and Papa are already up."

I heard the boys' footsteps on the stairs. The aroma of coffee drifted back into the bedroom.

"Come on, Mama," Jennifer said, pulling away and tugging at my gown. "You and Daddy get up."

I leaned over and kissed David on the cheek. "Wake up," I whispered. "It's Christmas morning."

"Hurry up!" Matt yelled.

"We're on our way," I called back to him.

I walked into the living room and gave everyone a Christmas morning kiss, poured myself a cup of coffee and settled down on the sofa. David sat beside me and slipped his arm around my shoulders.

The children were still going through their stockings. Under the soft lights of the Christmas tree and with sleep still in their eyes, they looked even younger, more vulnerable. I sipped my coffee and watched them, loving each of them so.

They presented us with gifts. Dave and Matt had made book-ends, and with Dave's help, Jennifer had woven potholders. We all "ooo'ed" and "ahh'ed" over our gifts, and they beamed at our appreciation.

The boys had asked for clothes, tapes of the latest rock groups, football books, and extra weights for their bench. Beginning in October, Jennifer had worked on her Christmas list. Some items were marked out. Others added. One did not change.

"What I want most of all," she told us over and over, "most of all in all the world," she always added, with that emphatic little nod of her head, "is Cabbage Patch twins."

I wrapped the strangely shaped box in bright red paper and late on Christmas Eve tucked it behind the lowest branches of the tree. When, with the first rip of paper, she saw the two funny little faces, her eyes widened and she laughed with delight and hugged them to her.

It was a good Christmas morning.

The day was clear and cold and the warmth from the fire-place held us together in the living room. One of our family gifts was a dart board and we spent most of the morning playing.

By late afternoon, eyelids were beginning to droop. David and Dad finally dozed off. Jennifer played with her dolls and Dave and Matt, stretched out on the floor, read their football books.

The skies were darkening as I put the roast in the oven. Mom started to set the table.

"We'd better eat soon," she smiled, "before everyone is asleep." She put her arm around my waist. "Hasn't it been a nice day?"

"The best," I answered her.

She glanced into the living room. "Hey," she whispered, "why don't you and I play a game?"

"You think we can get away with it?"

"We can try," she said.

Jennifer looked up from her dolls as Mom threw the first dart. "Nana, can I play?"

Mom looked at me and shrugged. "Sure you can," she said to Jennifer.

David opened his eyes. "Teams?"

Dad woke too and the boys closed their books. "Okay," I said. "Let's all play."

We were into our second game when the tones went off. I wasn't on duty, but paused to listen to my pager.

"ATTENTION LAKE OF THE WOODS FIRE AND RESCUE MEMBERS," our dispatcher announced. "WE HAVE A REPORT OF A 10–50 PI TWO MILES UP ROUTE 20 FROM ROUTE 3."

"It's going to be bad," I said, remembering the others. "There's something about that stretch of road." In the past three years, four people had lost their lives on that half mile section of straight highway.

"Aren't you glad you're not on duty?" David commented.

"Yeah," I said, trying to remember who was. Bob would go, and probably Joe and Kathy. Many of the others were away for the holidays.

Dad took his turn, then handed the darts to me. Only one of mine struck the target.

"MEDIC 29 IS EN ROUTE TO THE SCENE." Bob's voice.

It was Jennifer's turn. She threw the darts.

"Eighty-five, Mama," she announced proudly.

"How much?" I asked her.

"Eighty-five," she repeated. "Weren't you watching?"

"Yes, sweetheart," I smiled at her. "I was watching."

"SHOCK TRAUMA 29 STANDING BY AT THE STATION." Kathy's voice.

Bob reported Medic 29 on the scene. Seconds later he said, "BRING THE SECOND UNIT."

It was bad, but I felt better knowing we had a medic unit already there and a shock trauma unit responding.

"I guess we can relax now," I said.

They all looked at me blankly.

The game continued. I was in it, but not a part of it anymore. Something held my attention on this call. I was the only one listening to the voices, the only one wondering what Bob had found on that dark highway this Christmas night.

"It's your turn, Pat," Dad said.

I scooped up the three darts, aimed the first one, and missed.

Mom stepped into the kitchen to check the roast. "Dinner in about twenty minutes," she announced.

I threw the second dart.

"Hey, Mom," Matt said, "You got twenty points on that one."

"I'm on a roll," I told him. I took aim with my last dart.

"MEDIC 29 TO LAKE OF THE WOODS." Bob's voice again.

Then our dispatcher's. "GO AHEAD, MEDIC 29."

I lowered my arm to my side.

"Throw it, Mom," Dave said to me. "Get another twenty and we'll be ahead."

"SET THE TONES FOR ADDITIONAL CARDIAC TECHNICIANS."

I handed the dart to David.

"I have to go," I told him. "I'm sorry, but I really have to go."

"I know you do," he said. "Be careful."

I grabbed my pager and jacket and started toward the door. "I love you all," I called to them as I closed the door behind me and stepped out into the darkness.

Our firemen working traffic control guided me through the backup of cars. I eased over to the side of the road and got out. Flashing lights threw crimson circles over the wreckage. The two cars were locked together, their corrugated hoods merged into one.

I found Bob. "Where do you want me?" I asked him.

"Come on," he said. I followed him and watched as he leaned inside one of the cars, into the darkness of the back seat, where two of the victims were, the driver and a passenger. Before the collision, they had been in the front. Now they lay barely conscious, trapped by twisted metal.

I looked up to see a fireman carry a child from the second car and place her on a backboard on the long side bench inside the ambulance. A second patient lay on the gurney. Jay was there, holding a third patient, another child. He looked up and saw me.

"Pat," he called to me. "Come on with us."

"That unit's ready to leave," I said to Bob. "They have three patients and no CT. If it's okay, I'll go with them."

He glanced at the waiting ambulance. "Yeah, okay," he nodded. "Joyce is on her way, and it'll be a while before we'll have these two out of the car. Go ahead."

I stepped from the outside darkness into the luminous interior of the ambulance and closed the doors behind me. Paul called up to Jack, "Let's go," and we pulled away from the wreckage, slowly moving around the accident site, then through the congested traffic.

I was a latecomer and had no knowledge of what had happened before my arrival on the scene. "Give me a quick status," I said to Jay, as I knelt down to look at the boy in his lap.

"The girl seems okay," he told me, "but we haven't really had time to check her. This boy must be her brother. He's got a head injury. This eye," he said, pointing to the child's bruised and swollen right eye, "looked like this when we got here. It hasn't gotten any worse. His pulse is a little rapid, but he's breathing okay."

"Were they wearing seat belts?" I asked him.

He nodded. "Yeah."

"Thank God for that," I said. The boy whimpered when I raised his right lid. I checked both pupils with my pen light. Normal reaction. His pulse was a little rapid, but his blood pressure was fine. I hooked him up to the monitor just to keep a close check on his heart rate, though it appeared okay.

I stood up and moved next to Mac. He told me the man on the gurney was conscious and oriented. "He's complaining of pain in his left arm and leg," he continued. "We've bandaged a deep laceration over his left eye."

"Put oxygen on him and the boy," I told Mac. "I want to check the girl."

I knelt down and took her hand. Her blonde hair smelled fresh and sweet. Her flowered blouse and red skirt were crisp new presents from that morning. Her blue eyes met mine.

"My name is Pat," I said to her. "What is your name?"

She answered me, "Jennifer."

I smiled at her. "I have a daughter named Jennifer. She's eight years old. How old are you?"

"Seven," she replied.

"Is that your brother?" I asked, glancing back at the small boy in Jay's lap.

"Yes," she said, raising up to look at him. "Is he hurt bad?"

"No," I told her. "The young man with him is taking good care of him. What's your brother's name, honey?"

"Eric," she said, lying back down.

"Do you hurt anywhere?" I asked her, smoothing her hair back from her forehead, feeling her head for injuries.

"Just here," she said, rubbing her right arm.

I looked closely at her arm. There was no deformity. "Hold it real still," I told her. I took a cravat from the supply shelf. "I'm going to put it in a sling," I said. "This will make it feel better." I slipped the cravat on her arm, then knotted it beside her neck.

"Jennifer." The man on the gurney spoke to her.

"What, Daddy?"

"Are you and Eric all right?"

"We're okay, Daddy," she said. "Are you?"

"Yes," he said. Then he asked, "Jennifer, where's Mommy?"

She spoke to him in a calm, even voice, but her eyes were on me. "Mommy's all right too, Daddy," she said, looking at me as if she were waiting for an affirmation or a denial.

I could give her neither.

I moved back beside Jay. Leaning close to him, I whispered, "Jay, was their mother in the car?"

He nodded.

"Where is she?"

His eyes met mine and my question was answered. He moved

his head slowly back and forth, twice, perhaps three times, but by then I already knew their mother was dead.

"Pat." Her voice was so soft I wasn't sure she had spoken. I turned toward her. "Pat," she said again.

I moved to the bench and knelt beside her. She reached out for my hand and asked, "Will you tell me a story?"

I could do no more for her brother and father. Jay, Mac, and Paul were taking good care of them. "Yes," I said, moving closer to her, "of course I will."

I told her stories of Winnie-the-Pooh and his friends in the Hundred Acre Wood. Her favorite was the one about Pooh's eating too much honey and getting stuck in Rabbit's doorway. She laughed when I told her that Rabbit used Pooh's legs as towel racks. She never let go of my hand.

When we pulled up to the hospital ER loading dock, she began to cry and I held her close.

"I want my dolls."

I looked around the ambulance. "Where are they?" I asked her.

"They were in the car," she said.

"Jennifer." I wiped the tears from her face. "I'll get your dolls for you."

"You will?" she said. "You really will?"

"Yes, sweetheart, I really will."

Jack and Paul wheeled the father into the emergency room. Jay carried Eric in and then returned to help me with Jennifer. The doctor told me they would call the father's parents, who lived in Fairfax. It would be quite a while before they could get there.

The emergency room was crowded, and we had to put Jennifer on a gurney in the hallway. I couldn't leave her alone, so I looked around until I found a woman in the bay next to her. She was there with her husband, who had cut his hand. Her face was round and sweet, her eyes soft.

"Would you please talk with this little girl for a while?" I asked. "There's no one else to stay with her."

"Of course I will," she assured me.

I turned back to Jennifer. "I'll be back," I told her, "with your dolls."

As I walked away, I heard the woman saying, "Hello, dear, what's your name?"

Paul, Norm, and Jack had returned to the ambulance. I found Jay in the trauma room with Eric, watching the doctor examine him.

"Jay," I said softly, "we have to go now."

"Can I stay here with him, Pat?" he asked me. "The other unit's coming in. I can go back with them." He glanced back at Eric. "I just don't want to leave him yet."

I thought of Joe. "You're so much like your dad," I said. "Stay."

Our trip back was quiet. I rode up front with Jack. The streets of Fredericksburg glistened with the lights of Christmas. On lawns, Santa and his reindeer stood in suspended animation. Spotlights illuminated churchyard nativity scenes. Christmas trees standing tall and straight were framed in picture windows of the houses we passed.

A kaleidoscope of radiant colors flashed through the darkness. In home after home, I caught quick glances of the people inside, with children playing, families together.

I thought of my family. Mine, like Jennifer's, was incomplete. But my family, certain of my return, would switch on the porch light and keep my plate warm in the oven.

I turned to Jack. "I have to get her dolls."

He glanced at me. "Whose dolls?"

"The little girl's. Jennifer's," I said. "I told her I would bring her dolls to her. They were in the car."

"You're going back to the hospital?" he asked. "Tonight?"

"I have to."

When we turned back onto Route 20, Jack spoke again. "Pat," he said, "if you find them, look at them carefully . . . make sure there's no blood on them."

"I'm not sure I would have thought of that, Jack. Thank you."

Our firemen were still on the scene washing down the road. I stepped off the ambulance and looked for the car.

"Pat."

I turned and saw John.

"Where's the car the children were in?" I asked him.

"It's over there," he said, pointing to the other side of the road. "Why?"

"Have you all gotten the woman's body out?"

"Yes. Clyde came and took it to the funeral home. Why?"

"I told the little girl I'd get her dolls," I told him.

I turned and started across the highway.

He was right behind me. "Pat, you can't take something from the car," he said. "You've got to ask the deputy."

I stopped. "Where is he?"

"Over there with the wrecker."

I approached the deputy and introduced myself. Then I told him, "I want to get some dolls out of that car and take them to the little girl who was in the accident."

"Dolls?" the deputy said.

"Dolls."

"I don't have any problem with that," he said. "Just dolls. You're just taking some dolls?"

I nodded. "That's all."

He shrugged. "Okay, but you better hurry. The wrecker's about to tow it away."

The car had been pushed off the road. It rested on the grass away from where the firemen were hosing down the broken glass and the places where gasoline had spilled. Away from the revolving red and blue lights of the fire engine and the deputy's car, the car sat isolated, quarantined, a grim reminder that no day is really sacred.

I opened the car door and leaned inside. Reaching into the dark, I moved my hands slowly over the back seat, lightly over the particles of glass until I felt the soft, doughy arms of a doll. I pulled it to me and tucked it under my arm, then knelt and moved my hand down to the floor board. There, lodged under the front seat, was the second doll.

I stood and stepped away from the car and carried the dolls into the light. When I looked at them I saw they were twin Cabbage Patch dolls.

For the first time that Christmas night, I cried.

I walked to my car and laid them on the seat beside me and drove the twenty miles back to the hospital. I paused at the ER loading dock to inspect them. On one, at the very tip of a soft yellow hair ribbon was a trace of blood. I went into the bathroom and ran water over the stain, then scrubbed it twice with soap.

When I walked into the emergency room, Jennifer sat up. I held a doll in each arm so that she could see their funny little faces. "My dolls," she squealed. I handed them to her and she lay back down. She looked at each one, then at me. "Thank you," she said, smiling at me and hugging the dolls close to her.

"You're welcome, sweetheart."

The woman was still there. I thanked her for her kindness.

"I wish I could have done more," she said.

"I know," I told her. "We all do."

I leaned over Jennifer and kissed her softly good-bye.

When I turned into my driveway I saw the porch light glowing in the darkness. When I walked into my home, my family was there to greet me and my plate was still warm in the oven.

We later learned that Eric had suffered a mild concussion. Their father returned home the following day. Jennifer was released from the hospital that night and went home with her grandparents. It was then that she learned of her mother's death. She held on to her dolls into the night and through the dark days that followed.

I think of her often. I hope she somehow knows that even though her loss was immeasurable, the world still holds kindness. The world still holds love.


It snowed the next day and the next. We celebrated my forty-second birthday and built snow castles and played darts. In the evenings we bundled up and took long walks with Jennifer in front holding the flashlight.

Joe and I didn't have any calls on our duty day.

"Thank goodness," David said when six o'clock came and I was off duty. "I still shudder to think of you driving on anything other than dry pavement."

227

I laughed. "You're not the only one."

On New Year's Eve we went out with John and Yvonne. There were still some icy patches on the roads, so we didn't want to go far. A country band was playing at a local restaurant. "I'd rather drive on ice than listen to this," John grumbled. "Next year can we go hear some decent music?"

"Only if you'll let us beat you," I told him.

"Bullshit!"

I looked at Yvonne. "He never changes."

She smiled at him. "Never."

It was a wonderful night. Even John finally admitted he liked the band. At 11:50, the waitresses handed out hats and noise-makers. I kept a close eye on my watch.

"You can count the seconds and dance at the same time, can't you?" David asked.

"I think I can handle that," I told him.

"Then may I have the last dance of the year with you?"

I moved into his arms. "Seven minutes," I said.

"Hey, Pat." John tapped me on the shoulder.

I turned to him. "Do you want this dance with David?"

"Hell, no," he grinned. "He dances the way he races."

"You're getting drunk, Beery," David said, pulling me back to him.

"Pat!"

"What, John," I said over David's shoulder.

"They want you over there."

"Who does?"

"Some woman up there by the front door. She's having a baby."

I stopped. "What?"

"Go away, John," David said.

"Look," he shrugged, "they told me to come tell you and that's what I'm doing."

The restaurant owner came up behind John. "Pat," he said, "there's a woman here who's just gone into labor. Can you come with me?"

"What'd I tell you," John said.

I looked at David. "I'll be right back."

David looked at John. "You want to dance?"

"Bullshit."

The woman was sitting in the booth next to the front door. "My husband is calling the rescue squad," she said, "but the owner said you were a medical person."

I smiled. "Is this your first baby?" I asked her.

"Yes."

Her husband moved into the booth and put his arm around her. "They're on their way," he told her.

"It won't take them long to get here," I said. "Has your water broken?"

"No."

"When did your contractions start?"

"A half hour ago," her husband said. "They're about five minutes apart. That's pretty close, isn't it?"

"No, not for a first baby," I told him. "You've got plenty of time."

Her eyes widened. "Here comes another one."

Her husband looked at his watch. I looked at mine: 11:59.

I took her hand. "Short breaths, in and out of your mouth," I told her. I saw the reflection of the red lights in the window. Her contraction ended. She relaxed. In the background, I heard strains of Auld Lang Syne. "The rescue squad is here now," I told her. "They'll take good care of you."

Paul and Kathy came in and I gave them the information the young couple had given me. Then I walked outside with them.

"You want to come with us?" Kathy asked me. "This is your kind of call."

"No, thanks," I said. "Not tonight."

"Oh, yeah," she laughed. "It's New Year's Eve."

"Actually, it's New Year's Day," I told her. "Twelve o'clock slipped right on by."

"Happy New Year, Pat," she said.

I gave her a hug. "Happy New Year, Kathy. We're off to a great start, aren't we?"

She smiled. "We sure are," she said.

She stepped onto the ambulance and Paul eased it through the crowded parking lot. I stood alone in the crystalline clear night on the threshold of a new year. I watched the ambulance pull away, watched until the red lights disappeared and the siren's wail faded into the distance.

# Epilogue

WHEN I REFLECT back on that New Year's Eve, now nearly three years past, I find that so many of the memories of that night—of that time—have dimmed. It is not the inevitable passage of time that has shaded my recollections. Those shadows, instead, formed in the wake of my own passage through the changes and transitions of my life since then.

Winter was harsh that year. The bitter cold hovered outside our door. All of us had the flu. Sunshine, our yellow tabby cat, died. Then in early March, shortly after Jennifer's eighth birthday, David began to spend more and more time away from home.

"Why do you have to go away so often?" I asked him as he packed for his third trip in two weeks.

"I have to make a living," he answered, abruptly.

"But why so many business trips now?"

He shrugged. "Bad planning. That's all."

But that was not all.

For several months, even before New Year's, I had sensed a dissatisfaction in him. His affection would come in short bursts. He had grown impatient with the children and with me. He seemed preoccupied. Sometimes his gaze drifted away and I couldn't recognize what it was I saw in his eyes. When I asked him what was wrong, he would say, "Nothing."

But I loved him and believed that my love was stronger and more powerful than whatever was tugging at him.

I was wrong.

On April 1, David left us.

It was on a beautiful spring day. Jennifer was sick with chicken pox. It was the day before Matt's fifteenth birthday.

"Please don't go," I pleaded. "I don't understand why you're doing this."

"I'm not happy anymore," he said, finally. "I'm tired of taking care of people. I'm going to do what I want to do."

I watched him carry his suitcases to the car and drive away.

I told the children he'd gone on another business trip. I could not yet give words to the truth. It was almost two weeks later, at dinner one evening, when Dave asked, "Mom, when is Dad coming home?" that I told them.

"I don't think he is coming home," I said. I tried to give them a gentler explanation than he had given me. Still, Dave grew very angry. Matt left the table and went to his room. Jennifer cried, and I cried with her.

"It's mid-life crisis," Jean said when I told her. "He'll come back."

Joyce sent me notes that said "Thinking of You."

Joe would often stop by on his way home from work with a gallon of milk and ice cream for the children.

Kathy called me almost every day.

I phoned my parents and told them. They came the next day, Dad with his baseball glove and Mom with stacks of material and patterns for Cabbage Patch Kid clothes. Dave's anger quieted. Matt slowly came out of his shell. Jennifer laughed again. In the evenings, Dad helped me with all the paperwork of a home and family that had become my responsibility. When they left, we were stronger. We formed a tight circle of support and took one day at a time.

David rented a townhouse in Fredericksburg and bought a sports car.

"I know it's mid-life crisis," Jean said. "He'll get over it. He'll come back."

I called Bob. "I have to go off the squad," I told him.

"Not permanently," he said.

"I don't know. I just need some time. For the children . . . and for me."

"What will Norm and I do without you?" Joe said.

"You'll be fine," I told him. "There are other CTs."

In the beginning, my rescue squad work kindled my self-assurance which had, in turn, freed me to move through all the dimensions of my life unencumbered. Now my feelings of inadequacy entangled me in a web of self-doubt. How could I, then, attempt to salvage someone else's life when I couldn't hold mine together?

I had bills to pay, so I returned to teaching, finishing off the year for a third grade teacher who was expecting a baby.

Several days before I started work, I was in my room trying to piece a wardrobe together when I heard the tones go off. I stepped away from the closet and listened. The call was for a heart attack. I had lost track of the schedule and had forgotten whose day it was until I heard Joe's voice on the radio. He asked our dispatcher to tone out for a CT. It was my day, but there were other CTs.

It *was* my day. I turned off my pager.

I had not been in the classroom long before I found that each day I looked forward to seeing my third graders. They and my own children were helping to fill up the emptiness of my life. Still, I was saddled with anger and tears of self-pity continued to sting my eyes.

The children were divided into reading groups according to ability. I had six children for whom reading was quite difficult and began each day with them. We sat together in a circle around the reading table while the rest of the class worked on their written assignments.

We were reading a story about a little boy who makes a wish as he blows out the candles on his birthday cake. It was Shana's turn to read. She opened her book and flattened the pages with her hands.

"William . . . made . . . his . . . wish," she read.

"What do you think he's going to wish for?" I asked her.

"I don't know," she said, her eyes still fixed on her book. "Maybe a bike." The other children nodded in agreement.

"Is that what you wished for?" I asked.

She looked up at me. Her eyes were large and brown and as soft as her voice. "No, Ma'am," she said. "I ain't never had no birthday cake with no birthday candles. So I ain't never made no wish." Then she looked back down at her book and continued to read.

She said nothing more about the birthday cake, nor did I. That day after school I looked at her file and found that her birthday was May 30, a school day. On the night of May 29, Jennifer and I baked her a cake. When I arrived at school the next day, I stuck ten candles through the thick creamy icing, covered the cake with aluminum foil and pushed it under my desk.

After lunch, when the whole class was together and we had a while before recess, I asked Shana if she would tell them the story we'd read several weeks earlier about the boy who made a wish. She nodded and walked to the front of the room.

"There was this boy," she began, "and his name was William." The other children leaned forward in their desks to listen. "He had a birthday and when he blew out his candles . . ."

"Shana," I interrupted her. "I've got an idea. Let's show them."

"Show them?" she said.

I pulled the cake out from under my desk and placed it on the reading table beside her. Then I lit the candles. The joy I felt at that moment was equaled only by the look on her face. She blew out the candles with a burst of air so explosive it was as if she'd been saving it up for ten years. She stood with her head slightly bowed, the smile still on her face, while we sang Happy Birthday to her. I gave each child a cup of milk and Shana passed out the cake. Afterwards, she asked me if she could take the candles home.

Before she got on the bus that day, she walked over to me and stood quietly by my side. In one hand she held the candles. She reached out with her other hand and took hold of mine, and the tears which moistened my eyes did not sting. I remembered ". . . There's something about holding a hand . . . like holding a heart." I don't know what Shana wished for that day, but my own wish, a wish I didn't even know was there, came true.

I called Bob that night. "I miss the squad," I told him.

"And we miss you," he said.

For the remainder of the school year I responded to calls on weekends and agreed to continue my work as training officer. When summer came I returned to my crew.

"See," I said. "You made it without me."

"Not very well," Joe said, smiling. "Not very well at all."

After completing the training program at our August squad meeting, I set my notes aside, but remained standing. There was something more I wanted to say to them. I looked out at their faces as familiar to me as my own—faces I'd seen in darkness and in light, across shattered automobiles, in the confines of sickness and injury and death—the faces of my friends with whom I'd shared so much both within and beyond the lights and sirens.

"There are times in our lives which are difficult," I began, "and getting through them takes a lot of strength, sometimes more than we think we have." I paused for a moment, then continued, "I just want to thank all of you, individually and as a squad, for helping me find that strength."

After the meeting, after the last cup of coffee and the final moments of shop talk, I walked out into the warm night air. I felt good. I was happy, and whole.

Joe was behind me. "Good training, Pat," he said.

I stopped. "Thanks, Joe."

"And that was nice, what you said. I'm really glad . . . we all are, that you're okay now."

I smiled at him. "You know what Woody would say at a time like this, don't you?"

He nodded, then rested his hand gently on my shoulder. "Another save."

My mourning finally ended. The children were doing well and I was learning to smile and laugh and trust again. The healing was not yet complete, but I had survived.

Jean was wrong. David didn't come back. He moved into a bigger townhouse, bought a new sailboat, and openly shared his life with someone else. I also came to understand that nothing I could have done would have kept him with us.

I still keep a journal. I write less about each call than I did in the beginning. I pare down the details. If I forget to write about one, I know I can always go down to the fire and rescue building and dig out the old call sheets. But from call sheets I can only get medical information, and so often it's not the medical information that makes the call memorable.

The four-year-old girl had fallen against the living room coffee table. The cut required nothing more than a Band-Aid and a hug. Her parents signed the transport refusal form. Our paperwork was complete.

This family was from Puerto Rico, but had recently become American citizens. The parents spoke some English. The children, the little girl and her brother, could speak only Spanish. She sat on her father's lap. I knelt on the floor beside her to examine the cut. I showed her the Band-Aid before I put it on her forehead. Suddenly she smiled and pointed to my uniform.

"Nuestro bandera," she said, her dark eyes shining. She looked toward her parents. "Papa, Mama," she said, "nuestro bandera."

They smiled at her and nodded. "Si, nuestro bandera," her father said, pulling her close to him.

"What is she saying?" I asked him.

"Our flag," he said, proudly. The American flag stitched onto my uniform. "She is saying 'our flag.' "

That is why I keep my journal.

Since that New Year's Eve three years past, I have run close to 500 calls. That's not a lot considering the number of calls urban squads answer. Yet, that's 500 lives, 500 people who've been sick or hurt or dying, and the emergency medical care they received made the difference.

I don't remember many of the names. The faces stay with me longer. Still, eventually, I forget. Often, a person will come up to me and say, "Remember, you took me to the hospital?" Sometimes I remember, but sometimes I have to tell them, "I'm sorry. I don't remember. But you know, people look entirely different when they're lying down."

I still haven't delivered a baby, but I have stepped aboard the winged horse and ridden Pegasus from Wilderness to Charlottesville. Our patient, with head and chest injuries, had been trapped in her overturned pickup truck for almost an hour. When the Pegasus crew asked for a squad member to go with them, Joe and Norm pushed me forward. "It's yours," Norm said.

The chopper lifted off the ground for the twenty-minute flight. With our patient and the two paramedics and me in the back, there was barely room to move. We all wore earphones because of the noise of the engine and the blades rotating above us. We could only communicate through our mouthpieces. "Is it always this bumpy?" I said into mine. We were barely above the tree-tops and the helicopter shuddered and swayed with each gust of wind.

One paramedic was monitoring our patient. The other was filling out their call sheet. They both glanced at me and smiled. "Your first flight?" the one doing the paperwork asked.

I nodded.

"No." He shook his head. "It's not always this bumpy. We've got some real gusts today."

He was right about that. Some real gusts. I had already decided that I liked watching Pegasus from the ground much more than watching the ground from Pegasus.

We landed safely and moved our patient quickly into the trauma room. I gave the U.Va. medical personnel the information regarding the accident. She was later admitted with a concussion and pulmonary contusions.

An hour later, Joe arrived to take me home. "Well," he said, smiling broadly, "how was it?"

"Let me put it this way," I told him. "I was the only one who got off the helicopter and kissed the ground."

He almost believed me.

* * *

Four more people have died on that same stretch of Route 20. A sixty-year-old man and a young mother and her eight-year-old son were killed in a head-on accident there. It happened on Father's Day. Again our firemen had to cut open a car to remove the small body of a child.

The fourth fatality was a young man who was traveling to a new job in northern Virginia. He had made the decision to drive all night and was within two hours of his destination when his truck was hit head on by a car driven by a drunk driver. His jugular vein was severed and he was dead before we arrived on the scene. The driver and passengers of the car survived.

With each passing day, Wilderness less and less resembles its name. Housing developments are sprouting up like spring crops. Planning has begun for a shopping center almost within walking distance, and the highway department has installed a stoplight at Routes 3 and 20.

The dogwood and redbud still bloom in the spring, though, and my children and I can still pick wild strawberries in our back yard.

Wilderness, like all rural areas, is also no longer immune to the influx of drugs. Criminal convictions are published in the local newspapers, and in recent reports the majority of convictions were for possession and distribution of cocaine. The number of patients whose illnesses or injuries are directly related to drug and alcohol abuse has increased, and I can now understand a little of what Pete was talking about back at Station 22. I have been with some patients whose hands I don't want to hold.

Our rescue squad is still made up wholly of volunteers. We continue to serve our locale with eight regularly scheduled duty crews. Our gains have outweighed our losses. I think we're lucky. Surrounding squads are already supplementing their crews with paid personnel, and it's working well. One volunteer squad member from Stafford County said to me recently, "If I'm having a heart attack, I don't care if the EMT who takes care of me is volunteer or paid. I just want somebody to show up." That, after all, is what it comes down to: somebody to show up.

More and more, I fear the volunteer rescue squad is becoming the dinosaur of emergency medical care. A life span of little more than fifty years is not long enough for such a worthwhile organization. Julian Wise had the dream of neighbor helping neighbor and turned it into reality, but times have changed. Businesses are less willing to allow employees to leave for calls. Many people feel that if they are going to put in the long hours of training to become EMTs, they should be paid for it. Citizens are contributing less to volunteer squads. A bare ambulance alone can cost as much as $50,000. Add advanced life support equipment, communication systems, gasoline, maintenance, and basic medical supplies, and the cost is well over $90,000. The service is free, but it's not cheap.

I am still on Team 3. The duty roster lists us:

> EMT-CT — Pat Ivey
> EMT — Joe Broderick
> EMT — Norm Ensrud
> EMT — Purvis Beanum, our new crew member.

We're good together. I am their "fearful leader," but I'm not so fearful anymore. Buzzy would be proud of me. I haven't seen Buzzy for over two years. He's married now and still selling real estate in northern Virginia. Jean stays busy with her ever-expanding brood of grandchildren. Woody and Marge bought a camper and they head off for the beach or the mountains whenever they can. We still think of him when one of us says, "Another save." And we say it often.

I still remember Ed in his baseball cap with his pajama pants hanging from the legs of his uniform. Gentle, patient, and caring, he taught me what a leader should be. I also still think of Lou who never stopped believing in what I could become.

From my EMT class of nine years ago, only Bob and Joyce and I continue to run on a duty crew. We have taken and passed the exam for Cardiac Technician re-certification twice now, together. We have gone well beyond the average time served by rescue squad volunteers. We tell each other that we're tired. We sometimes grumble about calls that are too long, about too many calls or too few calls. We talk about going off the squad for a while. We've talked about leaving the squad for good, but we don't. They're still here and so am I. Lou tells me that after all these years, she still misses it. I know that's just how I will feel.

So much has come full circle: Linda and I searching for the little girl in woods and underbrush so near to where Matt and Justin were lost ten years ago.

This rescue squad I so hesitantly joined, with the desire to serve and to save, has, in turn, cared for and nurtured me. For through it, I am constantly reminded that it is only through turning our vision outward, toward others, that we can ever be truly happy, that we can ever find peace.

I am now an EMT Instructor. I teach others the skills necessary for emergency medical care and for "psychological first aid." In March, my first class completed the course. Those fifteen new EMTs came from all walks of life sharing one thing in common: the desire to help others. Some, like Norm, were already squad members. Others, like Purvis, soon joined. All of them will help increase the odds of survival for so many.

Sally Kelley was one of my students. She is a lovely woman, soft and gentle both in speech and manner. She came into class that first night and told me she didn't want EMT certification. "I just want the knowledge," she said. "I don't think I could be on the rescue squad. I couldn't do what you people do."

"I think you could," I told her.

She took a seat in the back of the classroom. Then slowly, as the weeks passed, she began to move closer to the front. I called on her occasionally and she always knew the answers. She was one of the first to sign up for the Emergency Room. In the end, she took the exam and scored the second highest grade in the class. In April, she joined the rescue squad and on a seasonably warm afternoon in early May, she ran her first call.

Our patient had suffered a stroke. Sally took his pulse, respirations, and blood pressure. She helped lift the gurney onto the ambulance and on our trip to the hospital, she held his hand. I sat on the seat opposite her, watching. When she looked at me and smiled, I saw in her face a reflection of my own so long ago. Doubt still lingered in her eyes, but there was confidence in her smile.

Giant steps had gotten her there just as they had for me. She had no idea of what might lie ahead for her, nor had I when I became an EMT. I could not crack open the door to the future. I couldn't catch just a glimpse of what was on the other side. I do know now that even if I could have seen what was there waiting for me, I would never have slammed the door shut and turned away.

I would have welcomed it eagerly, with open arms.

# ABOUT THE AUTHOR

PAT IVEY was born in Oceanside, California, in 1943, but grew up in Salem, Virginia. She graduated from Bridgewater College in Virginia with a BA in English and later studied Creative Writing at the University of North Carolina in Chapel Hill with Manly Wade Wellman. In addition to her work as a Cardiac Technician on the Lake of the Woods Volunteer Rescue Squad, she is now an Emergency Medical Technician Instructor. Her older son, David, attends James Madison University in Harrisonburg, Virginia, and she and her younger son, Matt, and daughter, Jennifer, live in Wilderness, Virginia.